THE
Stargazer's
GUIDE TO THE
Night Sky

Dr. Jason Lisle

Master Books®

The heavens declare the glory of God; and the
firmament sheweth his handywork.

—Psalm 19:1

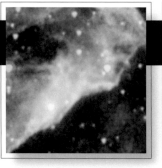
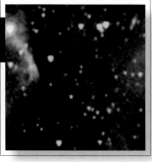

First printing: April 2012
Sixth printing: June 2022

Master Books, P.O. Box 726, Green Forest, AR 72638

Master Books® is a division of the
New Leaf Publishing Group, Inc.

ISBN: 978-0-89051-641-6
ISBN: 978-1-61458-194-9 (digital)

Library of Congress Number: 2011945896

Cover Design: Heidi Rohr Design

Interior Design: Diana Bogardus

Unless otherwise noted, Scripture quotations are from the New King James Version of the Bible.

Please consider requesting that a copy of this volume be purchased by your local library system.

Printed in China

Please visit our website for other great titles:

www.masterbooks.com

For information regarding author interviews, please contact the publicity department at (870) 438-5288.

Photo and Image credits:

r-right
l-left
c: center
cr: center-right
cl: center-left
b: bottom
br: bottom-right
bl: bottom-left
bc: bottom-center

t: top
tl: top-left
tc: top-center
bkg: background

Front Cover: Shutterstock.com
Back Cover: Chris Neville

NASA: pg 1, 3, 15, 21, 25t, 26, 27, 36(all), 37, 38(all), 39, 40, 41t, 43t, 43b, 57, 72, 73, 76bl, 79, 80, 91bkg, 93bkg, 94bkg, 115, 123t, 125, 128, 129, 130, 131, 132l, 132r, 133, 134, 135, 140, 141, 143, 145t, 150, 152, 154, 155, 156, 157, 158b, 160t, 161t, 161b, 162, 163, 165t, 169b, 171b, 175, 177, 178, 181, 183, 185t, 187b, 189, 191b, 194, 195, 202, 204r, 207, 210, 213b, 216

Jason Lisle: pg 8, 9, 10, 11, 15, 17, 19, 22, 25b, 29, 50, 51, 52, 54, 55, 56, 58, 59, 60, 61, 62, 63, 64, 66, 67, 69, 71, 90, 91c, 93c, 94c, 105b, 108, 124, 126, 136, 137, 138, 139, 142, 145b, 147l, 147r, 148, 149, 151, 153, 158t, 159, 160b, 168, 169t, 170, 171t, 172, 173b, 174, 182, 184, 185b, 186, 187t, 188, 190, 191t, 192, 193b, 196, 197, 198, 199b, 200, 201, 203, 209, 212, 213t, 214, 215, 218, 219, 220, 221, 222b, 223b, 224, 225, 226 (all), 234

Shutterstock: pg 5, 6, 7t, 7b, 14, 16, 19, 28, 30, 32, 33, 34, 42t, 43, 44, 45 (all), 46t, 46b, 84t, 87, 89t, 89b, 97, 99tl, 100bkg, 103, 107t, 107b, 112, 113, 116, 118, 123, 127

istock: pg 35, 84bl, 86, 101, 104, 120

wiki: pg 41c, 92, 96, 98, 167

NLPG: pg 42, 83, 166

dreamstime: pg 65, 68, 71t, 95, 99br, 100c, 105tl, 109, 110, 117, 144, 223t, 227, 228, 232, 238

Chris Neville: back cover, pg 235

Photo Researchers: pg 74t, 74bl, 74br, 75, 76br, 77, 82, 165, 173t, 193t, 199t, 204l, 208

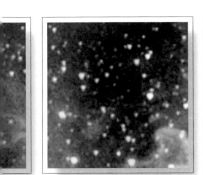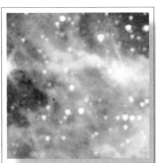

The Stargazer's Planisphere is included in the back of this edition to help you better enjoy God's amazing night sky. This chart helps you locate the positions of stars on any night of the year.

Introduction

There is something about the night sky that captures our imagination and evokes a sense of awe and wonder. And our appreciation of the magnificence of creation is enhanced as we learn more about the cosmos. As one example, the bright red star Betelgeuse is beautiful, whether you know anything about it or not. But when you consider that Betelgeuse is over 60,000 times the diameter of the Earth and lies at a distance of 3,000 trillion miles, somehow that just makes it all the more impressive.

We have all seen beautiful images of the universe obtained by professional astronomers. But what many people do not realize is that many of these celestial wonders are within the range of a small telescope. You just have to know where to look. In fact, there are many heavenly gems (such as star clusters) that look beautiful in binoculars. Even without any optical aid, there are countless celestial treasures that can be seen with the eye — if you know where and how to look for them.

This book is written for the person who has no experience in astronomy, but wants to learn how to best enjoy the night sky. If you have a small telescope, the star charts in this book will help you find the most spectacular celestial objects visible in such a telescope. If you are considering buying a small telescope at some point, this book will show you what things to consider. But even if you have no intention of ever owning a telescope, there are many cosmic wonders that can be seen by the unaided eye — or with low-power binoculars. And this book will show you how to find them. If you have ever looked up into the night sky and wanted to know more about what you are seeing, this book is for you.

I love astronomy. I always have. When I was very young, I would read all the astronomy books I could find. But what was really exciting to me was when I learned to find astronomical objects in a small telescope. My dad had a six-inch Newtonian reflector telescope — nothing fancy. But it is amazing what you can see with such a telescope, if you know the night sky. During the summer, when school was not in session, I could often be found outside on clear evenings, peering through that telescope. There is something very different about seeing an astronomical object with your own eyes. It just makes it so much more "real" than a textbook photograph. And it is this experience that I want to share with others.

I have worked at a number of observatories, and have led more telescope observing sessions than I can count. Through my education in astrophysics and through many years of experience, I have learned how to better enjoy the night sky. There are some simple tips and tricks that can make an observing session go from mediocre to spectacular. Whether you have a telescope, binoculars, or just your eyes, everyone can benefit from these guidelines.

This book is particularly helpful for observers in the Northern Hemisphere, especially those at mid-northern latitudes such as in the United States and Europe. However, Southern Hemisphere observers will still benefit from this book, and I have included several star charts for them as well. In fact, the general principles in chapters 1, 2, 3, 5, 6, 7, 9, and 12 apply equally well in either hemisphere. But the star charts in chapter 4, for example, apply mainly to the Northern Hemisphere (though they will still be somewhat useful for the Southern Hemisphere). This bias is due to the simple fact that I have lived entirely at mid-northern latitudes, and thus my experience is primarily with the portion of the sky visible from northern latitudes.

To maximize our enjoyment of the night sky, it is necessary to know how things move in the night sky. This is important so that we know when and where to look for a given target. To that end, chapter 1 is a basic introduction to celestial motions. Chapter 2 continues this theme with more advanced topics in celestial motions.

The basics of celestial motions are not difficult at all, once you have a mental picture of how things move in space.

Chapter 3 is all about the human eye. By understanding how the eye works, it is possible to greatly enhance your views of stellar objects. Whether you are looking through a telescope or viewing something with the unaided eye, chapter 3 will have some very helpful tips.

Chapter 4 is all about what you can see with the unaided eye. If you have ever wanted to know the names of constellations or bright stars,

Stargazing is great for all ages!

the charts in this chapter will make that easy to do. The chapter is organized by the time of year in which the various objects are visible. So if you are observing in mid-summer, you can skip to that section of the chapter. Chapter 5 is about celestial events, such as eclipses and meteor showers. It will tell you when and where to watch for these things.

Chapter 6 is an introduction to telescopes. In it, we discuss the various types of telescopes and the advantages and disadvantages of each. This chapter will be particularly helpful for people who wish to purchase a small telescope. In chapter 7 we then discuss tips on setting up and using a telescope to get the most out of it.

Chapter 8 is about the two largest celestial objects: the moon and the sun. This will be a great chapter whether

you view the moon by eye, with binoculars or with a small telescope. We also discuss how to safely view the sun. Chapter 10 is about stars — how they are classified and what to look for. Telescope users will find instructions on locating the best binary stars.

Chapters 9, 11, and 12 are particularly useful for people who have (or who are going to get) a small backyard telescope. (However, the information may be very interesting even to those who do not have a telescope.) In these chapters we discuss how to get the best telescopic views of planets (chapter 9), and deep-sky objects (chapter 11). Chapter 12 is for those who wish to take photos using their telescope.

It is my hope that this book will help readers to appreciate and enjoy the wonders of the night sky.

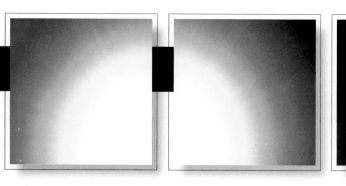

Chapter 1

Motions in the Sky—Basic

One of the most useful skills of the amateur astrono-mer involves a basic understanding of how things move in the sky. If you are going to really enjoy the night sky, it is important to know when various objects will be visible and where to look. So in this chapter we will explore the movement of celestial objects. We will answer questions like: Is Saturn visible this time of year? What constellations are visible at 10:00 tonight? What is the best time of night to see the constellation Orion? What phase will the moon be in next week? Why does the sun rise and set at different times during different seasons? When will the moon rise tonight? What is my current latitude? How do the stars change positions if I go from the Northern Hemisphere to the Southern? If the bright star Sirius is high in the sky directly in front of me, what direction am I facing?

All these questions are easy to answer when a person has a basic knowledge of motions in the sky. In fact, these questions can easily be solved "in your head" without a calculator. All that is needed is a basic mental picture of how the Earth, moon, and planets move in relation to the sun and stars. (A little bit of practice helps, too.) We will examine how the spinning of the Earth on its axis and the motion of the Earth around the sun affect the apparent position of objects in our sky. We will also explore the motion of the moon and the planets.

Celestial motions are not only interesting, they are very practical. As long as the sky is clear, I always know what direction I'm facing because of the position of the sun or stars. It's a useful skill to have when driving to some-where new, or going for a long hike. This directional awareness is second nature; I don't have to think about it. I can even tell the approximate time by the position of the sun, moon, or stars. And anyone can learn to do this. It's not hard at all.

When we understand celestial motions, it is very enjoyable to see the universe operate with the clock-work precision with which it was designed. It is fun to think, "Well, it's 7:00, so the moon should be low in the southwest right now," and then step outside and say, "Yes. Right where I expected." However, it is also very important to know about these motions if you want to look for something specific. If you want to look at Saturn tonight, you had better know when it is going to rise and set — or whether it's visible at all this time of year. Will your telescopic view of the Orion Nebula or your naked-eye view of the Milky Way be hampered by bright moonlight? You'd better know what phase the moon is in, and when it will rise and set.

◇Diurnal Motion

We begin by studying the most basic motion of objects

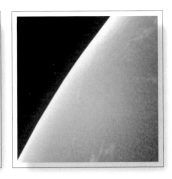

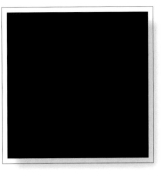
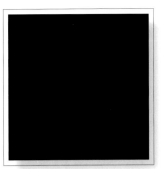

in our sky. It is common knowledge that the sun always rises in the east and sets in the west. However, the moon, stars, and planets also adhere to this pattern. This basic trend of east-to-west motion is due to Earth's rotation on its axis; things seem to go from east to west simply because the Earth is spinning in the opposite direction. This is called "diurnal motion." It is no different than someone spinning in a revolving chair; the world seems to be spinning the opposite way.

The Earth takes approximately 24 hours to rotate on its axis. Therefore, any object in the sky will take approximately 24 hours to make a complete circuit. If you see a bright star rising in the east, that star will be high in the sky 6 hours later, and will set in the west after an

additional 6 hours; the star will then be below the horizon (and thus not visible) for an additional 12 hours. These numbers are approximations only — we'll see why later. One application of this principle is that if you see a star (or planet) in a particular section of the sky tonight, rest assured that you will see it in almost the same spot in the sky the following night at the same time (24 hours later).

◇The Celestial Sphere

A very useful concept for understanding the positions and motions of stars is called the "celestial sphere." Ancient astronomers imagined that the stars were all pinned to the surface of a gigantic invisible sphere,

One-hour timelapse photography

1.1

The celestial equator (red) is the extension of Earth's equator into space. The celestial equator divides the visible universe into two hemispheres.

with Earth at its center. This sphere seems to rotate (east to west) relative to us, since the Earth is in fact rotating in the opposite direction. Of course, we now know that the stars are not on the two-dimensional surface of a sphere, but are at various distances throughout space. Nonetheless, the celestial sphere is a useful mental construct for understanding apparent stellar motion. There is no need to know the distance to different stars to understand their motion. Just imagine that they are all pinned to a giant, invisible sphere that spins around the Earth.

The celestial sphere has an equator and a North and South Pole – just like the Earth. By construction, the celestial poles and equator are perfectly aligned with Earth's. Imagine expanding Earth's equator out into space, so that it divides the universe into two hemispheres **FIGURE 1.1**. That dividing circle would represent

the "celestial equator." Likewise, imagine standing on the North Pole of Earth and looking straight up. That spot in the sky is the "North Celestial Pole" (NCP). It so happens that there is a star extremely close to the NCP; it's called the North Star or "Polaris." So, conveniently, the North Star is a nice physical representation of the NCP. A person standing on Earth's South Pole looking directly overhead would see the South Celestial Pole (SCP). But there is not a bright star at that location.

The celestial equator may be difficult to visualize as we stand on Earth's surface. However, if you lived on Earth's equator, the celestial equator would go right overhead. It would extend from due east to directly overhead to due west. Since the United States is north of the Earth's equator, the celestial equator appears shifted southward. In the USA, the celestial equator extends from due east, to a point somewhat south of

1.2

The celestial equator intersects the horizon at due east at an angle that is related to the observer's latitude. For this reason, stars rise in the east at an angle.

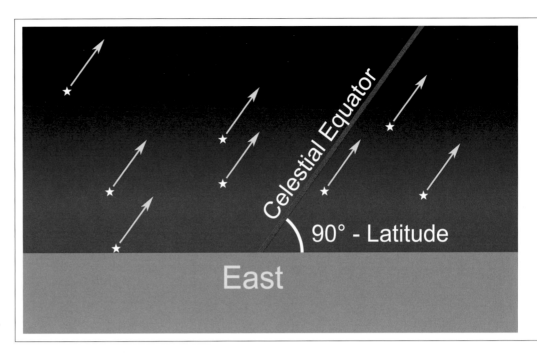

overhead, to due west. In fact, the angle at which the celestial equator intersects the horizon is exactly 90° minus the latitude FIGURE 1.2. At the North or South Pole, the celestial equator would be the same as the horizon.

Since we live on a rotating planet, from our point of view the celestial sphere rotates counterclockwise around the NCP. Thus, stars rise in the east and set in the west. Stars very close to the NCP never go below the horizon (so they do not rise or set), but they still circle in the same direction — counterclockwise around Polaris. The celestial poles themselves always appear in exactly the same location in space, as seen from a given location on Earth. However, since the celestial poles are at exactly opposite points on the celestial sphere, only one of them can be seen from any given location on Earth (except at the equator where both poles are barely visible, just touching the horizon). In the Northern Hemisphere, we can always see the NCP (i.e., the North Star is always visible in exactly the same spot), but we can never see the SCP since it is permanently below the horizon for us. Conversely, people living south of the Earth's equator can never see the North Star.

Some constellations are close enough to the celestial pole that they are visible all night, year-round, like Cassiopeia and Ursa Minor (for the USA). These are called "circumpolar" constellations FIGURE 1.3. Likewise, some stars (like Alpha Centauri) and constellations (such as

Crux) can never be seen from mid-northern latitudes because they are too close to the SCP, and thus never get above the horizon.

◇ The Greater Light to Rule the Day

For any given location on Earth, the local time is based on where the sun is in the sky. When the sun has reached its highest point in the sky, we set our clocks to noon. (To be precise, it's a bit more complicated than this. Time zones, daylight-saving time, and the uneven speed of Earth's orbit around the sun all cause the sun to be not exactly at its highest point at noon. But it's close enough for our purposes here.) On average, the sun rises at approximately 6 a.m., sets at approximately 6 p.m., and is farthest below the horizon at midnight. (Again, this is simplified.) We have defined time in such a way that it takes exactly 24 hours (on average) for the sun to make a complete circuit in the sky. Most of the sun's apparent motion is due to Earth's rotation on its axis, but not all.

The Earth actually takes 23 hours and 56 minutes to rotate on its axis once. For that reason, from our point of view all stars take 23 hours 56 minutes to revolve around Polaris and return to their original position. All stars do this except one — the sun. The sun takes 24 hours (on average) to return to a given location in the sky. The reason for the four-minute difference is that the Earth is orbiting the sun (and not the distant stars). It takes a full year for the Earth to orbit the sun once;

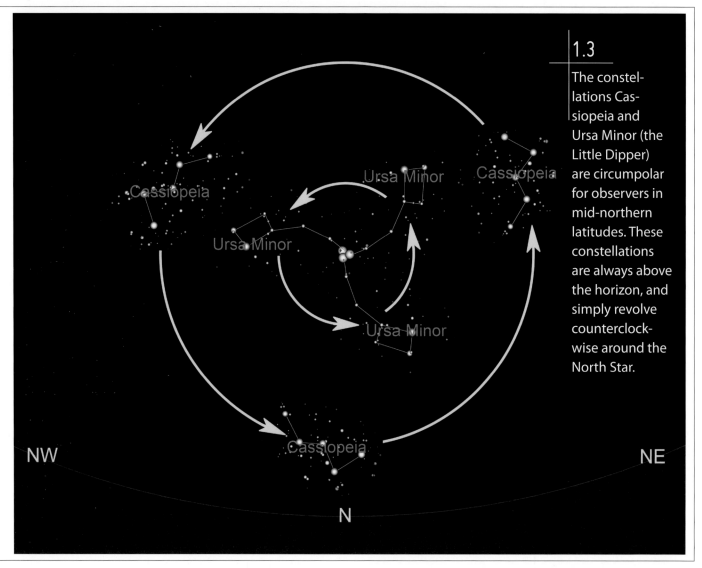

1.3

The constellations Cassiopeia and Ursa Minor (the Little Dipper) are circumpolar for observers in mid-northern latitudes. These constellations are always above the horizon, and simply revolve counterclockwise around the North Star.

but it moved a small fraction of that orbit in one day. So, whereas the Earth takes only 23 hours and 56 minutes to rotate completely, the sun is no longer in the same position it was one day ago since the Earth has moved around it just a bit. It takes an extra 4 minutes to "make up the difference." See FIGURE 1.4.

Since the 23 hours and 56 minutes period is how long it takes the Earth to turn as seen from a distant star, this is called a "sidereal day"; this represents the true rotation of the Earth on its axis. The 24-hour day is called a "solar day" (also called a "synodic day") since it is in relation to the position of the sun. From Earth's point of view, the sun travels eastward relative to the stars on a path called the "ecliptic." The ecliptic is actually the

plane of the Earth's orbit around the sun, and therefore appears to be the sun's annual path around the Earth as well. It is this slow motion along the ecliptic that causes the sun to rise 4 minutes later relative to the stars every day, or alternatively the stars appear to rise 4 minutes earlier relative to the sun.

Since we find it convenient to work by daylight, we have chosen to set our clocks by the sun, so there are 24 hours in one solar day. However, astronomers often prefer to set their time by the stars — sidereal time. There are 24 sidereal hours in one sidereal day. This is extremely convenient in astronomy, since a given star is always at the same location at a given sidereal time; we don't have to subtract 4 minutes off of every day.

But, in our standard solar time, the stars rise 4 minutes earlier every night, and the sun takes 24 hours to make a circuit. Conversely, in sidereal time, stars rise at exactly the same time every night; and the sun rises later by (an average of) 4 minutes per day. One minute of sidereal time is therefore slightly shorter than one minute of solar time. Since virtually all cultures of the world use solar time, this is what we will use throughout this book. But keep in mind that a sidereal day is 4 minutes shorter than a solar day; so stars take 23 hours 56 minutes to complete their circuit in the heavens — just 4 minutes short of a day.

The "4 minute" number is an approximation; but how does the number come about? The Earth takes one year to orbit the sun — that's about 365.25 (solar) days. Therefore, from the viewpoint of the Earth, the sun makes one complete revolution around the celestial sphere in one year. The Earth orbits the sun in the same direction the Earth rotates. This means, the sun "sees" one fewer Earth rotation every year than the stars do.

So, whereas there are 365.25 solar days in a year, there are 366.25 sidereal days (the Earth has actually rotated 366.25 times in one year). So the stars are effectively rising 24 hours (one full day) earlier after a period of 12 months. This means that stars rise 2 hours earlier per month, which works out to about 28 minutes per week, or just a bit less than 4 minutes per day.

If we understand the basic motion of the Earth on its axis, and the motion of the Earth around the sun, and if we gain a bit of familiarity with the constellations and bright stars, it is very easy to tell when an object of interest will be visible. Suppose you see a bright star high in the sky at midnight in the middle of December. You automatically know that it will be in that same position at 10:00 p.m. in January, and at 8:00 p.m. in February. You can also conclude that the star will not be easily visible in July, since it will be lost in the glare of the sun. If you see a star that is fairly close to the North Star, you can easily conclude that it will be visible year-round, at any time of night.

Here are some practical results of the above discussion. Since stars rise 2 hours earlier every month, they rise 12 hours earlier after 6 months — half a year. This makes sense since the Earth would then be on the opposite side of the sun. Therefore,

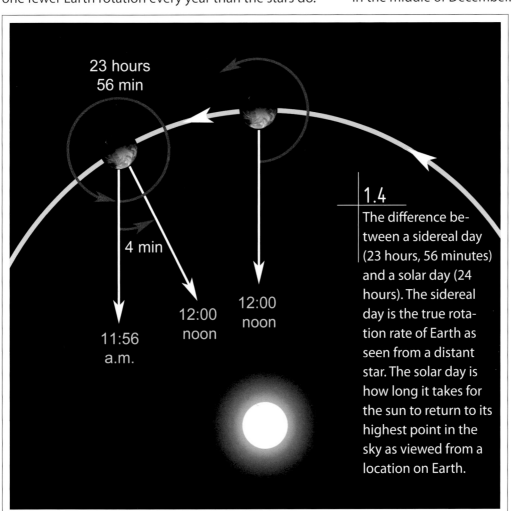

1.4

The difference between a sidereal day (23 hours, 56 minutes) and a solar day (24 hours). The sidereal day is the true rotation rate of Earth as seen from a distant star. The solar day is how long it takes for the sun to return to its highest point in the sky as viewed from a location on Earth.

23 hours 56 min

4 min

12:00 noon

12:00 noon

11:56 a.m.

stars and constellations that are visible in the evening sky in the summer are visible in the morning sky in winter (i.e., 12 hours later). Constellations that are high in the sky at midnight in spring cannot be seen in fall. If a constellation is low in the west just after sunset today, you know it probably won't be visible at all next month — it will set two hours earlier and will be lost in the sun's glare. These simple guidelines allow you to know where and when to look for the desired star or constellation.

Experience is the key. To someone who has never thought about motions in the night sky, the above discussion may seem abstract or confusing. But a little experience will make it very obvious what is going on. Simply try it. Go outside tonight, find a bright star, and make an estimation of its position. A week later, go out one half-hour earlier, and you will see the same star in the same position. Go out an hour or two later and see how that star has shifted to the west. It doesn't take long before these motions are very intuitive.

◇The Lesser Light to Rule the Night

In order to really get the most out of an astronomy observing session, it is crucially important to know the phase of the moon and approximately when the moon will rise and set. The rise and set times are determined primarily by the phase, so if you know one bit of information, you can estimate the others. It's important to know where the moon is for two reasons. First, the moon is beautiful (particularly in the first and third quarter phases) and makes a wonderful object to view in its own right. Second, and most importantly, when the moon is visible it tends to "wash out" anything else in the night sky. The moon is immensely brighter than any other nighttime object — it "rules" the night. The effect is particularly bad when the moon is near its full phase. The full moon is actually about nine times brighter than the first quarter moon. This effect will not significantly degrade your viewing of the planets, or bright stars. But globular clusters and nebulae are virtually destroyed by bright moonlight. Galaxies that are easy binocular objects under dark skies suddenly

become almost impossible to find when the full moon is out, even with the aid of a good telescope. It is astonishing how severe this effect is.

The moon orbits the Earth in the same direction the

Earth spins — counterclockwise looking down over the Earth's North Pole. However, the moon orbits much slower than the Earth turns — taking 27.5 days to orbit once. So, although the moon orbits from west to east relative to the background stars, it "loses" to the Earth's rotation and thus appears to move from east to west, just like the sun and stars. However, it appears to do this slightly slower than the sun and stars since its true motion through space is west to east. For this reason, the moon rises (on average) about 50 minutes later each day. So if you know when the moon was out last night, you know it will be about 50 minutes later tonight. Stars rise 4 minutes earlier every night, and the moon rises 50 minutes later. Alternatively, keeping time the same, the moon will be farther east (by about 12 degrees) than it was last night at the same time.

Many people are under the impression that the moon

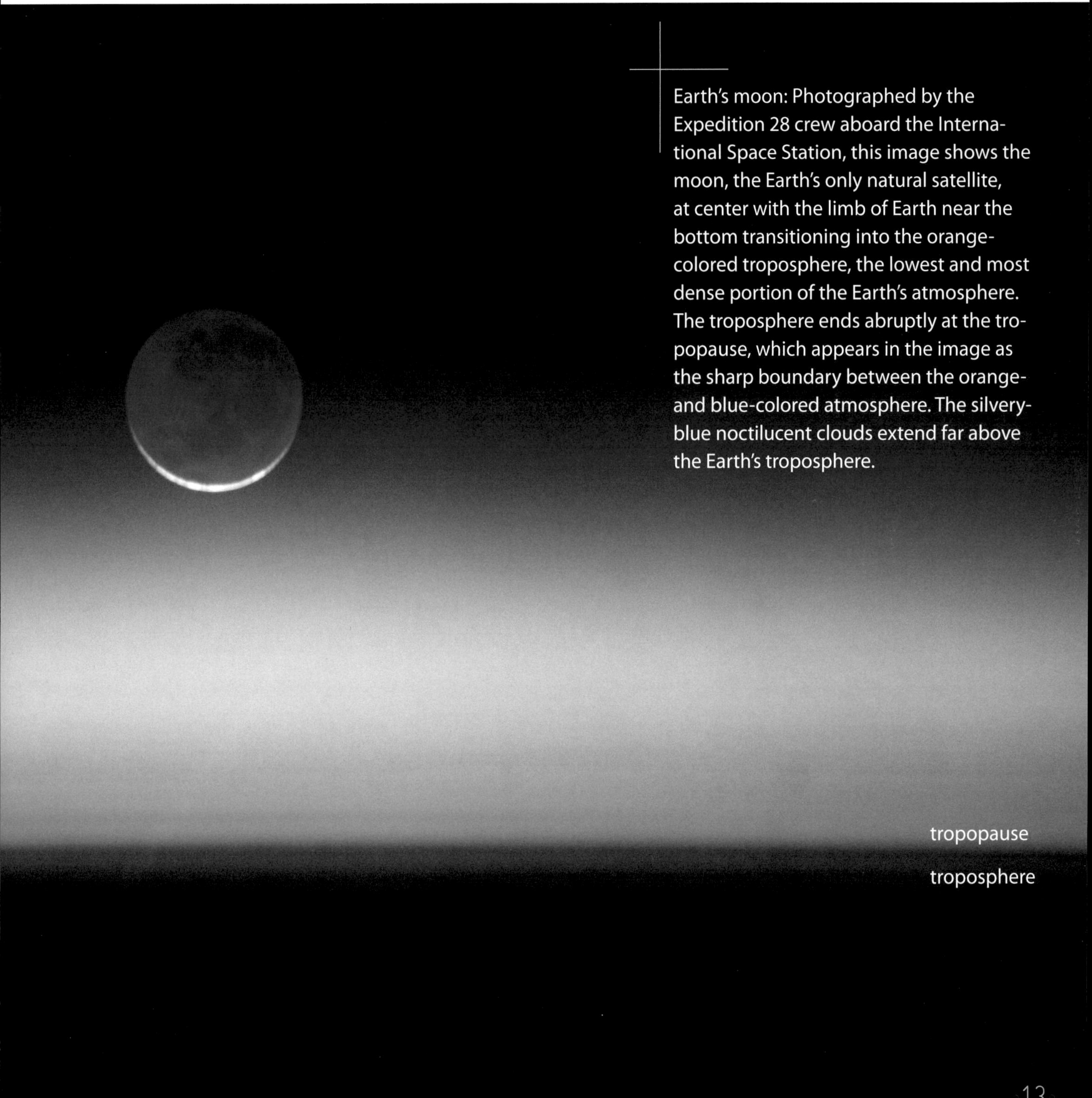

Earth's moon: Photographed by the Expedition 28 crew aboard the International Space Station, this image shows the moon, the Earth's only natural satellite, at center with the limb of Earth near the bottom transitioning into the orange-colored troposphere, the lowest and most dense portion of the Earth's atmosphere. The troposphere ends abruptly at the tropopause, which appears in the image as the sharp boundary between the orange- and blue-colored atmosphere. The silvery-blue noctilucent clouds extend far above the Earth's troposphere.

tropopause

troposphere

does not rotate since we always see the same side of the moon. But the moon does rotate; it simply rotates at the same rate that it revolves around the Earth — that's why we always see the same side. In fact, if the moon did not rotate, we would see the other side of the moon when it was on the other side of the Earth. The fact that the moon rotates at the same rate it revolves is not uncommon. Virtually all large moons do this; they are "tidally locked." Such a condition is very stable; if the moons were not tidally locked to begin with, they would eventually come to such a condition in time anyway. Since the moon rotates, it experiences day and night just like the Earth does. But since the moon rotates slowly, it takes nearly a month to go from one sunrise to the next.

Once when I was speaking at a university, an individual came up to me afterward and suggested that the moon and Earth should really be considered co-orbital planets. He suggested that the moon really shouldn't be considered a moon since the gravitational pull of the sun on the moon is about twice the pull of the Earth on the moon. This is in fact true. Effectively, the moon belongs more to the sun than the Earth as far

as gravity is concerned. In essence, both the Earth and the moon orbit the sun directly; however, the close proximity between the Earth and moon causes each of their orbits to be strongly perturbed by the other body. As far as I know, the Earth's moon is the only "moon" for which this is the case. It is ironic that the only "moon" that isn't truly a moon is called "the moon."

◇Phases of the Moon

As the moon orbits the Earth it goes through phases. A lot of people are under the impression that phases have something to do with Earth's shadow, but this is not so. Phases have to do with the percentage of the day side of the moon we can see from our position. The moon has a day side and a night side, just like the Earth. As the moon orbits the Earth (and rotates accordingly) we see different amounts of illumination from the sun, due to the changing angle of the sunlight. When the moon is closer to the sun than the Earth is (sort of "in between" the Earth and the sun), we see mostly the night side of the moon (the crescent and new phases); when the moon is farther away from the sun than the Earth is, we see mostly the day side

The moon is a great choice for a stargazer to begin

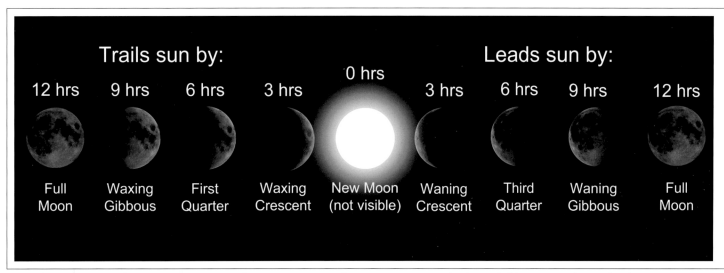

Trails sun by:

12 hrs 9 hrs 6 hrs 3 hrs 0 hrs

Leads sun by:

3 hrs 6 hrs 9 hrs 12 hrs

Full Moon | Waxing Gibbous | First Quarter | Waxing Crescent | New Moon (not visible) | Waning Crescent | Third Quarter | Waning Gibbous | Full Moon

1.5　Lunar Phases and Time: As the moon moves from west to east (right to left), it goes through phases as we see varying fractions of the sun's illumination.

of the moon (the gibbous and full phases). In between these two cases, when the sun is at a 90-degree angle relative to the moon, we see exactly half of the day side, and half of the night side of the moon (1st or 3rd quarter).

Phases are called "waxing" if we are seeing increasing percentages of the day side of the moon as time goes forward day after day; they are called "waning" if we see decreasing portions of the day side. The phases go in this order: new moon, waxing crescent, first quarter, waxing gibbous, full, waning gibbous, third quarter, and waning crescent. The moon is illuminated on its right side when in waxing phases; it is illuminated on the left when in waning phases (as viewed from the Northern Hemisphere of Earth). The practical application is this: if the moon is illuminated on its right side, it will be even brighter and fuller tomorrow night. If it is illuminated on its left side, it will be less illuminated tomorrow night.

It takes 29.3 days for the moon to go through all its phases. Note that this is slightly different than the orbital period of the moon (27.5 days). The difference is exactly analogous to the difference between sidereal and solar days on Earth. The moon takes 27.5 days to come back to its original position as seen by a star, but 29.3 days to come back to its original position as seen by the sun. The difference is because the Earth (and therefore the moon as well) has made a fraction of its orbit around the sun in one month. Since we usually prefer to use solar time, the 29.3 days period is the

more useful figure. This is where we get the idea of a month, and the word month is indeed derived from "moon."

Since it takes about one month for the moon to go through all its phases, it takes roughly one week to go through one-fourth of the cycle. If the moon is "new" today, it will be in first quarter phase in one week, full the week after that, third quarter the week after that, and then back to new the week after that. This is another one of those useful tidbits to keep in mind.

◇Phases and Times

It is very easy to tell roughly when and where the moon will be in the sky once you know its phase. A simple trick is to remember that the first quarter moon follows the sun by 6 hours (that is, it is now where the sun was 6 hours ago). The full moon follows (or leads) the sun by 12 hours — and is always opposite the sun in the sky. The third quarter moon leads the sun by 6 hours (or trails by 18 hours if you prefer). When the moon is new, it is roughly where the sun is; but, of course, you won't see it anyway FIGURE 1.5. Now let's go through some practical examples.

Suppose you want to look for some galaxies around 10:00 p.m. and don't want to be bothered by bright moonlight. If the moon is in "new" phase, that's great because you won't see it at all that night. But third quarter phase, or a waning crescent phase would also work — because the moon won't rise until after midnight. A

(thin) waxing crescent phase would probably also be okay, because the moon will set before 10:00 p.m.

Suppose you do want to look at the moon itself; probably the best phase would be first quarter. Here the moon is half illuminated from our perspective and the craters look the most vivid and beautiful. The first quarter moon would be high in the sky right after sunset and so you could start observing right away. If you are a morning person, then maybe third quarter phase would be your preference. The moon would be high in the sky just before sunrise, and would be beautifully "half" illuminated, though now on the left side instead of the right.

Suppose you remember seeing the moon in its first quarter phase last week, and want to know when it will rise tonight and what it will look like. Since it is one week later, the moon will be in its full phase. It will rise as the sun sets, and will set when the sun rises; so, you will be able to see the moon at any time of the night.

As one last example, let's imagine that it is 9:00 in the morning, and you want to know if the moon is visible.

Your calendar tells you that the moon was full 6 days ago. That means it is in the waning gibbous phase today — almost at 3rd quarter. It is therefore ahead of the sun by a little over 6 hours. So the moon is where the sun will be at around 3:50 p.m.; this is above the horizon in the southwestern sky. So, yes, you can see the moon at this time. Many people don't think to look for the moon in broad daylight, but it really can be seen if you know when (and where) to look.

◇Planets

The motion of planets is more complicated because their apparent motion in the sky is the combination of their true motion around the sun, plus the apparent shift in position due to Earth's motion around the sun. Fortunately, all the planets orbit in approximately the same plane: the ecliptic. For this reason the planets always form a nearly straight line along with the sun and the moon, and move along this line. Since the planets orbit the sun rather slowly (especially the outer planets), their motion is similar to that of the stars, at least for short time intervals (i.e., Saturn rises roughly 4 minutes earlier every evening, just like the stars).

The planets generally move eastward relative to the background stars; however, they occasionally move in the opposite direction. We will see why this is in a later section.

◇Seasons

The Earth's rotation axis is tilted relative to its orbit around the sun by 23.4 degrees. It is this tilt that is responsible for seasons on Earth. We notice two effects as a result of this tilt. In the summer, the sun is high in the sky and remains out for more than 12 hours per day. In the winter, the sun is low in the sky and remains out for less than 12 hours. Only at the equator is the sun out for 12 hours a day regardless of the season.

The height of the sun is directly connected with the amount of time it is visible per day. When the sun is higher in the sky as it is during summer, more than 50 percent of the sun's daily path is above the horizon. The sun is above the celestial equator in the summer. Therefore the sun remains up longer than 12 hours; in fact, it could be up as long as 24 hours for locations near the North Pole. When the sun is out longer, we receive more energy from the sun, and consequently have warmer temperatures. Also, since the sun is higher in the sky in summer, a given section of the ground receives more energy per unit area, and is thus warmer than in winter.

Although the Earth's tilt does not change (at least not significantly over the course of one year), the Earth is orbiting the sun. So, whereas the northern hemisphere is tipped toward the sun in summer, one half-year later it is tipped away from the sun FIGURE 1.6. It's not that the tilt has changed; rather the relative position of the sun has changed. Since the Northern Hemisphere is tilted toward the sun in summer, the Southern Hemisphere would necessarily be tilted away from the sun at this same time. This is why the Southern Hemisphere experiences the opposite season as the Northern Hemisphere for a given date.

It is a common misconception that seasons are caused by the changing distance from the Earth to the sun; many people suppose that we are closer to the sun in summer and farther away in winter. Although the Earth's orbit is slightly elliptical, the effect is fairly small and thus cannot account for seasons. Moreover, the Earth is actually closer to the sun in the (Northern Hemisphere) winter. So the changing Earth-sun distance cannot be responsible for seasons, even though this is very commonly believed.

◇Celestial Coordinate Systems

At this point we've explored how to estimate roughly where the sun, moon, and stars will be for a given time of night and a given time of year. It is now useful to discuss celestial coordinate systems, and some other terms relating to astronomical positions. These will allow us to understand and describe the position of the sun, moon, and stars with greater precision and will enable us to explore the motion of the planets and other celestial bodies as well.

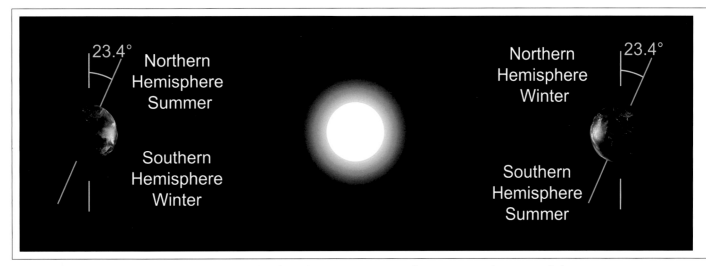

1.6   The seasons are caused by the tilt of Earth's rotation axis relative to its orbit around the sun

Two coordinate systems are widely used in astronomy. The first is based on our local horizon. The second is based on the celestial sphere. The local horizon coordinate system describes the position of an object in the sky with two coordinates: altitude and azimuth. If we wanted to, we could use a third coordinate to specify the distance; however, in most cases we don't need to know the distance. Two coordinates will do. These two coordinates are angular; they measure a separation in angle, not linear distance.

"Altitude" describes how high above the horizon an object is (in angle). A star that is touching the horizon has an altitude of 0°, whereas an object that is directly overhead has an altitude of 90°. An altitude could be negative — this would mean that the object is below the horizon and thus cannot be seen. The altitude of any object must always be between -90° and 90°.

Azimuth describes how far along the horizon an object is to the right of due north. So the North Star has an azimuth of (approximately) 0° because it is due north. A star that is directly east has an azimuth of 90°. A star that is due south has an azimuth of 180°, and a star that is due west has an azimuth of 270°. So, the azimuth of an object is always less than 360° and is always greater than or equal to 0°.

There are two other useful guides based on horizon coordinates. "Zenith" is defined to be the position directly overhead. So the zenith has an altitude of exactly 90°. The "meridian" is the great circle that runs through due north through the zenith, to due south[1] FIGURE 1.7. All stars reach their highest altitude when they cross the meridian, which marks the halfway point of a star's diurnal path.

It so happens that the width of your hand held out at arm's length (with your fingers and thumb together, not spread out) happens to cover about ten degrees of angle. This works for nearly everyone because people that have larger hands usually have longer arms as well. You can test this by holding your hand at arm's length "sideways" so that the side just touches the horizon. Then place your other hand above it — just

touching it, and place the first hand above it and so on, "walking" hand after hand until you reach the spot directly overhead. This should take nine hand widths — which is 90°. The altitude of the North Star is equal to your latitude on Earth. So if you live at latitude 40°, the North Star will be 40° in altitude — about four handwidths above the horizon FIGURE 1.8.

You can also use this method to measure angular separation. You might estimate that Jupiter is 20 degrees to the left of a particular star. This is a quick and easy way to describe to other observers exactly where you are looking.

Likewise, you can estimate the azimuth of an object by lining up hand after hand along the horizon starting from due north (due north is always easy to find because it is always directly below the North Star). Remember that azimuth is measured in angle along the horizon — not at any other altitude. The reason for this is that the angular separation of two different azimuths decreases as the altitude increases. For example, consider two stars on the horizon, one at azimuth 0° (due north), the other at 90° (due east). Their angular separation would be 90°.

However, suppose instead that the two stars are not on the horizon but instead have an altitude of 89° — almost directly overhead. Those two stars would be extremely close together — their angular separation would be less than 2° even though one has an azimuth of 0° and the other has an azimuth of 90°. One lesson to learn here is that you cannot easily (i.e., "in your head") estimate the angular separation of two objects from their azimuths and altitudes (except for some special cases). The branch of mathematics that deals with computing such angular separations is called "spherical trigonometry." It is a useful tool in astronomy, but is beyond the scope of this book.

It is customary in astronomy to use "degrees" to measure large angles. If an angle is smaller than one degree, it is measured in "minutes of arc" or "arcminutes" (or sometimes just "minutes" for short). One

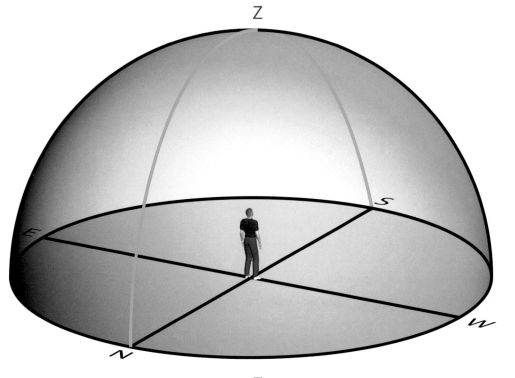

1.7
The meridian (green) passes from due north to the zenith (Z) to due south.

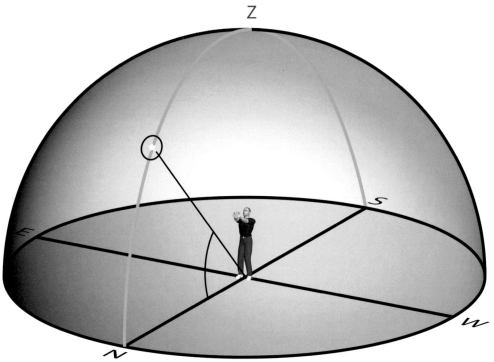

1.8
The altitude of the North Star is equal to the observer's latitude on Earth. This number can be estimated by noting how many hand widths (held at arm's length) it takes to go from the north horizon to the North Star. Each hand width is about 10 degrees.

Quick Method for Stargazing Measurements

1°-1.5°	5°	10°	20°

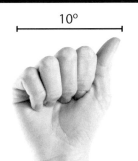
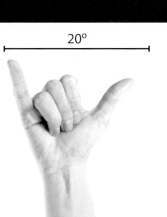

degree is equal to 60 arc-minutes. Furthermore, 1 arc-minute is composed of 60 "seconds of arc" or "arc-seconds." The symbol for 1 arc-minute is a single quotation mark or apostrophe; the symbol for arc-second is a double quotation mark. So 37 degrees, 46 arc-minutes, 56 arc-seconds is written as 37° 46′ 56″. Of course, it's no crime to write an angle as a decimal expression as well. We could write 37° 46′ 56″ as 37.78222°. Even though these two numbers are the same, note that the decimal expression is not .4656. You must divide by 60 to get the expansion. So be careful not to confuse arc-minutes with fractions of a degree. This can be a problem when people do not write down the symbols — especially in computer programs. For example, does 36 06 mean 36.06° or 36°06′? These are different quantities for the same reason that 0.7 hours is not the same as 70 minutes.

Another very useful tidbit is to know that the sun covers one-half of a degree — or 30 arc-minutes. The moon also covers roughly one-half of a degree. So the sun and the moon have approximately the same angular size. Your finger held at arm's length covers a little more than one degree — so it will appear twice as large as the sun or moon. This may seem surprising; psychologically, we "feel" that the sun and moon should be larger than this, but they're not. You will find that you can easily block the moon with your finger at arm's length (with one eye closed).

◇ Equatorial Coordinates

The horizon coordinate system discussed above is very useful for describing the position of a celestial object to other observers who are present. However, it is not useful for describing such positions to observers who are at a remote location. Suppose you are talking on the phone with your friend who lives in a different state, telling him how to find Mars. It's no good giving him an altitude and azimuth, because the object will appear at a different altitude and azimuth for him. Horizon coordinates are based on the local horizon, but different parts of the world have a different horizon. (Though, horizon coordinates may be "close enough" if

the remote observer is within a few hundred miles). Furthermore, as the Earth rotates, the horizon coordinates of a star change. It would be nice if we had a coordinate system where a star's position is relatively permanent.

The Cassiopeia region as imaged in infrared wavelengths.

The "equatorial coordinate system" overcomes these two problems. Equatorial coordinates are the same for everyone on Earth, and they do not change with time; that is, a star's equatorial coordinates remain the same throughout the night, even though its altitude and azimuth change. Otherwise, equatorial coordinates are very similar to horizon coordinates.

Equatorial coordinates are based on the celestial sphere. In particular, they are based on the celestial equator — hence the name. The angular distance of a star above the celestial equator is called its "declination." If the star is below the celestial equator, its declination is negative. Declination is exactly analogous to altitude except it is based on the celestial equator instead of the local horizon. The NCP has a declination of exactly 90°, whereas the SCP has a declination of -90°. The North Star would thus have a declination of almost 90°.

For Northern Hemisphere observers, it is very easy to estimate the declination of an object. Simply use your hands at arm's length (as described above) to measure the angular separation of the object from the North Star, then subtract this number from 90°. Interestingly, at the Earth's North Pole, declination and altitude are the same for all objects; the North Star would be at the zenith — directly above the observer.

Declination is also analogous to latitude. If you are located at latitude 40°, and you know of a star that has a declination of 40°, that star will pass directly overhead when it crosses the meridian. Stars with a declination that is less than your latitude will pass south of zenith when they cross the meridian, and stars with a greater declination will pass north of zenith.

Stars or constellations whose declination is greater than the quantity of 90° minus your latitude will never go below the horizon. These are the "circumpolar" stars and constellations that we mentioned previously. Circumpolar stars or constellation never rise nor set because they never reach the horizon. Rather, they simply revolve counterclockwise around the North Star. Observers in the continental United States can always see the Little Dipper as well as the constellation Cassiopeia on a clear night since these constellations have a high declination. They are close to Polaris, and never set. The downside of this is that stars or constellations with a declination less than your latitude minus 90° can never be seen. For mid-northern latitude observers, this would include the Southern Cross (Crux) and Eta Carina.

For every patch of sky that is circumpolar, there is an equal and opposite patch of sky that can never be seen from the same latitude. At the North Pole, or South Pole, all the visible stars and constellations are circumpolar, but half of the sky is forever hidden. At the equa-

tor, all of the sky can be seen (throughout the course of a day), but no constellations are circumpolar.

Right ascension (RA) is the other equatorial coordinate. This coordinate describes how far along the celestial equator an object is. So it is analogous to azimuth; but there are some differences. The first difference is that (unlike all other celestial coordinates) RA is measured in hours — not degrees. A complete circle in RA would consist of 24 "hours" rather than 360°. These are "hours" of angle not of time. I know it's confusing. I wouldn't have set it up that way; but that's just the convention. (And despite the confusion, there really are some good reasons for it.)

A second difference is the starting point. Whereas the starting point (0°) for azimuth is due north, the starting point (0h) for right ascension is the position of the sun at the vernal equinox. Unfortunately, this is a bit hard to picture. I find that RA is the most difficult coordinate to estimate by eye for this reason. It may help to know that the zero point is below the great square of Pegasus.

A third difference is that RA increases as you go left (to the east), whereas azimuth increases to the right. So if star A is to the left of star B, then star A has the greater RA (unless we passed 24h along the way). A fourth difference is that the RA coordinate moves with the stars — not the Earth. Think of the equatorial coordinate system as being "attached" to the celestial sphere as the Earth rotates inside it. So as a star rises, passes the meridian, and sets, its RA remains constant. Therefore, which RA coordinates can be seen depends on the time of day and the time of year **FIGURE 1.9**.

Suppose that it is the vernal equinox; this means the sun has an RA of exactly 0h. Also, suppose that we see the moon rise three hours after the sun does. Then the moon would have an RA of 3h. So now we can see why the RA coordinate is measured in hours, and why it increases as you go left.

You can roughly estimate the RA of an object by measuring its angular distance along the Celestial Equator (going to the left) from Pegasus (zero hours) — (or another object for which you already know the RA), and then divide the angle by 15 to convert to hours (since 360°/15 = 24 hr). This is similar to measuring the azimuth by estimating the angle along the horizon, but it's a bit harder because the celestial equator is not visible as the horizon is, and also because the starting

point isn't as obvious (as due north is). You will probably never have to estimate RA and Dec by eye to find an object; there are several other ways in which they are useful.

◇Using RA and Dec Coordinates

Often, astronomical publications such as *Sky & Telescope* magazine will give the equatorial coordinates of an object of interest, such as a newly discovered comet. There are several ways in which you could use the listed RA and Dec coordinates to find the object. First, if the object is fairly bright, you may not need to know its position very precisely. In this case, you could simply estimate the position in the sky by eye — finding the declination by the distance from the North Star, and the RA by the distance to the left of Pegasus as previously discussed.

Alternatively, many computer programs can display the RA and Dec as a grid, or as labels for various objects. You could use such a program, or any map of the

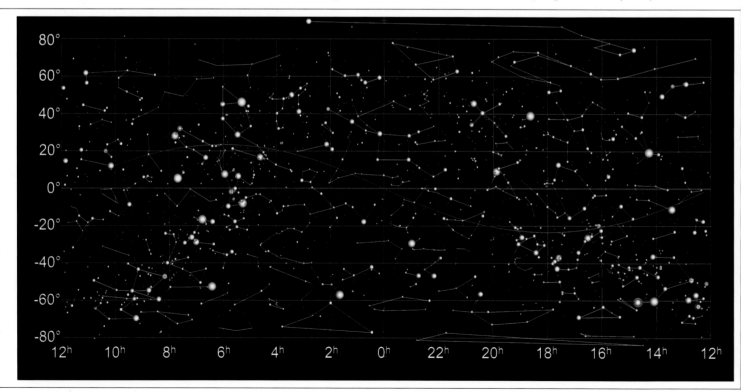

1.9   The equatorial coordinate system. The vertical axis shows the declination; the horizontal axis shows the right ascension.

night sky that shows equatorial coordinates, to locate your object. You can use FIGURE 1.9 in this way. You may find, for example, that the coordinates point you to a spot 2 degrees above Orion's central Belt star (Alnilam). You'll know exactly where to look.

Some telescopes have "setting circles." Once calibrated on an object whose RA and Dec you know, you can use these circles to find any other RA or Dec. This method requires that the telescope is properly aligned with the NCP. Moreover, this method does require a bit of practice, and a bit of patience. Note that some setting circles use "hour-angle" instead of RA. This coordinate is related to RA by the sidereal time. This isn't used very often these days and so it won't be discussed further here.

Additionally, many telescopes now have built-in computer controls which (once calibrated) will automatically point to the correct RA and Dec. This is probably the most useful purpose you will have for equatorial coordinates. Simply punch in these numbers and the telescope will move to the correct location. One disadvantage of this method is that you do not get a "feel" for where the object is actually found in the heavens when the telescope does all the work for you. So it can be a little "too easy." Also, most telescopes I've used do not calibrate perfectly. They'll get you close to the object, but it's best if you have a pretty good idea where the object is anyway.

◇ Experience: Both Real and Virtual

The best way to get a feel for motions in the sky is to get outside and watch. Whenever you are outside, take a moment to look up and note the position of celestial objects. Even before you get into your car on the way to work, take the time to notice the position of the sun, and think about whether or not the moon is above the horizon. If it is, try to see it. It is really amazing what you can see when you take just a moment to look.

Another great way to get a feel for stellar motions is with the virtual experience provided by computer software. There are a number of fantastic planetarium-style programs — many of them free. Try one of these programs and watch what happens when you speed up time. Try watching the diurnal pattern of the stars over the course of a night. Or try skipping ahead from one day to the next to notice how the stars and moon change positions from night to night. It's like traveling through time, and it will quickly give you a feel for how the night sky works.

Another useful tool is a planisphere, also called a "star wheel." At the writing of this book, the best planisphere available is called a "Miller Plansphere" and should cost less than $10. Some (like the Miller version) are made of plastic, others of paper. These star wheels make use of the fact that the stars appear to rotate once around the Earth each night, and also make one complete rotation each year (by virtue of rising four minutes earlier each night). By lining up the date with the time on the planisphere, you can see what the stars will look like at any given date and time. It won't do planets or the moon, since their motion is more complex. But the planisphere is a great instrument to quickly find out which constellations will be visible at a given time on a given date.

◇ A Review of Celestial Motions

The above sections are all you really need to know about motions in the sky to find anything you want to find. By noting the time, you can estimate in your head where the sun is. By looking at a calendar you can check the phase of the moon and estimate when it will rise and set. By looking up the coordinates of an object, or finding it on a star chart, you can estimate very roughly when it will rise and set. A computer program or an astronomy magazine such as *Sky & Telescope* can give you the current location of the planets, or any bright comets. You could at this point skip to another chapter to learn about what interesting things to find, and how specifically to find them.

But if you would like to learn a bit more detail about estimating when and where things will rise and set, read on. You may have noticed for example, that the sun does not always rise exactly at the same time, or in the same location. Sometimes the full moon is high in the sky, and other times it is lower. These issues are also something that you can learn to estimate "in your head" without the use of a computer or calculator. The next chapter is designed to clarify and reinforce the information we've already discussed, and enhance the precision of our estimations of celestial motions.

Chapter 2

Motions in the Sky—Advanced

Let's review what we have covered previously, and refine our estimations. We begin with diurnal motion. Stars rise in the east and set in the west, or revolve counter-clockwise around the north celestial pole (NCP) (or clockwise around the south celestial pole [SCP] for the Southern Hemisphere) due to Earth's rotation. Stars always reach their highest point when they cross the meridian. A star is said to "transit" when it crosses the meridian. The word "transit" also has other uses in astronomy, which we will cover later. But context always makes it clear which definition to use.

The exact path a star takes depends on its declination and the observer's latitude. For mid-northern latitudes, if a star has a declination of zero (it would be on the celestial equator), it will rise directly east (azimuth = 90°), reach the meridian (about 6 hours later) somewhat south of zenith, and set due west (azimuth = 270°). It will be above the horizon for about 12 hours (or to be precise, 11 hours 58 minutes, since stars rise 4 minutes earlier every day).

◇Solar Motion and Seasons Revisited

The sun's declination is zero on the vernal equinox (March 21) or autumnal equinox (September 21) — so the sun is above the horizon for exactly 12 hours. Every place on Earth gets 12 hours of sunlight, and 12 hours

of darkness on the equinox.[1] (That's where the word "equinox" gets its name — it means "equal night.") In spring and summer, the sun's declination is higher than 0°, whereas in autumn and winter, the sun's declination is less than 0°. This is because the Earth orbits the sun, and is tipped on its axis. The sun reaches its highest declination of 23.4° on the summer solstice (June 21) — the longest day of the year (Northern Hemisphere). This number (23.4°) is the tilt of Earth's axis relative to the sun, so it makes sense that this is the farthest the sun could be from the celestial equator. The sun reaches its lowest declination (-23.4°) on the winter solstice (Dec 21) — the shortest day of the year.

If we took a picture of the sun every day at the exact same time of day starting in January, we would notice the sun climbing higher and higher until it came to a stop on June 21 — the summer solstice. (Solstice means "sun stop.") The sun would then sink lower every day until the winter solstice, at which point it would begin climbing again. Another way to see why this happens is to plot the ecliptic relative to the celestial equator. The ecliptic appears as a sine wave on such a graph FIGURE 2.1. The sun moves leftward along the ecliptic over the course of one year. Recall that the celestial equator is aligned with Earth's equator, whereas the ecliptic is aligned with Earth's orbit. Since Earth's

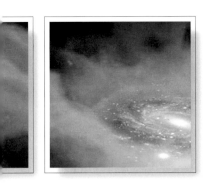

equator is tipped relative to Earth's orbit by 23.4°, the celestial equator is tipped relative to the ecliptic by 23.4°.

Since the sun reaches a maximum declination of 23.4°, anyone located at a latitude higher than 23.4° can never see the sun directly overhead; it will always pass south of zenith. This latitude is called the Tropic of Cancer. Likewise, anyone living below a latitude of -23.4° (the Tropic of Capricorn) can never see the sun directly overhead. Someone observing from the Tropic of Cancer would see the sun directly overhead at noon on the summer solstice.

Another latitude of interest is 66.6° (which is 90° minus 23.4°); this is called the Arctic Circle. Anyone observing from this latitude will experience 24 hours of sunlight on the summer solstice. The sun would never go below the horizon on this day; it would just touch the northern horizon at midnight. Conversely, on the winter solstice, the sun would never rise; it remains below the horizon — just touching the southern horizon at noon. Likewise the Antarctic Circle (at latitude -66.6°) experiences a similar effect in the opposite time of year.

◇ Sunset and Sunrise

On the day of the spring or autumn equinox, the sun will rise due east and set due west for any location on Earth. If we neglect atmospheric refraction, the effects of time zones, daylight-saving, and the solar analemma

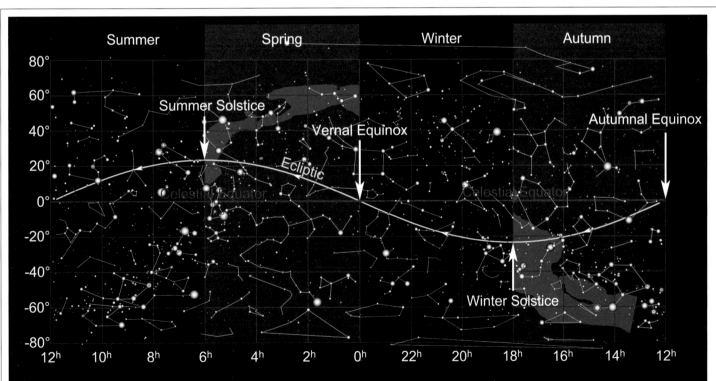

2.1   The celestial sphere. The celestial equator is shown in red, and the ecliptic is shown in yellow. The sun appears to move leftward along the ecliptic relative to the background stars, taking one year to make a complete loop. The location of the sun at the equinoxes and solstices is indicated. These times mark the boundaries of the seasons.

(all of which we will cover later), the sun will rise at 6 a.m. on the equinox, and set at 6 p.m., regardless of the latitude of the observer (except on the North or South Poles where the sun skims along the horizon).

For the Northern Hemisphere seasons of autumn and winter, the sun will rise *south* of east *after* 6 a.m., and will set *south* of west *before* 6 p.m. for any latitude on Earth (neglecting the aforementioned technicalities). Once again, the poles are exceptions to this since the sun does not rise or set there. The equator is a partial exception: the sun does rise south of east and sets south of west just like any other latitude, but the sunrise and sunset times are unaffected at the equator. But aside from these exceptions, the Northern Hemisphere experiences later sunrises and earlier sunsets in the fall

and winter. Therefore, the Northern Hemisphere has shorter days in these two seasons than in the summer and spring. How much shorter the days are depends on the date and latitude; as we go farther north or as we approach the winter solstice, the days get shorter and shorter. Moreover, since the sun is shifted toward the south, it appears lower in the sky in winter and fall than in summer and spring.

For the Northern Hemisphere spring and summer the sun rises *north* of east *before* 6 a.m., and sets *north* of west *after* 6 p.m. Since the sun sweeps a larger path in the sky (more than 180 degrees), the days are longer than 12 hours. As before, the Arctic Circle is an exception, only because the sun may not set at all when close to the solstice. Days are longer in spring and

Omega
Centauri
NGC 5139
Hubble
Space
Telescope

The moon as viewed from space

summer; the severity of the effect increases as you go farther north, and as you get closer to the date of the summer solstice. The above times should be considered approximations; but the trends are very noticeable. Extremely high latitudes experience extreme variations in day length, whereas latitudes close to the equator do not.

◇Lunar Motions Revisited

The moon orbits roughly in the ecliptic — not the celestial equator. (Recall, the ecliptic is the path of the Earth around the sun, and the apparent path the sun traces out relative to the background stars.) This makes the moon rather unique; essentially all other large moons of the solar system (and many of the smaller ones as well) orbit in their planet's celestial equator — not the ecliptic. (There is only one other large moon that breaks the rule: Triton, which orbits neither in the ecliptic nor celestial equator of its planet.) Since the moon orbits in the ecliptic, we can now estimate not only when it will rise and set, but where. We can also more accurately predict moonrise and moonset times.

Probably the best way to grasp this principle is to plot the ecliptic relative to the celestial equator as in **FIGURE 2.1**. Since the moon orbits the Earth from west to east (right to left as seen in the northern hemisphere) it

moves along the ecliptic the same way the sun appears to move, but 13 times faster.[2] So in the same way that we can think of a full moon as trailing the sun by 12 hours, we can also think of it as trailing the sun by 6 months — half a year. Therefore, since the sun is high in the sky (at the highest points of the ecliptic) during early summer, the full moon will be low in the sky (at the lowest points of the ecliptic). The summer full moon will rise later than 6 p.m., set earlier than 6 a.m., rise south of east, and set south of west. In other words, it will behave exactly as the sun does in the *winter* (minus 12 hours).

Conversely, the full moon in winter will be very high in the sky (as the sun is in summer). It will rise north of east and set north of west and will be out for more than 12 hours — just like the summer sun. The full moon is the second-easiest case because it acts just the opposite of the sun. The easiest case would be new moon, which behaves exactly as the sun does, rising and setting at the same time and in roughly the same place. But of course you will never see a new moon (except as an eclipse shadow).

The other phases of the moon require just a bit more thought. Consider the first quarter moon. It "trails" the sun by 6 hours (in terms of transit time), as in **FIGURE 1.5**. But in terms of its position on the ecliptic, it "leads" the sun by three months FIGURE 2.1. That is, in three months the sun will be in the spot on the ecliptic where the first quarter moon is today. So when will the first quarter moon make its highest arc in the sky? The answer is: on the spring equinox. This is because the sun makes its highest arc in the sky on the summer solstice, and the spring equinox occurs three months earlier. So the first quarter moon will rise earlier and set later than other times of the year and will be farther north than usual when the date is around the spring equinox. Conversely, the first quarter moon will rise later and set earlier (and will swing farther south) when the date is near the autumnal equinox. Using these principles, you can refine your mental estimate of when and where the moon will rise and set.

◇Eclipses

For the purposes of estimating the approximate time and position of moonrise and moonset, it is fine to think of the moon as being exactly on the ecliptic. But to be more precise, the moon's orbit is tilted just slightly – about 5° relative to the ecliptic. That's not much, but it makes a huge difference when it comes to eclipses. An eclipse is when the shadow of one object falls upon another. For our purposes here, there are two types of eclipses. A solar eclipse happens when the moon's shadow falls upon the Earth (i.e., the moon "blocks out" the sun). A lunar eclipse occurs when the Earth's shadow falls upon the moon, causing the moon to appear dark, and often a bit reddish.

If the moon orbited exactly in the ecliptic, there would be two eclipses every month: one solar, one lunar. At new moon, the moon would be positioned exactly between the sun and Earth, thereby blocking the sun for a short time. Two weeks later, when the moon reached its full phase, it would be exactly opposite the sun; thus the Earth would be directly between the sun and the moon and would cast its shadow on the moon. But since the moon's orbit is tilted slightly relative to the ecliptic, it often slips "just above" or "just below" the sun at new moon. And likewise, the full moon often slips just above or just below Earth's shadow. Remember, the sun and moon cover only 1/2° in angle, so a 5° tilt in the moon's orbit relative to the ecliptic means that the new moon can "miss" the sun by as much as ten diameters as it passes by. Given this information,

Edge of the moon

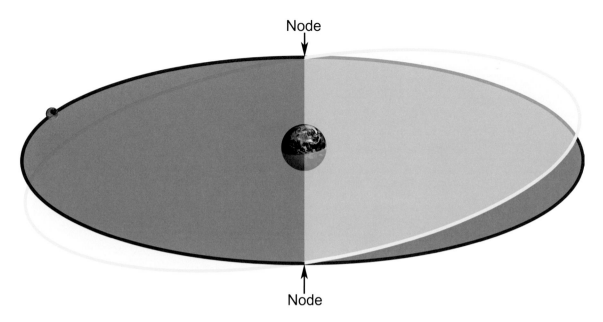

Node

Node

2.2   The ecliptic – the plane of Earth's orbit around the sun – is shown in yellow. The plane of the moon's orbit around the Earth is shown in blue. Solar and lunar eclipses are only possible when the sun and moon simultaneously cross the nodes – the location where the two planes intersect.

it may seem surprising at first that eclipses ever occur. But we can see that they do once we consider the apparent movement of the sun along the ecliptic.

If we plot the moon's orbit relative to the ecliptic **FIGURE 2.2** it will intersect at two points (just as the ecliptic intersects the celestial equator at the vernal and autumnal equinoxes). These two points of intersection are called "nodes." In fact, the term "node" is the generic term for the two points of intersection on any two great circles, but here we will limit it to the points of intersection between the moon's orbit and the ecliptic. As the moon orbits, it will eventually cross one of those nodes; then two weeks later it will cross the other one. Likewise, the sun completes its apparent orbit along the ecliptic once every year. Therefore, it too will cross one of those nodes at some point, and will cross the other one six months later. If the sun and moon happen to cross these nodes at the same time, an eclipse occurs. If they cross the *same* node at the same time, a solar eclipse occurs. If they cross *opposite* nodes at the same time, a lunar eclipse occurs.

Unfortunately, this is one of those things that cannot be easily estimated "in your head." The timing and positioning for an eclipse to occur is quite precise, whereas the methods we've discussed in this chapter are only approximate. So you'll need a computer program to

compute eclipse dates and times; alternatively, a good astronomy magazine often lists the upcoming dates. We will list a few of the better upcoming eclipses in the chapter on celestial events. Since the sun crosses the nodes twice per year, there are only two times of the year when eclipses are possible; and they are separated by six months.

◇ Precession of Lunar Nodes

You could of course just memorize the dates when the sun crosses the nodes of the moon's orbit, and at least estimate the two annual seasons when an eclipse *might* occur. For example, suppose the sun crosses a lunar node on August 7. You could then find if the moon will be new or full within a few days of that date, and then predict a solar or lunar eclipse respectively. This does work, but there is an added complication; the lunar nodes move. This means that the moon's orbit around the Earth does not remain in exactly the same plane. Although it is always tilted about 5° relative to the ecliptic, the *direction* in which it is tilted slowly changes over the course of 18.6 years. So the nodes (the points of intersection between the moon's orbit and the ecliptic) gradually move westward along the ecliptic. This motion is called "precession." Due to precession, the sun does not cross the nodes on the same date every year; the date changes. This is one reason why it is so challenging to predict the exact timing of eclipses without the use of a computer.

After 18.6 years, the nodes have made a complete revolution around the ecliptic and return to their original location. Combining this period with the period of the moon around the Earth relative to the sun, and other factors beyond the scope of this book, we find that eclipses have a tendency to repeat themselves on an 18.031-year cycle — the Saros cycle. That is, the configuration of the sun, moon, and Earth is about the same every 18.031 years. So if an eclipse occurs on a particular date, a very similar eclipse is likely to occur 18.031 years later. The cycle is not exact, because the orbital period of the moon is not an integral fraction of the cycle of the nodes. Nonetheless, you may find that eclipses do come in a (very approximate) 18-year pattern.

◇Lunar Eclipses

The lunar eclipse can only occur when the moon is in its full phase, and when it lies precisely on the node of intersection between its orbit and the ecliptic. During a lunar eclipse, the Earth's shadow falls on the moon, completely blocking all direct sunlight and causing the moon to grow dark. Everyone on the night side of Earth can see a lunar eclipse when it happens (barring clouds). So if a lunar eclipse happens any time after sunset and before sunrise for your time zone (which is the case for about half of lunar eclipses), you will be able to see it so long as the weather cooperates.

Since the sun is essentially the only light source for the moon during its full phase (the stars and planets contribute essentially nothing), it may be surprising that the moon can be seen at all when eclipsed.

Sequence capturing a total lunar eclipse

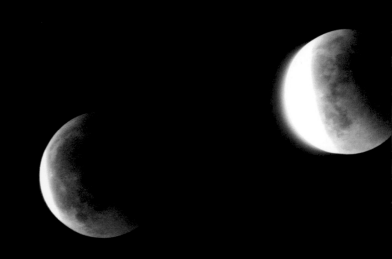

However, the Earth's atmosphere refracts ("bends") a small fraction of sunlight around the planet, which gives the moon a small amount of illumination. Interestingly, the amount of sunlight refracted around the Earth changes quite drastically from year to year, and is not always completely predictable. When the Earth has more particulate matter in its atmosphere (say after the eruption of a powerful volcano), it is often the case that very little sunlight is refracted, and the moon tends to be very dark during eclipse. When the Earth's atmosphere is relatively free of particulates, it usually refracts quite a bit more sunlight (especially at the red end of the spectrum), and the eclipsed moon can appear fairly bright orange, or reddish.

An interesting aspect of lunar eclipses is that you can actually see the moon orbiting over the course of the eclipse. Since the moon orbits from west to east, you can watch it enter Earth's shadow from the right (west) side, slowly move into full shadow, and then exit out the left side. The process lasts a few hours. It is intrigu-

ing to see such drastic changes in the moon's appearance in so short a time.

It must also be noted that the Earth (as well as the moon and everything else) actually has *two* shadows. It has a darker inner shadow called the "umbra" and a lighter outer shadow called the "penumbra." You can illustrate this with your hand using sunlight, or a sufficiently large artificial light source. The shadow of your hand on the ground or a wall is not completely sharp; it has an inner darker region, and an outer lighter region. The same phenomenon can be seen during a lunar eclipse. As the moon moves into Earth's shadow, before it is totally eclipsed, you will notice a fainter outer shadow (the penumbra) surrounding the central dark umbra.

The umbra represents the region where sunlight is blocked completely (aside from the trace amount that is refracted by the atmosphere). So a person standing on the moon during an eclipse could not see the sun at all if standing in the umbra. The penumbra is

Total solar eclipse
in March 29, 2006
in Cappadocia,
Turkey

the region where only part of the sun is blocked. So a person standing on the moon in the penumbra would see part of the sun (say, the left portion) with the rest (the right portion) being blocked by the Earth. Since the Earth's umbra is much larger than the moon, during a total lunar eclipse the moon will fit entirely in Earth's umbra and will be quite dark.

Lunar eclipses were used as one of the earliest scientific lines of evidence that the Earth is round. The ancient astronomers knew enough about motions in the sky to understand that the Earth is between the sun and moon during a lunar eclipse. They could also see that the Earth's shadow on the moon is always a circle. Therefore, the Earth is a sphere. (The notion that Christopher Columbus was the first to postulate that the Earth is round and that his journey was designed to prove it is nothing but a myth.)

◇Solar Eclipses

Solar eclipses are actually a bit *more* common than lunar eclipses, yet paradoxically you are far *less* likely to ever see one. The reason is that whereas lunar eclipses are visible to everyone on the night side of Earth (statistically about 50 percent of Earth's population) a total solar eclipse is only visible to the small fraction of people that are directly beneath it. So a person in Arizona may experience a total solar eclipse while a person in Maine does not. The reason is this: the moon's shadow on the Earth (the umbra) is only about 93 miles across. So only people within a 93-mile diameter will experience total blockage of the sun (though people outside this radius may experience a partial eclipse; i.e., they are in the moon's penumbra). As the Earth rotates and as the moon orbits the Earth, this 93-mile umbra will move across the surface of the Earth, creating a 93-mile-wide path. Only people within this path will experience a total solar eclipse. The maximum time that a total solar eclipse can last is 7 minutes 31 seconds.

During a total solar eclipse, the bright surface of the sun (the photosphere) is completely blocked by the moon, revealing the outer, fainter regions of the sun. The chromosphere (a colorful region extending just beyond the photosphere) becomes visible. The solar corona also becomes visible — the corona is fainter

Partial solar eclipse during sunrise January 4, 2011 in Catalonia

but extends much farther into space than the chromosphere. These regions of the sun are always present, but can only be seen (by eye) during a total solar eclipse.

Statistically, any given spot on the Earth experiences a total solar eclipse once every 400 years or so. So if you wait for a solar eclipse to come to your area, you may have a very long wait indeed! Bottom line: if you want to see a total solar eclipse, most likely, you will have to travel to one. On the other hand, if you are satisfied with seeing a partial solar eclipse, you may not have to go anywhere. The moon's penumbra is much larger than the umbra, and can extend over an entire continent; so partial solar eclipses are fairly common.

◇Annular Eclipses

The moon's orbital path around the Earth is not a perfect circle, but a slight ellipse with the Earth at one focus.[3] The moon is therefore sometimes closer to Earth, whereas other times it is farther away. When the moon is closer to the Earth, it appears slightly larger than the sun. This leads to long-lived solar eclipses — up to 7.5 minutes maximum. However, when the moon is farther from the Earth, it appears slightly smaller than the sun. Even when it passes directly in front of the sun from our vantage point, it is not able to block it completely, but leaves a thin "ring" — or "annulus." This is an annular eclipse. During an annular eclipse, the moon's umbra does not reach the surface of the Earth; it stops short.

◇Libration

Observing the moon through binoculars or a small telescope is a very enjoyable endeavor, and a great way to begin observational astronomy because it is very easy to pick up (see chapter 8). Beginners will very

quickly learn to identify the various maria and bright craters, and will enjoy watching the moon go through its phases. Since the moon orbits at the same rate it revolves around the Earth, we always see the same side of the moon, which makes it easier to learn the features. But experienced observers will notice that we don't always see exactly the same side. The moon seems to "wobble" a bit from week to week, exposing regions that were not visible on the previous week. So although only 50 percent of the moon's surface is visible at any one time, by watching the moon over the course of time, you can actually see up to 59 percent of its surface, due to this wobbling motion.

This wobbling effect is called "libration." Recall that the moon's orbit is not exactly circular, but is in fact slightly elliptical. When the moon swings closer to the Earth, it speeds up in its orbital motion. When the moon is farther from Earth, it slows down. However, the rotational spin of the moon remains constant. Therefore, although the average spin of the moon on its axis matches its orbital period around the Earth, there are times when the moon is orbiting a bit faster than its

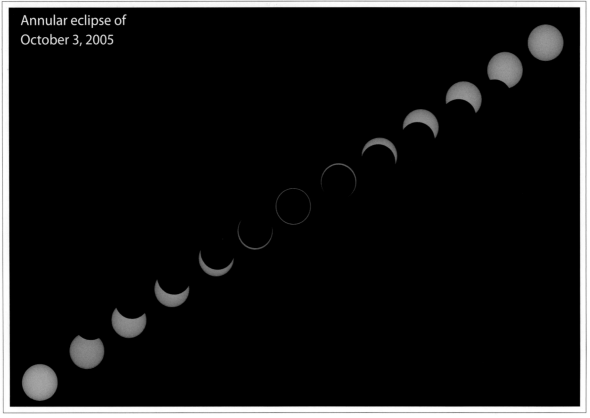

Annular eclipse of
October 3, 2005

Solar System: not to scale.

rotation, and other times when it is orbiting slower. This causes the apparent wobble left and right over the course of one month. One of the easiest ways to see this effect is to note the position of Mare Crisium. This lunar feature is sometimes very near the left limb of the moon, and other times it appears farther in. The change is due to libration. This is one of the easiest effects of libration for beginning observers to see (see chapter 8 for more details and for illustrations of libration).

There is also a north-south type of libration. This is due to the fact that the moon's orbital plane does not exactly match its rotation axis. So sometimes the moon is slightly "below" its rotation axis as it orbits the Earth and we can see a bit more of its North Pole. At other times, the moon is slightly above its rotation plane, and we can see a bit more of its South Pole. This causes a slight up-down wobble, not quite as noticeable as the left-right libration.

◇Motion of the Planets

The motion of the planets can seem rather complicated to the beginner. The apparent path of each planet appears complex because we are on a planet orbiting the sun, watching other planets orbiting the sun. However, if we were to observe the planets from a fixed location far above the solar system, their motion would be straightforward. Planets orbit the sun in slightly elliptical paths with the sun at one focus of the ellipse.

For most planets, the ellipse is very nearly a circle, and the human eye cannot distinguish the difference. Only the orbits of Mercury and Mars are noticeably elliptical to the eye. So, for our purposes here, we will consider the orbits to be circles.

◇The Superior Planets

Let's first consider the motion of the superior planets; these are planets that orbit farther from the sun than Earth does. The superior planets are Mars, Jupiter, Saturn, Uranus, and Neptune. Since these planets orbit the sun slower than Earth does the Earth occasionally passes them as it orbits the sun. When such a configuration occurs, the outer planet and the sun will be in opposite directions as seen from Earth. So the superior planet is said to be in "opposition." Opposition is the best time to observe the superior planet for three reasons. First and foremost, the planet is as close to the Earth as it can get at opposition. It will appear larger, brighter, and more distinct in a telescope. This is particularly evident for Mars. Second, since the planet is opposite the sun, it rises at sunset, and sets at sunrise, and is therefore out all night. Third, the planet will cross the meridian at midnight. So it is very high in the sky at the time when the sky is the darkest.

Since the Earth is in the process of passing a superior planet at opposition, the outer planet will seem to move backward in the sky for several weeks from our

Mars

Jupiter

Saturn

Uranus

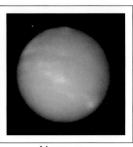
Neptune

perspective. So while planets normally move from west to east relative to the background stars (which is their true motion through space), during the weeks surrounding opposition, they will move from east to west relative to the background stars. This is called "retrograde motion." It is most obvious for the planet Mars, but can be seen in all the superior planets during opposition.

Another configuration of interest is called "conjunction." This is when a planet is "behind" the sun; that is, the superior planet and Earth are on opposite sides of the sun. When a planet is in conjunction, it cannot be seen. The planet need not be *directly* behind the sun to be in conjunction; its orbital path may cause it to pass just above or just below the sun. However, it still cannot be seen because it is lost in the sun's glare. A conjunction simply means the planet is as close in angle to the sun as it can be. In general, the word conjunction simply means a "meeting" of two celestial objects. We might say, "Mars is in conjunction with the star Regulus," meaning that Mars is passing very close to Regulus. However, when the word "conjunction" is used with only one object, it is presumed that the other object is the sun. So if your astronomy magazine indicates that "Mars is in conjunction this month," you will not be able to see that planet.

All the planets orbit the sun in the same direction: counterclockwise as seen from above the Earth's North Pole. Planets that are closer to the sun orbit it faster than those that are farther away. Since the Earth takes one year to orbit the sun, planets that are closer to the sun take less than one year to orbit, whereas those that are farther from the sun take more than one year. The

planets Uranus and Neptune, being the most distant planets, are the slowest of all. Their motion is essentially star-like. It takes several years for these planets to move from one constellation to the next. If Neptune crosses the meridian at midnight on a particular date, then the following year it will be only slightly to the east of the meridian on that same date. If we wait a few more days, then it will once again cross the meridian at midnight.

Recall from the previous chapter that the stars rise four minutes earlier every evening. So in one year they rise 24 hours earlier, making a complete circuit. The superior planets do the same thing except it takes them a bit more than a year to complete the circuit since they orbit in the same direction as the Earth. This is called the synodic period of a planet. For the purpose of observing planets, the synodic period is more useful to know than the planet's actual period around the sun. The synodic period tells you what time of year the planet will be in a good viewing position based on when it was in such a position in the previous year. The planets Uranus and Neptune have a synodic period just over one year. So if they're easily visible in September of one year, then they will also be easily visible in September of the following year. They will undergo opposition perhaps only a few days later than they did the previous year.

Saturn has a synodic period of about one year and two weeks. So whatever its date of opposition was last year, just add two weeks to get the opposition date for this year. Jupiter has a synodic period of about one year and one month. So if it is in opposition in July of one year, it will be in opposition in August of the following year.

Jupiter's opposition date is perhaps the easiest to remember of all the planets; just add one month each year.

Mars is the strangest of all the superior planets, because it has a synodic period of 2.1 years. While all other superior planets can be seen clearly once per year, you have to wait two years for a good view of Mars. Moreover, the apparent size of Mars changes much more drastically than any of the outer planets. Mars is small, and so normally appears rather unremarkable in a small telescope — a small red disk. But since Earth comes very close to Mars during opposition, Mars appears spectacular for a couple months every 2.1 years.

◇ The Inferior Planets

Mercury and Venus are the two inferior planets — those planets whose orbits lie closer to the sun than Earth does. Since they orbit closer than the Earth does, they orbit faster than the Earth does. In fact, I find this makes it rather difficult to keep track of where Venus and Mercury currently are, particularly Mercury, which is usually lost in the sun's glare.

Whereas the outer planets are best seen at opposition,

the inner planets can never be at opposition. Recall that "opposition" means the Earth is in between the planet and sun, which never occurs for inferior plants. Inferior planets are best seen in the configuration called "greatest elongation." This configuration denotes the greatest possible angular separation between the sun and planet as seen in our sky. Mercury and Venus are never far from the sun in angle. The best time to look for these planets is just after sunset or just before sunrise around the date of their greatest elongation. Eastern elongation means the planet is as far east from the sun as it can be, and the planet is best seen (in the *western* sky) after sunset. Conversely, western elongation means the planet is as far west from the sun as it can be, and the planet is best seen (in the *eastern* sky) just before sunrise.

Venus can often be seen several months before or after greatest elongation. Since it is farther from the sun than Mercury, its angular separation from the sun in our sky can be quite large. It's hard to miss Venus; it is brighter than any nighttime star. Venus can even be observed during the day with binoculars — or even the naked eye if you know exactly where to look. However, Mercury is never far from the sun's glare and is rather tricky to spot. Mercury is only visible within a

While cruising around Saturn in early October 2004, NASA's Cassini Mission captured a series of images that have been composed into the largest, most detailed, global natural color view of Saturn and its rings ever made. The images were taken over the course of two hours on Oct. 6, 2004, while Cassini was approximately 6.3 million kilometers (3.9 million miles) from Saturn.

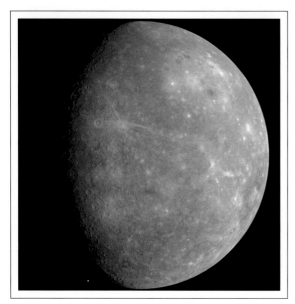

Mercury

Venus (Color coded to show elevation)

week or two of greatest elongation, and is always very close to the horizon at twilight.

Some elongations are better than others. Since planets always lie along the ecliptic, and since the angle the ecliptic makes with the horizon changes with seasons, the planet will be higher above the horizon when the ecliptic lies at a steep angle. This is called a "favorable elongation." The favorable eastern elongation occurs in early spring, whereas a favorable western elongation occurs in early autumn.

Like the superior planets, Mercury and Venus are in conjunction with the sun when they are lined up with the sun. However, the inferior planets have two types of conjunctions. They are in conjunction when they are on the far side of the sun (such that the sun is in between the planet and Earth). This is called "superior conjunction" and is just like the conjunction that outer planets have. However, the inferior planets can also be in conjunction when they are in between the sun and the Earth. This is called "inferior conjunction." The outer planets cannot undergo inferior conjunction, because they are farther away from the sun than Earth, and thus can never be in between the Earth and the sun.

Occasionally during inferior conjunction Mercury or

Venus will cross directly in front of the sun. This is called a solar transit. The planet appears as a tiny black disk silhouetted against the solar sphere. It is a bit like a miniature annular eclipse. Solar transits of the planet Venus occur only twice per century, always separated by eight years. Solar transits of the planet Mercury occur 13 or 14 times per century.

◇ Comets

Occasionally our night sky is graced by the appearance of a bright comet. Comets are icy objects and generally have extremely elliptical orbits. They might spend many years (perhaps hundreds of years) in the outer regions of the solar system, swinging by the inner solar system for only a few months. During these months solar energy vaporizes some of the icy material forming a tail that streams away from the comet and may extend millions of miles into space.

The motion of a comet is very difficult to predict in your head. Many comets do not orbit in the ecliptic, and their direction is not necessarily in the same direction as the planets. From the perspective of Earth their path can seem somewhat erratic. They may appear in any part of the sky and their motion is not intuitive. They may be visible for a few weeks or months, and then diminish as they return to the outer solar system. It's been said that comets are a bit like cats: they have tails and they do what they want. The best way to predict a comet's motion is to use a computer program, or a sky chart such as in *Sky & Telescope* magazine.

◇Meteor Showers

Meteor showers are generally caused by the debris left behind by a comet. This debris travels in a fairly well-defined path. If and when the Earth intersects this debris path, a meteor shower occurs. Since the Earth takes one year to orbit the sun, it will intersect a given debris field at roughly the same date every year. Therefore, most meteor showers are annual. The most impressive, reliable meteor shower is the Perseid meteor shower. This shower occurs every year around August 12. Over 60 meteors per hour may be seen at around the time of the shower's peak.

Occasionally, the Earth passes through a particularly dense patch of cometary debris. This can result in an especially intense meteor shower, producing thousands of meteors per hour. Such a display is called a "meteor storm" and is quite rare. Most meteor storms are unpredictable. However, there is one that occurs somewhat regularly. The Leonid meteor shower which peaks every year around November 17, and normally produces a meager display of about 20 meteors per hour, produces a meteor storm roughly every 33 years. The period is not exact, and the storm does not always occur. We will revisit the topic of meteor showers (and the Leonid meteor storm in particular) in chapter 5.

◇The Analemma

Imagine that you were to set up a wide-angle camera, permanently pointed at a particular direction in the southern sky. Then imagine taking a picture once per day at exactly noon, capturing the precise position of the sun. If you then played the resulting pictures in sequence, the sun would trace out a thin figure-eight shape. This shape is called the "analemma" and sometimes appears on globes. From this, we can see that the sun appears to move up and down in the sky, and slightly left and right throughout the course of a year. The up and down motion is due to the Earth's tilted rotation axis: our celestial equator is tilted 23.4° relative to the ecliptic. Therefore, the sun can be as much as 23.4° degrees above the celestial equator (at summer solstice) or as much as 23.4° below the celestial equator (at winter solstice). Thus, the analemma is about 47° tall. The tilt of Earth accounts for the up-and-down annual motion of the sun.

The left-and-right annual motion is caused by the Earth's slightly elliptical orbit around the sun. The Earth's orbital motion is slightly faster when Earth is nearer to the sun, and slower when it is farther away. But the rotation of Earth on its axis remains constant. So, sometimes the day (from one solar transit to the next) is a bit longer than 24 hours, and sometimes it is just a bit shorter. The average day is 24 hours exactly. This accounts for the horizontal width of the analemma.

Halley's Comet: March, 1986 The comet is visible from Earth every 75 or so years.

A series of many 30-second long exposures spanning about six hours one night using a wide-angle lens. Combining those frames which captured meteor flashes, this dramatic view of the Perseids of summer was produced.

It also partly accounts for why the sunset and sunrise times vary throughout the year. If the Earth's orbit around the sun were a perfect circle, its orbital speed would be constant and the latest sunset and earliest sunrise would occur on the summer solstice. But the varying orbital speed shifts the sunrise and sunset times a bit.

On average, the sun will transit (cross the meridian) at noon. It will cross a bit earlier or later due to the aforementioned effects of Earth's varying orbital speed. However, we must also consider the effects of time zones and daylight-saving time. For societal convenience, the Earth has been divided into various time zones, where all clocks within the region are synchronized regardless of the position of the sun. People that are roughly in the center of their time zone will see the sun on the meridian (on average) at noon.

Those on the eastern side of the time zone will see the sun reach the meridian sooner. They will experience early sunrises, and early sunsets. Conversely, those on the western side of the time zone will experience late sunrises and late sunsets. Some locations also observe daylight-saving times, in which all the clocks are shifted one hour forward relative to the true solar time for several months. With daylight-saving time in effect, celestial motions happen one hour later than they would otherwise (e.g., the sun crosses the meridian around 1:00 p.m. on average.)

◇Precession of the Equinoxes

Today, the Earth's rotation axis happens to be lined up fairly well with the North Star. But this has not always been the case. The Earth's tilt relative to its orbit remains at 23.4°; however, the direction in which it is tilted changes with time. This means the North Celestial Pole (NCP) actually drifts over the centuries. If we were to map the path of the NCP with time, we would find that it traces out an exact circle, and would therefore eventually travel back to the North Star in 26,000 years at its present speed. So it is a very slow phenomenon. Nonetheless, ancient star charts confirm that the NCP has drifted substantially with time.

This motion of the NCP means that the celestial equator drifts along the ecliptic with the same period (i.e., it would take 26,000 years to make a complete cycle). The constellation in which the sun is found at equinox (the intersection of the celestial equator and the

Tutulemma: Solar Eclipse Analemma. Credit & Copyright: Cenk E. Tezel and Tunç Tezel (TWAN)

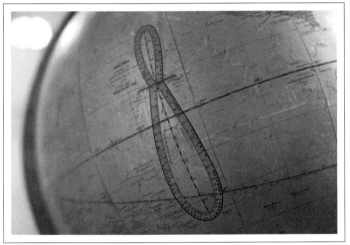

Globenmuseum Vienna

ecliptic) therefore shifts with time. This phenomenon is therefore called the "precession of the equinoxes."

We learned earlier that star positions are defined in terms of their position on the celestial sphere — the declination being the angle from the celestial equator, and the right ascension being the "hours" along the celestial equator. But we now see that the celestial equator itself is not fixed, since it is defined by the Earth's tilt, which precesses with time. Therefore, the coordinates of stars must be constantly adjusted for this. The change is small over a few years, or even a decade. But over the centuries, the right ascension and declination of the stars will change significantly. Again, this is not due to any actual motion of the stars, but rather due to the motion of our defined coordinate system.

Therefore, to be really precise, when we record the coordinates of a star, we must also mention the date at which those coordinates are recorded. This is called the "epoch." So, for example, you might see a star's position recorded as the following: RA 12hr37' DEC: 49°57' epoch 2000. This means that these coordinates are accurate for the year 2000, but must be converted if we are substantially far from that date. For most backyard observing, you won't have to worry about the epoch. Most computer software will automatically do the conversion anyway. But it is a good thing to know if you are dealing with a very precise position, and older coordinates.

It is interesting to note that we are rather privileged to have a star almost directly above the NCP. Since the NCP drifts with time, this has not always been the case. In fact, there has been only one other time in history when human beings have had a North Star. This was around the year 2800 B.C. To put this in perspective, this is around the time in which the Bible indicates that Noah lived, before the great flood. Noah would also have had a North Star – but not the same one we have. During Noah's time, the star Thuban (which lies in between the handle of the Big Dipper and the bowl of the Little Dipper) would have been very close to the NCP. At no other time in history have human beings had a North Star.

◇Putting It into Action

These are the basics of celestial motion. If you have studied this chapter carefully, you know the qualitative essentials that any astronomer knows about motions in the night sky. Granted, this chapter is not designed to give you the details of how to make exact calculations of stellar or planetary positions. There are other books that will show you how to compute such things. Some books even contain computer code that you can use to write your own programs. But the fun is in understanding the basic motions of the night sky on a qualitative level, and making rough correct predictions about where things will be. No equipment is necessary to do this. So give it a try!

Chapter 3

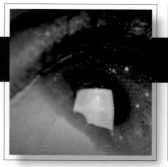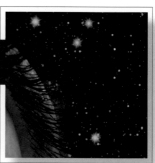

Understanding the Eye

To get the most out of an observing session, it is necessary to know the basics of how the human eye functions. The eye has a cornea and lens which bend light and bring it to a focus, producing an image on the inner back side of the eye. This back part of the eye is called the retina, and it is packed with light-sensing receptors, which transmit electrochemical signals to the brain. The human eye has two different types of light-detecting cells: rods and cones. During the day, we use primarily the cones. There are three different types of cones: one which is very sensitive to red light, one which is sensitive to green light, and one which is sensitive to blue light. These three cones are wired together such that our brain receives information on the

relative amounts of light received by each of the three cones; this combined information we perceive as color.

◇ The Cones

Our cone system is similar in many ways to a color video camera. We perceive color images of any sufficiently illuminated object in our field of view. However, unlike a video camera, our light-sensing receptors are not evenly distributed; they are far more concentrated near the center of the back of our eye. When you play back a video, the left side of the screen is just as crisp as the right side or the center. Not so with your eyes. You have much sharper vision near the center of your field of view than the periphery. If you glance away from this book, you will still be able to see the book in your peripheral vision, but you can no longer read the words. They are not crisp because you have fewer cones on the periphery of your field of view than you do dead center.

The uneven distribution of cones in the human eye is a design feature. The center (in terms of field of view) of the retina where the human eye has the highest density of cones is called the fovea. The fovea has no rods; it is packed full of cones only. This high density of image receptors gives people exceptionally clear images of anything that is directly center in their field

Retina   **Rods**

Cones   **Lens**

Optic Nerve   **Rods**

Basic structure of the eye

of view. The lower number of cones throughout the rest of the retina gives people a very wide field of view, without sending an overwhelming amount of information to the brain.

Since we spend most of our waking hours in a well-illuminated environment, we are fairly familiar with how our cones work. For example, we instinctively know that we must look directly at something for maximum clarity. However, when stargazing, we use primarily our rod system. This is because the rods are far more sensitive to light than cones, and are thus able to detect much fainter objects. The rod system is quite different from the cone system, and it is useful to understand the differences to maximize our observing experience.

◇The Rods

Unlike cones, the rods do not have the threefold red-green-blue sensors. Therefore, rods cannot detect color. This is why color is difficult to determine under poor light conditions. At night, our vision is much like an old black-and-white television. To the extent we can see any color at all at night, it is because our cones are able to detect *some* light even at night; they simply cannot detect light as faint as the rods can. Colors therefore appear much less vivid under low illumination than they do under high illumination. For this reason, views of faint objects (such as a nebula) through a telescope will appear much less colorful than textbook photographs.

Rods themselves cannot distinguish color at all. However, rods are most sensitive to blue-green light, and are not at all sensitive to red light. It is easy to demonstrate this. Suppose during the day there is a blue car parked next to a red car and both are about the same brightness. At night, under low illumination, neither car will

appear to have any color. They will both appear "grey," but the red car will appear a much darker grey than the blue one. The rods are not able to see it as well. Indeed, red objects look almost "black" at night. This is important for a number of reasons. For one, consider what kinds of objects you will want to look at through a telescope. Since you'll be using primarily your rods in telescope observation, this means that a red object will be harder to see than a blue one of equal brightness. If you have a beautiful textbook photo of a red and blue nebula, you will only see the blue parts with your telescope — and they will appear grey.

The rod system is more complex and less intuitive than the cone system. Rods do much more than simply transmit an image to the brain. Some sets of rods are designed to detect only horizontal lines; others detect only vertical lines. Some sets of rods are sensitive to motion of a particular speed and direction. In other words, those

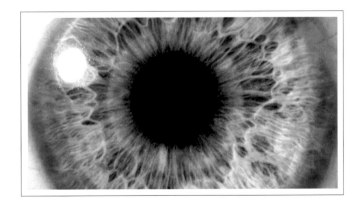

particular rods only transmit a signal to the brain if they detect a *moving* image. Sometimes when I am trying to observe an object that is just fainter than my ability to see, I can move the telescope slowly, and then I suddenly find I am able to see the moving faint object, whereas I could not clearly see it when stationary. It's a strange experience, but it really works.

◇Averted Vision

Recall that the fovea is in the center of the retina (with regard to our field of vision). The fovea is packed full of cones; and to make room for them all, there are absolutely no rods. For this reason, under low light levels, you will not be able to see something that is directly center. As far as your night vision is concerned, you have a "blind spot" at the center of your vision. To demonstrate this, find a very faint star or other faint source of light in your peripheral vision. Then look directly at it. It will disappear! Looking slightly away from it will cause it to reappear. I like to think of this as Murphy's Law of night vision: if you look at it, you won't see it.

Therefore, when looking at faint objects through a telescope (which is the vast majority of celestial objects), you must avoid the instinctive tendency to look directly at the object. On the other hand, you don't want to look very far away from the target either because the eye has a low density of rods on the periphery of its field of view. The density of rods is highest in a circle not far away from and surrounding the fovea. Therefore, the best place to look is just slightly to the side of the target object; use "averted vision." You will have to experiment a bit the first few times to figure out how

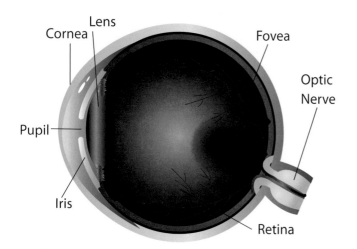

Averted vision involves looking at an object in low light slightly off center. This is becasue near the center of the retina is the *fovea*, and this creates a "blind spot," since it is not as sensitve to light.

far away to look to get the best view. Too far away and you will not have a crisp view. Too close and you will not see the target at all, or it will be very faint. Finding the best place to look will become second-nature after you do this a few times.

The importance of using averted vision cannot be overstated. It can make the difference between seeing a beautiful spiral galaxy, and seeing nothing at all. You will want to use averted vision on almost everything in the night sky: globular star clusters, nebulae, galaxies, and so on. The only exceptions will be very bright objects, such as bright stars, planets, and the moon. These exceptions you can look at directly.

◇Dark Adaptation

The human eye has an ingenious way of adapting to a tremendous range of lighting conditions. You can see clearly on a bright sandy beach in sunlight, and you can also see stars at night under light conditions that are a billion times fainter. By knowing a bit about how the eye adjusts to light and dark conditions, you can enhance your ability to see in the dark. This will improve your ability to see faint objects in a telescope or with the unaided eye.

There are two ways in which the eye adjusts to changes in ambient illumination. The eye can make quick adjustments by contracting or relaxing the iris. The iris is the colored part of the eye. It surrounds the pupil — the center of the eye that allows light through. By contracting the iris, the pupil is made smaller, letting less light through. A sudden increase in ambient lighting will cause the iris to contract. You can demonstrate this by looking in a mirror and shining a flashlight on your eye. The pupil will almost instantly shrink in size to compensate for the extra light. Removing the flashlight causes the pupil to dilate again. The iris is able to make quick adjustments to compensate for minor changes in lighting; however, it is not enough to compensate for the enormous changes in lighting that take place between day and night. For such large changes, a different system kicks in.

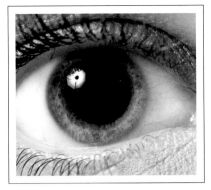 

Examples of the iris and pupil being expanded and contracted to see in various levels of light

The retina itself is able to compensate for very large changes in brightness, using an ingenious negative feedback mechanism. It's not as fast as the iris, but it is able to adjust to a much larger range of lighting. Here is how it works. We will focus on the rod system, but the cones use the same type of system.

The rods contain a chemical (rhodopsin) that is light sensitive. When photons (particles of light) strike this chemical, they cause it to twist and break, which releases energy. This release in energy causes the rod to send an electrochemical signal to neighboring cells, which eventually sends the signal on to the brain (under the right circumstances). The details are complicated, but the point is this: the light-sensitive chemical (rhodopsin) is destroyed in the process. So if another photon strikes the rod after the rhodopsin is depleted, no energy would be released and no signal would be sent. Rods therefore have a process which restores the rhodopsin — they "reset the mousetrap" so that it is once again ready to send a signal upon receiving a photon.

The rods are constantly restoring the rhodopsin, and light is constantly breaking it down. But consider what happens when there is a lot of light hitting the rods. The photons are hitting the rods faster than the rods can restore the rhodopsin. So the first photon registers, but then the next ten (for example) do not because there is insufficient rhodopsin. In other words, under high illumination conditions, the retina becomes relatively insensitive to light due to the depletion of rhodopsin. Only a small fraction of the incoming photons generate signals to the brain, and so the brain is not overwhelmed by too many light-signals in a bright environment.

Now consider what happens when there is very little light. In this case, the rods are able to build up a lot

of rhodopsin because there are very few photons to break it down. But since a lot of rhodopsin is available, even one photon is likely to trigger a signal to the neighboring cell. Since the photons are infrequent, by the time the next one hits, the "mousetrap" has been reset and a new signal is sent. So, whereas under bright conditions only a small fraction of photon strikes are reported, under low light conditions, nearly 100 percent of photon strikes are reported to the next cell. The cones have a similar system but use different chemicals.

Pretty clever isn't it? The retina is constantly and continually adjusting to the ambient light. But this takes some time. Perhaps you have walked out from a dark movie theater into bright sunlight and it nearly hurts at first. This is because a large supply of the light-sensitive chemical was generated in the retina for the dark movie conditions, and now nearly 100 percent of the light is triggering the rods and cones. But after only a few minutes, the chemicals become depleted and you find that you are able to see without pain. Your eyes have become light-adapted. In astronomy, we are much more interested in the reverse process: dark adaptation.

With dark adaptation, the rhodopsin is able to build up more quickly than it is broken down by incident light. As more rhodopsin builds up in the rods, you find that you are able to see fainter and fainter objects as higher percentages of the light are signaled to the brain. One important thing to know about dark adaptation is that it takes a lot longer than light adaptation. It may take 30 minutes to become dark-adapted enough to do some serious astronomy. But it takes only seconds of exposure to a bright light to light-adapt. Don't lose your night vision by exposure to bright lights!

◇The Dark Adaptation Process

Cones also dark-adapt in a similar fashion to the rods. But they are not as sensitive to light in the first place, so they are not able to "go as low" as the rods. When you first step outside at night and begin to dark-adapt, both your rods and cones will begin increasing their

Using a red light at night helps you see without impacting your dark-adapted vision

light-sensitive chemicals. But after about four minutes, your cones will be about as dark-adapted as is useful to you. Although they continue to adjust after that, the rods will "take over" at that point and become more useful to you than the cones. The rods will continue to adapt for the next half hour. The way that they adapt is such that their detection threshold is an exponential decay. In other words, they adapt very quickly at first,

and then get slower and slower as you get closer to your best, ideal night vision.

As a general guideline, it takes about 30 minutes to dark-adapt. The rods will continue to become even more sensitive beyond that time, but they will do so at a very slow rate. Nonetheless, if you want to become as dark-adapted as you can possibly get, it will take about two hours! After that, you will not notice any signifi-

On average it takes half an hour to "dark-adapt", and by two hours, you will be seeing the best you will be able to. Eating carrots can boost Vitamin A production which will help in the dark adaptation process.

cant improvement. For most purposes, 30 minutes is fine. But if you want to see some really faint object that is near the limit of visibility, you will have a better chance if you are in darkness for about two hours. The difference between 30 minutes of dark adaptation and two hours is slight, but there is a difference.

◇Dark Adaptation Tips

Given that it takes so much time to dark-adapt, there are some things to consider when preparing for an observing session. First of all, once you dark-adapt, don't lose it or it will take another half hour to get it back again. Therefore, make sure you've done everything for which you need light before you start your observing session. By all means, use that bright flashlight when setting up your telescope, and studying up on your star charts. But then, once you have started observing, do not turn on a bright light again until you are finished. Don't go inside (if the lights are on) once you have started observing. This means that things like bathroom breaks are not a good idea. "Go before you come," as they say.

Eat carrots. Yes, it really works! Carrots contain carotene which is converted by the body into vitamin A. This vitamin is used by the retina to generate a portion of the rhodopsin. A healthy dose of vitamin A will improve the retina's ability to dark-adapt. You can also take vitamin A supplements. Be careful not to go over the medically approved limit though, because a vitamin A overdose is harmful.

Use a flashlight with a red beam. Remember that rods cannot detect red light very well, but cones can. As far as the rods are concerned, a red flashlight is nearly invisible. Therefore, you can use a red flashlight to read something using your cones, without light-adapting the rods. You can use this method to check a star chart without spoiling your night vision. The redder the beam, the better will be the flashlight. Red LED lights are good because they produce a very pure color. Note that rods are not completely blind to red light, so a red light will have some effect. It is not as good as no light at all, but red light is far less destructive to night vision than any other color.

A really nice thing to remember about your eyes is that you have two of them! And there is a neat trick that allows you to make use of this. If you are doing telescope observing, you will primarily be using only one of your eyes. This is the only one you really need to worry about staying dark-adapted. So if you do need to turn on a light for any reason, keep one eye closed. I use my left eye for reading, checking star charts, bathroom breaks, etc., and I use my right eye for telescope viewing. I usually combine this with the previous tip. I use a red flashlight for checking charts, and only with my left eye. That way both eyes are always relatively dark-adapted, and my right eye is always perfectly dark-adapted. In any case, make sure that at least one of your eyes stays dark-adapted for the entire observing session, for the best views.

Which eye to pick? Keep your *dominant* eye dark-adapted. Most people have better vision in one eye than the other. And the brain automatically draws most of its information from that dominant eye. To find out which eye is dominant, look at a distant object and hold out your finger at arm's length so that it is just below the distant object. Now close one eye. If your finger appeared to move so that it is no longer under the object, then you closed your dominant eye. Otherwise, your open eye is dominant. Use your dominant eye for all telescope viewing. One possible exception would be very bright objects like the moon. I like to use my nondominant eye on the moon because the moon is so bright that it will light adapt that eye. That way I can keep my good eye dark-adapted. Some astronomers use an eye patch to cover their dominant eye if they need to go inside or turn on lights for any reason. Red glasses can also be used, but a patch is better. Remember that it is better to have no light at all than red light.

◇Don't Hold Your Breath

Sometimes there is a tendency for people to hold their breath when they are looking at a faint astronomical object. Don't do this. The slight deprivation of oxygen will (temporarily) reduce your night vision. You won't be able to see as faint if you are holding your breath. Also, it's best to leave your other eye open. So if you are looking through the telescope with your right eye, avoid the temptation to close your left eye. Believe it or not, your brain will quickly learn to ignore the information from the other eye, and it won't be an issue.

Chapter 4

Astronomy with the Unaided Eye

Astronomy is not limited to those with access to telescopes. There are many things in the universe easily visible without any optical enhancement at all. In this chapter we cover astronomical phenomena that can be enjoyed without any equipment other than your eyes. These include astronomical targets such as bright stars, constellations, and star clusters. As with the rest of this book, this chapter is geared more for observers living at mid-northern latitudes. However, much of the information will also be useful for southern hemisphere observers, though the described positions will be shifted to the north.

◇ Constellations, Asterisms, and Bright Stars

It is enjoyable to know the names and locations of some of the brighter stars in our night sky. Some of the particularly bright stars show obvious color. The brighter stars can be imagined to form various shapes in our night sky: the constellations. There are 88 official constellations. They are purely a matter of convention. In modern usage, the constellations have official boundaries and completely fill the night sky. In other words, there are no "gaps." Every point in the night sky belongs to one, and only one constellation.

Stars are named based on their brightness, and the

constellation in which they are found. They use the lowercase letters from the Greek alphabet first, then the Roman alphabet, though the latter is not common today. The letter is followed by the Latin possessive form of the constellation name. For example, the brightest star in the constellation Centaurus is named Alpha Centauri. The second-brightest star in that constellation is Beta Centauri, and so on. Of course, stars can change brightness with time, and our ability to measure the brightness of stars has improved with technology. So there are a number of cases where the Greek letter does not reflect the true order of brightness. But generally speaking, the brightest star in the constellation is the Alpha.

Bright stars often have a proper name as well, like "Rigel," "Vega," and so on. In these cases, it is acceptable to use either the Greek letter system or the proper name; however, the proper name is usually preferred. So Alpha Lyrae is another name for the star "Vega." Fainter naked-eye stars are usually named by the Flamsteed system. This uses a number, followed by the Latin possessive form of the constellation name. The numbers are in order of the star's right ascension within the constellation, going from west to east. So, 1 Centauri is the westernmost star (naked-eye) in the constellation Centaurus.

The constellation of Orion

We do not know who first named the constellations, but we do know that many of them are very ancient. The constellation Orion is mentioned in the biblical Book of Job, which is thought to have been written around 2000 B.C. In addition to the official constellations, there are several asterisms that are useful to know. Asterisms are groups of bright stars that are not one of the official 88 constellations. An asterism could be a part of a constellation; the Big Dipper is an asterism that is part of the constellation Ursa Major. Or an asterism could combine stars from several constellations; the summer triangle contains stars from three constellations: Lyra, Aquilla, and Cygnus.

It is useful to know some of the constellations, asterisms, and bright stars for several reasons. First, it helps you to understand how you are oriented: what direction you are facing, and so on. Second, many binocular objects, as well as telescopic deep-sky objects (discussed in chapter 11) can be located by star hopping using the constellations. Third, these constellations and bright stars are beautiful in their own right. So let's discuss some of the more interesting constellations and bright stars as they are found at various times of the year.

4.1 The winter sky with labeled constellations: mid-January around 9:00 p.m. standard time. This map is for observers at north latitude 40°. Observers at latitudes farther north will see these stars shifted southward; observers farther south will see these stars shifted farther northward.

◇Winter

We begin with the winter evening sky FIGURES 4.1 and 4.2. One of the advantages of winter observing is that the nights are long; therefore, you can begin observing quite early. Let's consider the evening sky around 9:00 in mid-January. The constellation that will dominate high in the south is Orion — the hunter FIGURE 4.3. Orion's belt consists of three bright blue stars in a straight line, relatively close together at equal distances. From east to west, they are named Alnitak, Alnilam, and Mintaka. Alnitak and Alnilam are both blue supergiants, class O9 and B0 respectively.

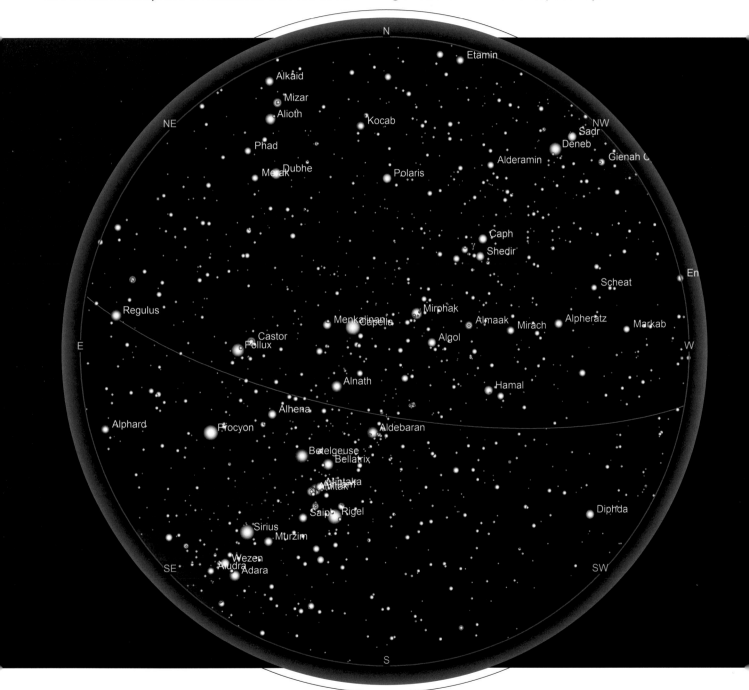

4.2   The winter sky with labeled bright stars: mid-January around 9:00 p.m. standard time. This map is for observers at north latitude 40°. Observers at latitudes farther north will see these stars shifted southward; observers farther south will see these stars shifted farther northward.

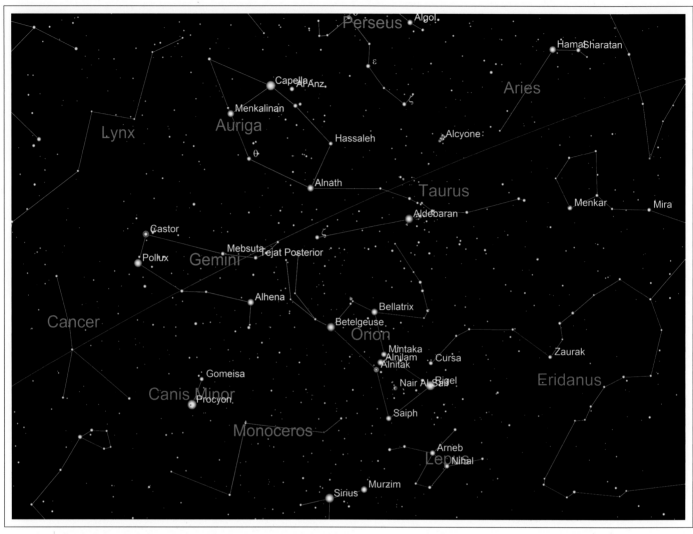

4.3   The constellation Orion and surrounding region

Mintaka is a blue bright giant, class O9. (See chapter 10 for information on stellar classification.) So these are some of the hottest, brightest stars in the night sky. Mintaka is less than half a degree from the celestial equator. So it is very useful in helping a person to picture where the celestial equator is in the night sky. This also means that Mintaka rises virtually due east and sets almost due west.

Surrounding the belt stars are four stars which form a tall quasi-rectangle. These represent Orion's shoulders and legs. The upper east star in this box is Betelgeuse [**bet**-l-jooz, or **beet**-l-jooz]. It is a red supergiant, and appears noticeably red to the unaided eye. Betelgeuse is

roughly six hundred times the diameter of the sun. The upper west star is named Bellatrix; it is a blue giant. The lower west star is named Rigel — a blue supergiant. The lower east star is named Saiph, also a blue supergiant. The brightness of these stars makes Orion stand out more than any other winter constellation.

Just below Orion's belt lies Orion's sword. It consists of three stars, fainter and closer together than the belt stars, and oriented more vertically. The center star of this sword is actually the combined light of the Trapezium and the Orion Nebula (see chapter 11). Binoculars will reveal the cloudy appearance of the nebula.

Northwest of Orion lies the constellation Taurus — the bull. The brightest star in Taurus by far is Aldeberan, a red giant. It is noticeably red in color, and similar to Betelgeuse. However, Aldeberan is not quite as bright nor quite as red as Betelgeuse. Aldeberan marks the eye of the bull. It is found amongst a cluster of much fainter stars which form a "V" shape. (Aldeberan marks the upper left endpoint of the "V.") This "V" represents the face of the bull. It is in fact a true cluster of stars called the Hyades. Aldeberan is not actually part of the cluster; it just happens to be lined up with it, but much closer to Earth. The Hyades cluster is one of the largest naked-eye open star clusters.

Another one of the best naked-eye star clusters lies just to the west of the Hyades. It is called the Pleiades or the "seven sisters" FIGURE 11.3. This cluster consists of a few hundred stars, though only six or seven are visible to the unaided eye. They form a shape resembling a tiny little dipper. Several dozen stars in this cluster are visible in binoculars, making it one of the best binocular targets in the winter sky. Through binoculars, the blue color of the stars can be seen.

Directly north of Orion is the constellation Auriga, which is usually drawn as an uneven Pentagon. The brightest star in Auriga is named Capella. It is the sixth brightest star in Earth's night sky. Though it appears to the eye (and in the telescope) as a single star, it is actually a multiple-star system. The brightest two stars in the system are both yellow giants, comparable in temperature to the sun, but much larger. For binocular and telescope viewers, Auriga contains a number of fairly prominent open star clusters.

West of Auriga and north of the Pleiades is the constellation Perseus. It has a sort of wishbone shape to it: two groups of three stars with the brightest star in the middle in each case. The second-brightest star in this constellation is named Algol. It doesn't stand out in any obvious way, but it may be the most interesting star for naked-eye astronomy. Every 2.87 days, like clockwork, Algol drops in brightness for a few hours, and then goes back to its normal brightness. The change in brightness is very noticeable to the unaided eye; Algol goes from its normal brightness of magnitude 2.1 down to 3.4. (See chapter 10 for a description of the magnitude system.) This makes it about as faint as the stars around it, whereas it is normally noticeably brighter.

For this reason, Algol is often called the "Demon Star." The reason for the periodic change in brightness is now understood: Algol is an eclipsing binary. Though it appears as a single star in even the most powerful telescopes, it is in fact two stars in a very tight orbit. The stars' orbital plane is nearly edge-on relative to us. So every 2.87 days, the faint star passes in front of the bright one, blocking some of its light. (There is also a very slight drop in brightness when the bright star blocks the faint one; however, this is not noticeable to the unaided eye.) Several other eclipsing binaries are now known. But Algol is the best, most noticeable example, and was the first to be discovered. You can look up on the Internet, in *Sky & Telescope* magazine, or with computer software to find out when Algol will be at minimum.

To the east of the Auriga is the constellation Gemini: the twins. Two stars dominate this constellation: Castor and Pollux. They are comparable in brightness, but not identical. Pollux is the one farther south. It is slightly brighter than Castor, but also slightly redder. Pollux is now known to have at least one orbiting planet. In fact, it was the first extrasolar planet discovered orbiting a bright star. Castor is a complex multiple-star system, though the eye perceives it as a single star.

South and slightly east of Orion we find the constellation Canis Major — the big dog. This constellation is dominated by the bright star Sirius. Sirius is the brightest star visible in Earth's nighttime sky. Any "star" brighter than Sirius is actually a planet. Sirius is a main-sequence star, class A1 — slightly hotter, larger, and brighter than the sun. This gives it a slight bluish color. It appears very bright because it is a relatively nearby star, only 8.6 light-years away. It is the fifth-closest star system to our solar system. Since it is in the constellation Canis Major, Sirius is sometimes referred to as "the Dog Star."

East of Orion in between Sirius and Pollux is the small constellation Canis Minor — the little dog. It is dominated by a very bright star named Procyon. The constellation is unremarkable, aside from the fact that Procyon is considerably brighter than any other stars in it. This gives Procyon a very isolated appearance.

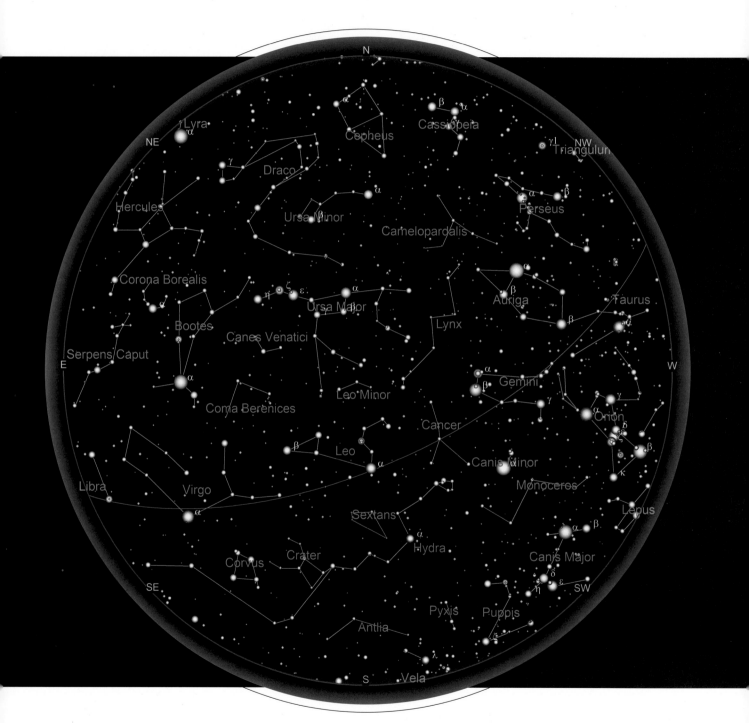

4.4 The spring sky with labeled constellations: mid-April around 10:00 p.m. (daylight-saving time). This is the appearance of the night sky as observed at (north) latitude 40°. North is up. The ecliptic is shown in yellow.

◇Spring

In mid-April, the constellation that dominates the evening sky is Leo — the lion FIGURES 4.4, 4.5, 4.6. It will be visible very high in the south at around 10:00 p.m. (daylight-saving time). The mane of the lion is represented by a group of stars resembling a sickle, or a backward question mark on the west side of the constellation. The bottom star in the sickle is Regulus; it is the brightest star in Leo. Regulus is a multiple-star

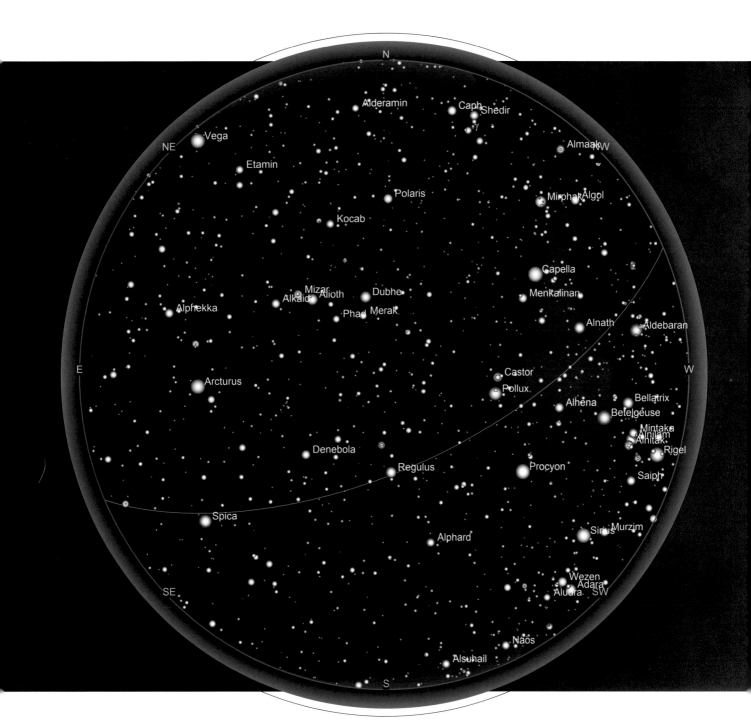

4.5   The spring sky with labeled bright stars: mid-April around 10:00 p.m. (daylight-saving time). This is the appearance of the night sky as observed at (north) latitude 40°. North is up. The ecliptic is shown in yellow.

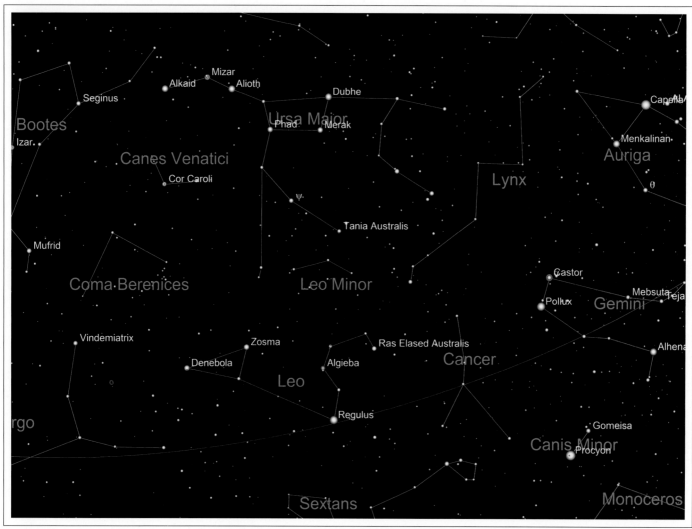

4.6   The constellations Leo, Ursa Major, and the surrounding region

system. The two main pairs of stars can be seen separately in a backyard telescope. Regulus is very close to the ecliptic. So planets and the moon often undergo conjunction with Regulus, and occasionally occult it.

On the east side of Leo are a group of three stars which represent the hips and tail of the Lion. They form a right triangle. The eastern vertex of the triangle is marked by the star Denebola — "tail of the Lion." Denebola is the second-brightest star in Leo.

Just west of Leo is the faint constellation Cancer. Cancer lies just about halfway in between Gemini and Leo. The constellation has the shape of an upside down letter "Y." None of the stars in this constellation are brighter than magnitude 3.5, which makes the constellation difficult to see under light-polluted skies. Cancer is the home of the open star cluster M44 — the Beehive Cluster (also called "Praesepe"). This cluster is located in between and slightly west of Delta and Gamma Cancri, the two most central stars of Cancer FIGURE 11.6. The Beehive appears as a faint glow to the unaided eye. It is a spectacular binocular object. The Beehive Cluster makes it worthwhile to learn how to identify the constellation Cancer.

East and slightly north of Leo is the constellation Coma Berenices. The constellation itself is rather unimpressive, consisting of only faint stars. However, it is home to a stunning naked-eye star cluster, located close to the western border of the constellation FIGURE 11.4. The Coma Berenices star cluster requires fairly dark skies to see, because it is comprised of only faint stars. However, there are a lot of them. At a rural location, you will have no difficulty whatsoever seeing this lovely star cluster with the unaided eye.

Spring evenings are a great time to observe the constellation Ursa Major — the Big Bear. Although the constellation is circumpolar for northern latitudes and can therefore be seen year round, it is highest in the sky in late spring. Look very high due north and find the Big Dipper. It is one of the most recognized asterisms. The Big Dipper is part of the constellation Ursa Major. The Dipper itself forms the back half and tail of the bear. (And no, I've never seen a bear with such a long tail. So don't ask.) South of the Big Dipper are the back legs of the bear. The front portion and the head of the bear are to the west (in spring evenings).

While you are there, you might as well take the time to find Polaris — the North Star. This is the one star that doesn't move noticeably with the time of night or the time of year. It's always going to be right there. But the Big Dipper makes an excellent guide to find the North Star. The two stars on the edge of the bowl of the Big Dipper (Merak and Dubhe) point directly to the North Star. Polaris is about five times the distance between these two stars away from Dubhe.

The North Star is not particularly bright, but it is fairly isolated from any other stars of comparable brightness. Polaris is the last star in the handle of the "Little Dipper" — Ursa Minor (the little bear). This time of year, the other handle stars of the Little Dipper extend east from Polaris and curve slightly toward the Big Dipper. The two stars on the edge of the bowl of the Little Dipper (Kocab and Gamma Ursa Minoris) are only slightly fainter than Polaris; the rest of the stars in this little constellation are much fainter.

A fun naked-eye target in Ursa Major is the optical double, Mizar and Alcor. Mizar is the center star in the handle of the Dipper FIGURE 4.6 and FIGURE 10.3. Very close to it is a fainter star named Alcor. Most people can see it with the unaided eye. Binoculars will make the separation really obvious. The really interesting thing is that Mizar itself is a true binary; it is made up of two stars which appear as one to the eye. So you are actually looking at *three* stars: Mizar A, Mizar B, and Alcor. A small backyard telescope is able to split Mizar into its two component stars.

Another star of interest near the Big Dipper is Thuban. Thuban is almost exactly halfway between Mizar and Gamma Ursa Minoris (the end of the bowl of the Little Dipper). Thuban is interesting because it used to be our North Star around the year 2800 B.C. Earth's axis precesses with time, and so it wasn't always lined up with Polaris. (See chapter 2 for details.) Thuban is part

Big Dipper

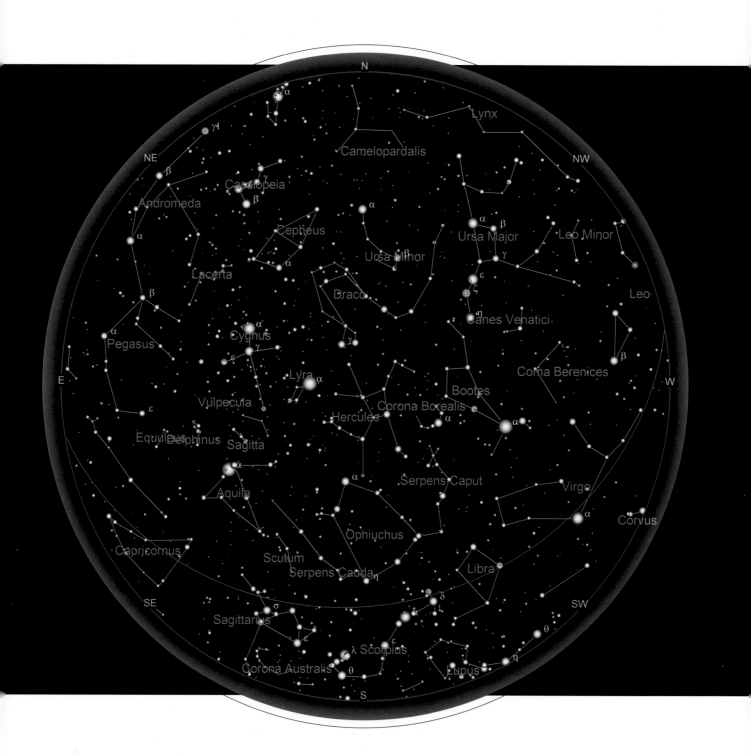

4.7 The summer sky with labeled constellations: mid-July around 11:00 p.m. DST.

of the constellation Draco — the dragon, which winds in between Ursa Major and Ursa Minor.

The constellation Boötes [boh-**oh**-teez] is found just to the east of Coma Berenices. Boötes is shaped like a kite. It even has a little tail (Eta Boötis). The brightest star in Boötes is Arcturus. It forms the base of the kite.

Arcturus is a red giant star, and the color is quite noticeable: not as red as Betelgeuse, but at least orange. Arcturus is the fourth brightest star in Earth's night sky, and the brightest star north of the celestial equator. So it's hard to miss.

Arcturus has the third-highest proper motion of any

4.8   The summer sky with labeled bright stars: mid-July around 11:00 p.m. DST.

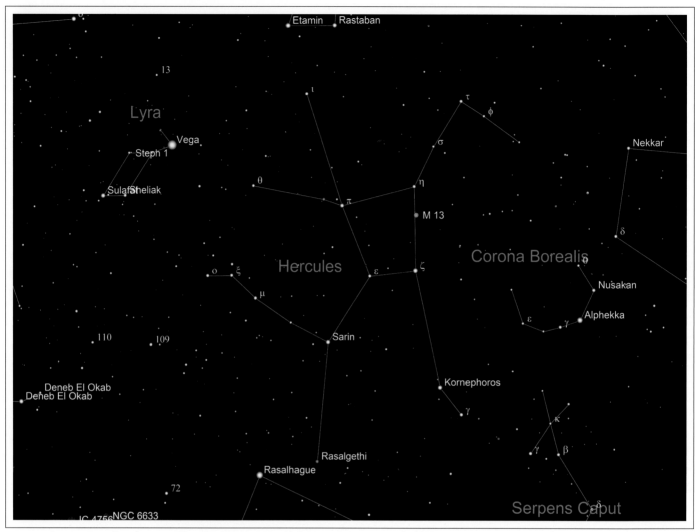

4.9   The constellation Hercules and surrounding region

star. Proper motion is the angular speed of the star through the galaxy relative to the background stars. Arcturus moves about the width of the full moon every 800 years. Another way to find Arcturus is to star hop from the Big Dipper. The three stars in the handle of the Big Dipper form an arc. If you continue to follow that arc beyond the handle, it will "arc" to "Arcturus." Then you can "spike on to Spica," which is farther south.

Spica is the blue star in the southeastern sky, early in the spring evening. It never gets terribly high for mid-northern latitude viewers. Later in the spring, or later in the evening, it will rise a bit farther and swing south. Spica is the brightest star in the constellation

Virgo, and marks the lowest point of the bright stars in that constellation. Virgo is a fairly large constellation, and is rather unremarkable to the naked eye. However, telescope observers would do well to become familiar with Virgo, as it has some wonderful deep-sky objects, including the famous Virgo galaxy cluster.

◇ Summer

During summer, mid-northern latitude observers will need to begin their observing sessions a bit later, due to the late sunsets. Let us consider the evening sky in mid-July, around 11:00 p.m. daylight-saving time FIGURES 4.7 and 4.8. At this time, the bright star Arcturus is still visible, but is now high in the west. Arcturus is like a beacon which draws the eye to the constellation Boötes. Just east of Boötes is a small constellation called Corona Borealis — the Northern Crown. This constellation forms an almost perfect little half-circle of stars.

High overhead at this time of year, just to the east of Corona Borealis, is the constellation Hercules FIGURE 4.9. The stars of Hercules are not terribly bright, so it can be a little bit challenging for beginners. The important shape to recognize is the keystone: a trapezoid consisting of Eta, Pi, Epsilon, and Zeta Herculis. This is usually (though not universally) considered to be Hercules' torso, with Pi and Eta Herculis representing the shoulders, and Epsilon and Zeta Herculis representing the hips. The most notable thing about this keystone is

that it contains the best globular cluster in the northern celestial hemisphere: M13. This globular cluster is located one-third of the way down from Eta to Zeta Herculis. It is very faintly visible to the unaided eye on a clear night, and appears as a fuzzy glow in binoculars. It is a fantastic telescope object.

This is the best time of the year to observe the constellation Scorpius, which is found low in the south FIGURE 4.10. Scorpius is dominated by the bright red supergiant Antares. Antares is noticeably red to the unaided eye; it appears similar to Betelgeuse but is not quite as bright. The name "Antares" literally means "against Mars" as if to say that this star rivals Mars due to its brightness and reddish color. Antares is within a few degrees of the ecliptic. So planetary conjunctions with

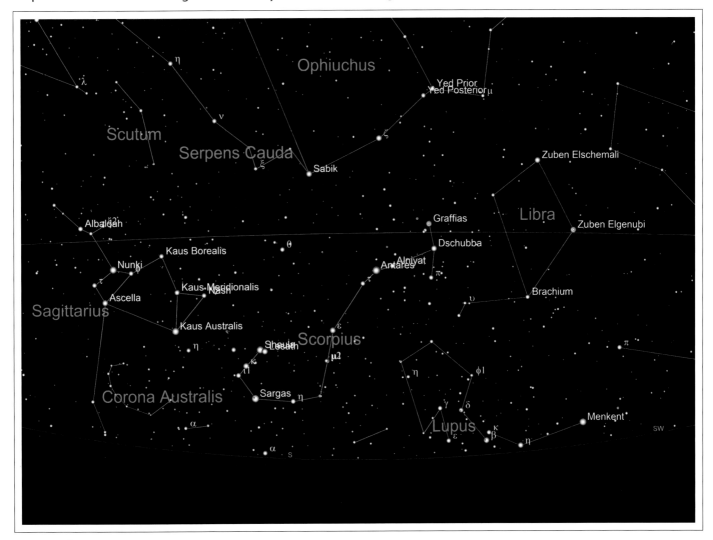

4.10　The constellation Scorpius and surrounding region. The horizon shown here is for latitude 40°.

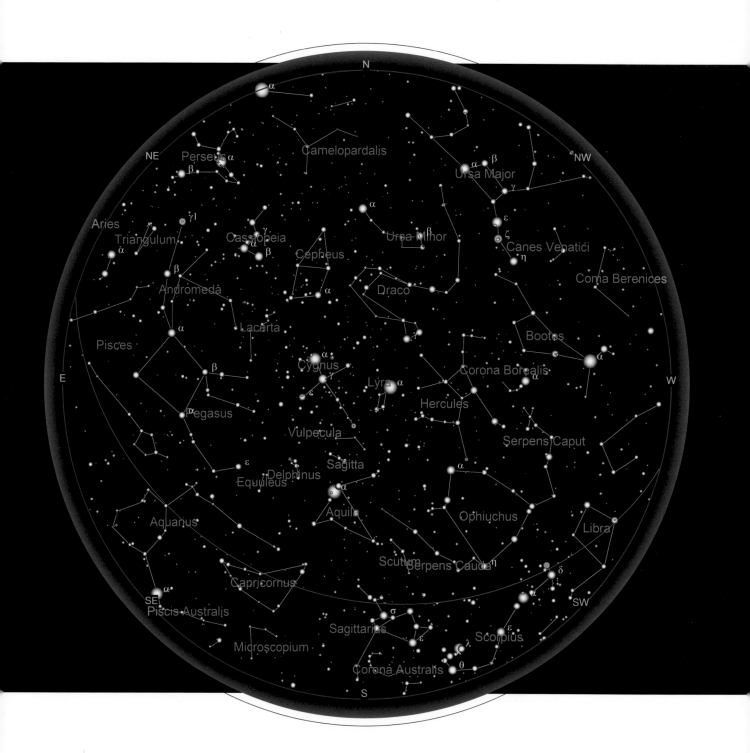

N

NE

Perseus α
β

Aries

Triangulum
α

Andromeda
β

Pisces

E

α

Pegasus

α

Cassiopeia γ
α
β

Cepheus

Lacerta

β

ω

Cygnus α

Vulpecula

ε

Delphinus

Equuleus

Aquarius

Capricornus

SE

Piscis Australis

Microscopium

Camelopardalis

Ursa Minor

Draco

γ

Lyra α

Hercules

Sagitta

Aquila

Scutum
Serpens Cauda η

Sagittarius
σ

ε

Corona Australs
θ

S

Ursa Major
α β
γ

ε
ζ
Canes Venatici
η

Coma Berenices

Bootes
α

Corona Borealis
α

Serpens Caput

α

Ophiuchus

Libra

δ

α
SW

ε

Scorpius
λ

NW

W

4.11 The late summer sky with labeled constellations: mid-August around 11:00 p.m. DST.

Antares are common. It is occasionally occulted by the moon.

The southeastern region of Scorpius is home to a number of interesting star clusters, some of which are visible faintly to the unaided eye. M6 (the Butterfly cluster) and M7 (the Ptolemy cluster) are two such examples. They are found just north of, and just northeast of Lamba Scorpii respectively (see chapter 11 for details). They are superb binocular targets. M7 is the larger and brighter of the two. A number of smaller, telescopic open clusters are also found in this region of the sky. This part of the sky is very close to the center of

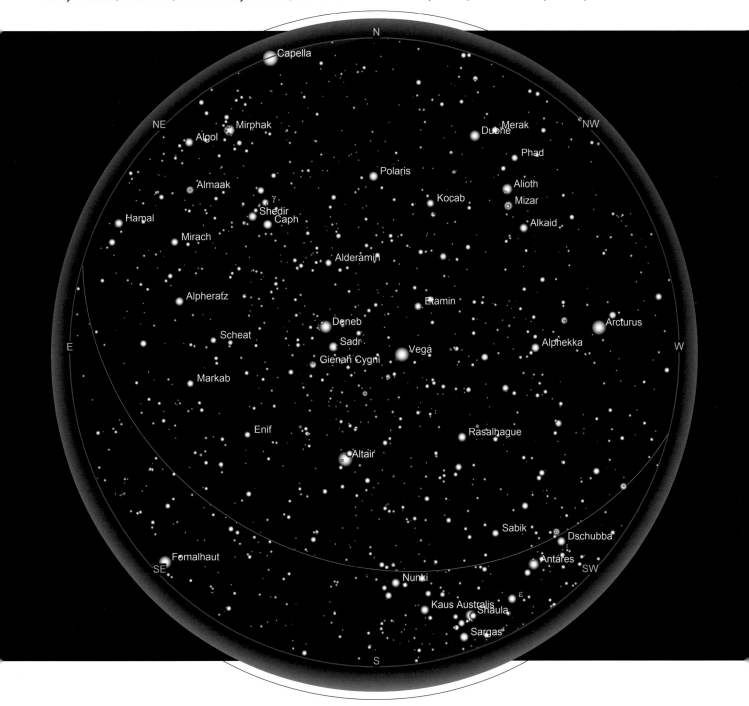

4.12   The late summer sky with labeled bright stars: mid-August around 11:00 p.m. DST.

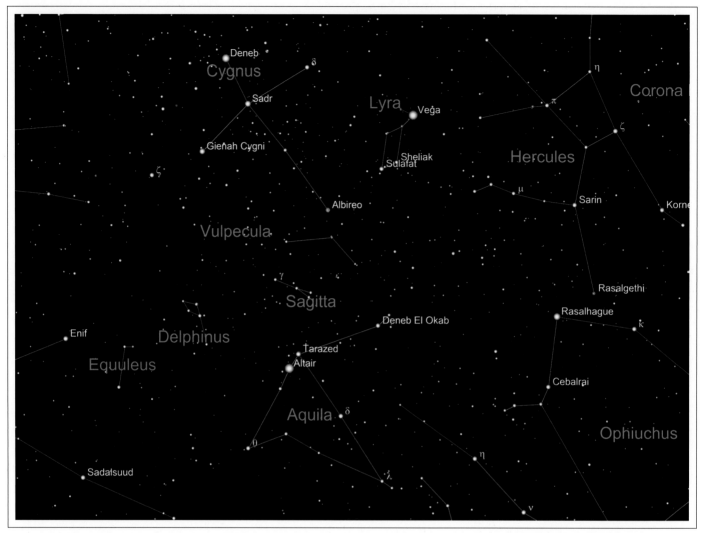

4.13 | The summer triangle (Vega, Altair, and Deneb). The Milky Way passes directly through the summer triangle

our galaxy, which is why so many star clusters can be found here.

North of Scorpius and south of Hercules is the constellation Ophiuchus. It is a very large constellation, consisting of stars no brighter than magnitude 2. It is relatively unremarkable. However, telescope observers will find a few globular and open star clusters in and around Ophiuchus.

◇Late Summer

The late summer evening sky is so rich I decided it deserved its own category. By late summer, I mean

mid-August around 11:00 p.m. **FIGURES 4.11** and **4.12**. Of course this is the same as mid-July around 1:00 a.m. Either way, the constellations described in the previous section are still visible, but are now farther to the west. The Milky Way shines brightly overhead at this time. Under dark rural skies, the Milky Way is a wonderful sight. The naked eye can easily detect dark patches of dust along the Milky Way, as well as light patches which correspond to star clusters and bright nebulae. These are always splendid binocular objects.

The Milky Way streams right through one of the most well-known asterisms: the Summer Triangle **FIGURE 4.13**. It consists of three bright stars: Vega (the brightest),

Altair, and Deneb (the faintest of the three, but still far brighter than anything nearby). Vega and Deneb are the two stars on the north side of the Summer Triangle. Vega is noticeably brighter than Deneb and is west of it. Altair lies at a greater angular distance to the south.

These three stars are a great lesson in perspective. Vega is about 25 light-years away and is the fifth-brightest star in Earth's night sky. Altair is only 17 light-years away; it's one of the closest stars to our solar system. Deneb, on the other hand, which appears only a bit fainter than these two stars, is about 1,500 light-years away! Clearly, Deneb must be very intrinsically bright to even compete with Vega and Altair. In fact, Deneb is a blue supergiant and one of the most luminous stars so far discovered. It's about 60,000 times intrinsically brighter than the sun.

The summer triangle is an asterism, not a constellation, because each of its three stars is already assigned to one of the official 88 constellations. Let's explore the constellations belonging to the stars of the Summer Triangle, beginning with Vega.

Vega is the brightest star out this time of year for mid-northern latitude observers. It belongs to the constellation Lyra — a small constellation consisting of about six easily visible stars. Four of these form a faint, but nearly perfect parallelogram just below Vega. The fifth star is Epsilon Lyrae, just east and slightly north of Vega. And the sixth star is Vega itself, which is far brighter than any of the others.

Epsilon Lyrae is an interesting naked-eye star. It is actually a double star, and if you have good vision you can actually resolve both stars without the aid of binocu-lars. If you can't split them, don't be discouraged; I find only about one in three people can. I'm in that blessed third, but then again I know exactly what I'm looking at, and I have pretty good vision (for the moment at least). Binoculars will allow you to clearly see both stars. And with a telescope at high magnification (on nights of good seeing), you can see that each of these two stars is also a double. So with a decent telescope, you can see all four stars. For this reason, Epsilon Lyrae is often called the "Double-Double." See chapter 10 for additional details on Epsilon Lyrae.

Deneb is the brightest star in the constellation Cygnus — the swan. Deneb is the "tail" of the swan (that's what the name means). The "wings" lie just southwest of Deneb, rather close to it. The head of the swan is marked by Albireo, quite a bit farther to the southwest, about half the distance to Altair. This reflects the long neck and short tail of a swan. Cygnus is also sometimes called "the Northern Cross." These same stars form a nearly perfect cross, with Deneb at the top. Cygnus is therefore the Northern Hemisphere counterpart to Crux — the Southern Cross.

Albireo, the head of the swan, or the bottom star of the cross, appears as one star to the eye. However, it is actually binary. Albireo is one of the best, most colorful binary stars for a backyard telescope. It is a blue-and-yellow star, easily resolved even at low magnification. I find I can usually resolve the two components even in binoculars. (See chapter 10 for details.)

Altair is the brightest star in the constellation Aquilla, the Eagle. Beta and Gamma Aquilae are just to the southeast and northwest of Altair respectively. The wingtips of the Eagle are represented by Theta and

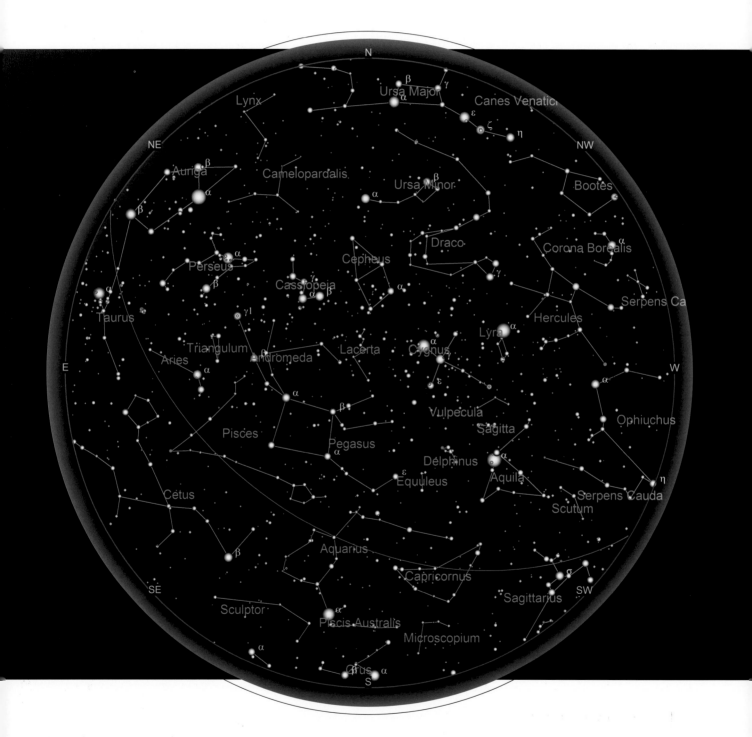

4.14   The autumn sky with labeled constellations: mid-October around 10:00 p.m. DST.

Zeta Aquilae. Lambda Aquilae and the nearby stars mark the tail. Since the Milky Way passes through the west side of Aquila, there are a number of star clusters in this constellation. Most of them are too faint to be seen with the unaided eye, but are good telescope targets.

The constellation Sagittarius is located south and slightly west of Aquila. It is low in the south in the late summer evening sky. The shape of Sagittarius is difficult to describe, so I won't attempt it. It is the group of medium brightness stars (around magnitude 2) in the south, just east of the central band of the Milky Way. The central core of our galaxy is actually within

4.15   The autumn sky with labeled bright stars: mid-October around 10:00 p.m. DST.

the boundary of this constellation, on the west side, so it is loaded with deep-sky gems. To the naked eye, you can see many bright patches of the Milky Way in Sagittarius. These are all star clusters and nebulae. Many of them look nice in binoculars or a backyard telescope, so telescope users will want to become very familiar with this constellation.

Just below Sagittarius is the constellation Corona Australis — the Southern Crown. It is about the same size and is similar in shape and brightness to Corona Borealis (the Northern Crown). This constellation is close to the southern limit of visibility for mid-northern latitudes, so this is the only time of the year when you can see it in the evening sky.

◇Autumn

We now turn to the evening sky in mid-October, at around 10:00 p.m. daylight-saving time FIGURES 4.14 and 4.15. The Summer Triangle is still visible, but is now in the western sky. Very high in the south to southeast is the constellation Pegasus FIGURE 4.16. The most recognizable part of this constellation is the asterism called the Great Square. The stars comprising the Great Square are not as bright as those in the Summer Triangle, but they are the brightest ones in the area. So it is not difficult to see. The square is comprised of Markab

(Alpha Pegasi), Scheat (Beta Pegasi), Algenib (Gamma Pegasi), and Alpheratz (Alpha Andromedae).

Pegasus really doesn't have much to see in terms of naked-eye astronomy. But it is relatively easy to find, and that makes it a great jumping-off point for finding other constellations (such as Andromeda). The orientation of Pegasus turns out to be really convenient. Amazingly, the square is aligned with the celestial sphere. So Scheat is almost directly North of Markab (they have the same Right Ascension). Likewise, Alpheratz is almost directly north of Algenib. Both Algenib and Markab are at declination +15, so they are both almost exactly 15 degrees above the celestial equator. Alpheratz and Scheat are both just under declination 30. You can easily envision the celestial coordinate system just by looking at Pegasus.

The star on the northeast corner of the Great Square is Alpheratz — the brightest star in the constellation Andromeda. Andromeda is shaped like a curved bullhorn extending northeast from Alpheratz and curving north. This bullhorn is comprised of an upper and lower arc, both of which begin at Alpheratz. The lower arc extends to delta Andromedae, Mirach (Beta Andromedae), and ends at Almaak (Gamma Andromedea). Almaak is a very colorful telescopic binary star, similar to Albireo but tighter. The upper arc is com-

M31 Andromeda Galaxy

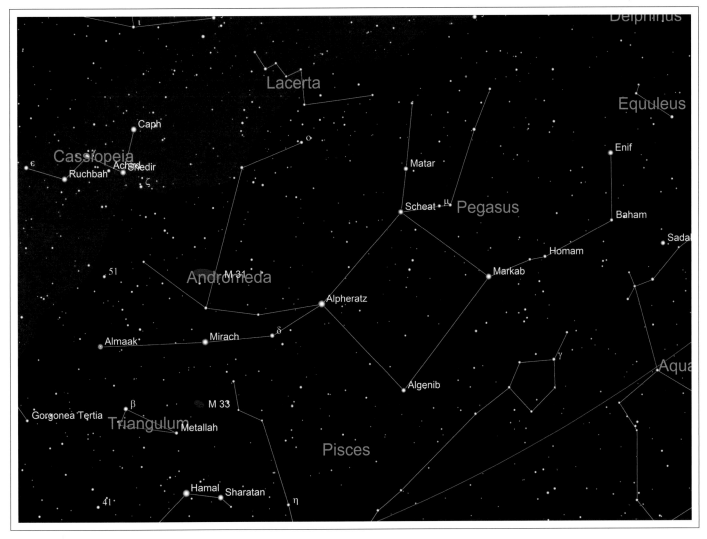

4.16   The constellations Pegasus and Andromeda

prised of fainter stars, one for each of the stars on the lower arc, and ends in Phi Andromedae.

Andromeda is well-known because it contains the brightest galaxy in the northern celestial hemisphere: M31. This galaxy (often called "the Andromeda Galaxy") is the only one that is easily visible to the unaided eye under moderately dark skies for Northern Hemisphere observers. Find Mirach (the second-brightest star in Andromeda) on the lower arc. Then hop up to Mu Andromedae on the upper arc, just northwest of Mirach. Then go up once more to Nu Andromedae. M31 is located just over one degree west from Nu Andromedae. That faint glow is the combined light of several hundred billion stars at a distance of 2.9 million light-years. It's the farthest and largest object that can be (easily) seen with the unaided eye. It is a spectacular binocular object. With binoculars (and

sometimes just by eye) you can see the orientation of the disk of M31.

This is also a good time of the year to view Cepheus and Cassiopeia. These are both circumpolar constellations for mid-northern latitude viewers, so they can be viewed year-round. But they are highest in the sky during the autumn. Cassiopeia will rise even higher later in the evening (or later in the fall). It is shaped like a "W" or an "M" depending on your perspective.

This is also the best time of year to observe the constellations Aquarius, Pisces, and Aries. However, these constellations are rather unremarkable and contain no impressive naked-eye targets. Our goal in this chapter has been to cover the most interesting constellations and bright stars, as well as objects of interest visible to the unaided eye.

Chapter 5

Celestial Events

In this chapter, we address celestial events that can be observed with the unaided eye. These include conjunctions, massings, eclipses, meteor showers, and so on. In addition, we will touch on atmospheric phenomena that are often visible to the amateur astronomer, such as lunar halos, coronae, and mock suns. We will also address manmade celestial targets: satellites.

◇Conjunctions and Massings

A conjunction is when one celestial body passes closely by another. Since planets orbit the sun, they often undergo conjunctions with stars that are near the ecliptic. The moon also does this; and since it orbits quite fast, it does this quite often. Planets can also undergo conjunctions with the moon or with each other. These events are often quite beautiful to the unaided eye — particularly conjunctions between the brighter planets. It is a delight to see two bright objects so close together in the night sky. You can look up when these events will occur on the Internet, or in an astronomy magazine such as *Sky & Telescope*. You can also use computer software to compute when conjunctions will occur.

As an example, Venus is in conjunction with Jupiter on the morning of April 30, 2022. It is within 15 arcminutes of Jupiter on this date, and the two make a spectacular pair in the eastern morning sky. The

two are still relatively close on the week surrounding that date. But since the actual "passing" occurs on the 30th, this is the date of conjunction. If no other object is mentioned in the conjunction, then it is meant to be the sun. For example, "Jupiter is in conjunction this month" means that Jupiter is in conjunction *with the sun* and you won't be able to see it. Planets often undergo conjunction with bright stars, but only those which are very close to the ecliptic, such as Regulus. Venus is in conjunction with Regulus on July 9, 2018 in the evening sky.

A massing occurs when three or more objects come close together in the sky. For example, a massing of Mars, Jupiter, and Saturn occurs in the morning sky of March 26, 2020. Since planets don't move all that fast, a massing of planets will generally last a week or more. Of course the group is in its tightest formation for only an instant. Massings may include the moon. There is a massing of Venus, Saturn, Mars, and the moon in the eastern sky on the morning of March 28, 2022. Since the moon does move rather quickly, massings involving the moon last only one day.

Conjunctions of Jupiter and Saturn occur approximately every 20 years. Jupiter is in conjunction with Saturn on December 21, 2020, and then again on October 30, 2040. Conjunctions between Venus and other objects

are fairly common since Venus is a fast-orbiting planet. A close conjunction of Venus and Mercury occurs on May 28, 2021. Venus and the moon conjunct on July 12, 2021 and Venus conjuncts with Mars on the very next day. A very close conjunction with the moon occurs on November 7, 2021. Venus conjuncts with Mercury on December 29, 2021, and again with Mars in March 10, 2022. It conjuncts with Saturn on March 28, 2022, and with Jupiter on April 30, 2022. All of these take place within one year.

A triple conjunction occurs when a planet passes by another celestial object three times in a row. This occurs when the first conjunction takes place just before the planet begins to undergo retrograde motion. The planet then backs up in the sky from our perspective, and passes the object again. The planet then reverses again back to its normal prograde direction, and passes the object a third time. Saturn, for example, undergoes a triple conjunction with the star Delta Geminorum on September 11, 2033; December 24, 2033; and May 29, 2034.

◇Occultations and Transits

An occultation is when one celestial object passes directly in front of another, blocking the background object from our sight. If the foreground object is smaller (in angle) than the background object, then the event is called a transit, rather than an occultation. A planet can occult a background star. This is not terribly common with bright stars because planets have such small angular size. But they do occur. One example is the occultation of Regulus by Venus on October 1, 2044.

The moon has much larger angular size. Thus, lunar occultations are quite common. However, they do not always happen at a convenient time (e.g., the middle of the day, or when the moon is below the horizon). Nor do they happen for all locations on Earth. Since the moon is relatively close to the Earth, observers at different locations on Earth observe the moon at slightly different positions in space. It is therefore possible for observers in North America to see the moon occult a star, while observers in South America see the moon pass just north of that same star. The details and timing of the event depend strongly on the location of the observer.

The moon can also occult a planet. This is visible to the unaided eye, but the best way to enjoy it is through a telescope at modest magnification. I once observed a lunar occultation of Saturn through a telescope, and

5.1 A lunar occultation of Saturn, September 18, 1997. The moon is in a waning gibbous phase. Saturn is essentially touching the invisible right limb of the moon. The image was taken using an 8-inch telescope at the Sommers-Bausch Observatory in Boulder, Colorado.

Solar Eclipse Seen in Baja California: This photo mosaic shows a view of the sun from Baja California during an eclipse on July 11, 1991, with the moon sliding in front of the sun.

it was really breathtaking **FIGURE 5.1**. Such occultations are fairly common. But again, they won't necessarily be visible from all locations on Earth.

Planets can also occult or transit other planets, though this is quite rare, and happens only a few times per century. The next one will happen on November 22, 2065, when Venus will transit Jupiter. (Venus will appear smaller than Jupiter at the time, so the event is a transit rather than an occultation.) Such events can be seen with the unaided eye, and are just stunning in a telescope. A spectacular transit of Mars in front of Jupiter will occur on December 2, 2223. I sure hope it's not cloudy that night.

◇Eclipses

We have already covered eclipses in some detail in the chapter on celestial motions. Here we are more concerned with how to safely observe them, and when

to look. But in light of the above discussion, there is one thing we should point out about the phrase "solar eclipse." The terminology is somewhat inconsistent. Solar eclipses are actually "occultations" of the sun by the moon, whereas annular solar eclipses are actually "transits" of the moon across the sun. But they are

⬎ Solar Eclipse

October 14, 2023	western states, along with Central and South America
April 8, 2024	northeastern and central United States and parts of Mexico
July 22, 2028	Australia and New Zealand
November 25, 3030	South Africa and Australia

never referred to as such. The moon is the exception to the rule. Only lunar eclipses are true eclipses — where we observe the shadow of one body falling on another.

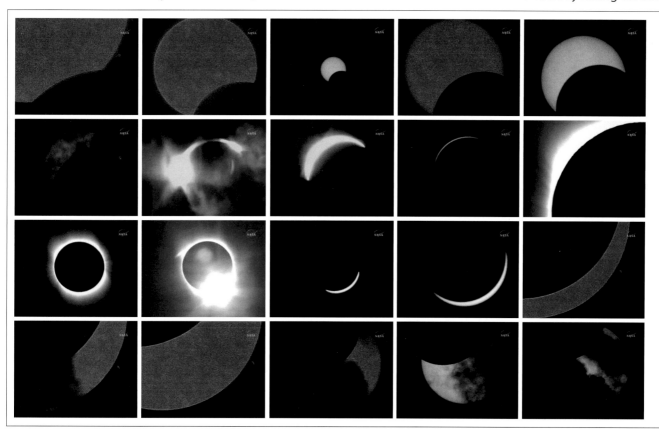

Solar Eclipse Image Sequence: Visible in parts of Canada, northern Greenland, the Arctic, central Russia, Mongolia, and China. The eclipse swept across Earth in a narrow path that began in Canada's northern province of Nunavut and ended in northern China's Silk Road region.

Eclipse glasses
Credit & Copyright: Max Alexander

phases of an eclipse, or for any annular eclipse, it is never safe to look directly at the sun. The ultraviolet radiation is very destructive to the retina, and can cause permanent damage. Fortunately, there are several safe ways to view an eclipse during the partial phases.

First, consider using eclipse glasses. There are inexpensive glasses specially designed to let you look safely at the sun. They block virtually all ultraviolet light, and reduce the visible light greatly so that you can look comfortably at the sun. Eclipse glasses often appear black or silver. You cannot see anything with them, except the sun.

For a total solar eclipse, you will probably have to travel somewhere if you want to see one. They are only visible (as a *total* eclipse) for a path on Earth that never exceeds 93 miles in width. So you will have to check some astronomy databases or software to find when the next solar eclipse will occur within the distance you are willing to travel.

During the total phase of a total solar eclipse, *and only at that time*, it is safe to look directly at the eclipse. The photosphere of the sun is entirely blocked by the moon at that point, and you may look directly at the chromosphere and corona. During totality, the brighter stars will become visible. However, during the *partial*

Likewise, there are filters for purchase that can be fitted over binoculars or a telescope which let you look safely at the sun. Make sure the filter is designed specifically for that purpose. Also make sure that the filter does go over the open end of the telescope — not over the eyepiece (in contrast to all other telescope filters). In other words, the sunlight must go through the filter *before* it enters the telescope. (Unfortunately, some

An amateur astronomer in Papua, New Guinea uses a solar filter to view a solar eclipse safely, avoiding damage to the eyes. Credit & Copyright: Jay Pasachoff

Group observing an annular solar eclipse, showing one amateur astronomer, at right, using a pinhole camera to safely observe the sun. Credit & Copyright: Jay Pasachoff

Example of the projection method. A solar eclipse projected on a white card using a pair of binoculars on a tripod. Credit & Copyright: Laurent Laveder

↘ Projection Method:

1   Point the telescope or binoculars directly at the sun as if you were going to look at it — but don't of course!

2   You can use the shadow of the telescope/binoculars to aim it at the sun; don't sight down the telescope as you would with a star.

3   Then put white paper a few feet away from the eyepiece. When centered, the telescope/binoculars will project an image of the sun on the paper.

4   You then focus the telescope/binoculars until the image is nice and sharp.

5   You can change the distance of the paper from the eyepiece; moving the paper farther will make the image of the sun bigger, but fainter.

6   You will have to adjust the focus whenever you change the distance.

CAUTION! Never look directly at the sun with your binoculars or telescope!!

places do sell "solar filters" for the eyepiece of a telescope; do not use these — they are unsafe.)

Another way to safely view the sun during a solar eclipse (or anytime) is by using the projection method. This works on a six-inch or smaller telescope, and works very well with binoculars as well. If you use binoculars, leave the lens caps on one side (e.g., the left side) so it acts like a single small telescope.

I have successfully used the projection method on telescopes larger than six inches, but there is a danger in doing so. Once you exceed about six inches of aperture, internal heat can become a problem. Specifically, you run the risk of cracking the eyepiece. To safely use

a larger telescope for solar viewing, you can always stop down the aperture (to six inches in diameter). You might very well get away with using a larger telescope without reducing the aperture (I have); but if the eyepiece cracks, don't say I didn't warn you.

For a given location on Earth, total lunar eclipses are far more common than total solar eclipses. The reason is that they are visible for everyone on the nighttime side of Earth. You usually don't have to go more than a few years between good lunar eclipses. No special equipment is needed for lunar eclipses. They are enjoyable naked-eye events. If you watch the entire eclipse from beginning to end, they typically last a few hours. The moon will turn orange, brown, very dark brown,

⬂ Lunar Eclipse

July 27/28, 2018	eastern Africa, western Asia
January 20/21, 2019	United States
May 15/16, 2022	eastern United States
November 7/8, 2022	western United States
March 13/14, 2025	United States
September 7/8, 2025	Asia
March 3/4, 2026	Alaska, eastern Russia

or anything in between, depending on the particulate matter in Earth's atmosphere during the eclipse.

◇ Meteor Showers

One of the best celestial events for naked-eye astronomy is the meteor shower. A meteor is a bright streak in the night sky, sometimes called a "shooting star" or a "falling star." It is caused by a small bit of matter falling from space and burning up as it is heated by atmospheric resistance. There are numerous small rocks and dust particles orbiting the sun. Sometimes their orbital path brings them close enough to be pulled in by Earth's gravity. They travel at thousands of miles per hour. So when they strike the atmosphere, they are heated almost instantly by air resistance and usually vaporize in seconds.

The term "meteor" refers to what you see — the bright streak. The rock causing the streak is called a "meteoroid." If the rock reaches Earth's surface, it is called a "meteorite." Only about one in a billion meteoroids is large enough to reach the surface of the Earth before entirely vaporizing. On a clear, moonless night in a rural setting, you will generally see a few meteors. But on certain nights of the year, you might see hundreds. This is a meteor shower: a period of enhanced meteor activity. A meteor that is not associated with a meteor shower is called a "sporadic."

Many meteor showers are annual, and therefore predictable. For example, the Perseid meteor shower always happens around August 12, and generates hundreds of meteors. The reason for this (which we covered briefly in the chapter on celestial motions) is that the Earth intersects a particular meteoroid stream at a given point in its orbit. And since the Earth takes one year to orbit the sun, it intersects the same debris stream one year later. These meteoroid streams are almost always associated with comets. They are produced as the comet's material is launched from its surface by solar heating. Eventually the debris spreads out over the entire orbit of the comet. For this reason, only comets with an orbital path that comes close to Earth's will produce annual meteor showers. Often, when the comet returns to the inner solar system, it is correlated with a better meteor shower that year. This is presumably because the density of debris is higher near its source comet. This happened with the Perseid meteor shower in and around the year 1992, when its progenitor comet Swift-Tuttle returned to the inner solar system.

A Perseid Aurora

Credit & Copyright: Jimmy Westlake (Colorado Mountain College)

Two meteor tracks of the Perseid meteor shower

Credit & Copyright: Pekka Parviainen

A typical meteor shower shows little activity per hour

During a meteor shower, meteors may occur in any part of the sky. However, they will all appear to be moving away from the same point in space. This point is called the "radiant." This point represents the direction in which the Earth is intersecting the meteoroid stream. Meteor showers are named based on the constellation in which their radiant is found. So the radiant for the Perseid meteor shower is found in the constellation Perseus. This doesn't necessarily mean that there will be any more meteors in that constellation than elsewhere. It simply means that wherever the meteor occurs, it will be moving away from the radiant.

If two or more meteor showers have a radiant in the same constellation, then the shower is usually named after the nearest bright star within that constellation. For example, the Eta Aquarids meteor shower and the Delta Aquarids meteor shower both have a radiant in Aquarius. Using the name of the star will distinguish between the two.

Meteors can have distinct color — particularly the brighter ones. The color depends on the composition

of the meteoroid, and the speed with which it travels through the Earth's atmosphere. They can be white, blue/green, orange, red, purple, or yellow. Since meteors from a given shower tend to have similar compositions and trajectories, they tend to have a similar color. However, it is possible for the color to change as various layers of the meteoroid are vaporized away, revealing a somewhat different composition in the next layer. It is common for very bright meteors to have a green core with an orange tail.

A particularly bright meteor is called a "fireball." There is some ambiguity as to how bright the meteor must be to be classified as a fireball. Most astronomers would say it must be brighter than Venus, so magnitude -4 or less. (See chapter 10 for a description of the magnitude system. The magnitude system is such that more positive values represent fainter objects.) Some fireballs are brighter than the full moon. The term "bolide" is also used to describe certain extraordinary meteors, though there is some ambiguity here. A bolide may refer to a meteor brighter than the full moon, or an exploding meteor. The latter is very rare. I have only seen a handful in my life. But there are cases where internal gas pressure can split a meteor into multiple components. Meteors brighter than the full moon can be (and have been) seen during the day.

Bright meteors often leave a visible trail which glows for about a second. This is called a "train." Occasionally a train will last longer than a second (sometime much longer) in which it is called a "persistent train." During the Leonid meteor shower of 2001, I witnessed a number of trains which lasted for several minutes. One of the brightest ones lasted about 15 minutes, and became distorted by the wind.

◇Meteor Shower Observing

The three most important things for getting the most out of a meteor shower are: dark skies, dark skies, and dark skies. This means you will want to be in a rural location, as far away from city lights as possible. It also means you will want to pick a moonless night, or at least observe during a part of the night when the moon isn't out, or is a very thin crescent. Of course, meteor showers happen when they happen; the Perseids are always on August 12–13, whether the moon is full or new. So what should you do if this year, the full moon falls on August 12–13? I would suggest you skip the meteor shower, and go to bed early. Seriously, nothing spoils a meteor shower like bright moonlight. Instead of seeing a hundred meteors, you'll see maybe three. It just isn't worth it. Remember, they are annual. So you will get another shot next year. On the other hand, don't pass up a good meteor shower that falls on a moonless, cloudless night (because next year it might not).

Clearly, dark adaptation will be essential to viewing the fainter meteors (which are more common than bright ones). So once you are dark-adapted, avoid turning on any lights. Use only a red flashlight, and even then only when essential. Be patient. Even the *best* annual meteor showers only produce an average of one meteor per minute. Meteors often come in spurts. You won't see any for several minutes, and then you'll get three within a single minute, for example.

Orient yourself so that you can see as much of the sky as possible. Get away from any tall trees, buildings, or other objects that will obstruct part of the night sky. Remember, the meteors can happen anywhere in the sky. So if part of your sky is obstructed, you will miss the meteors that occur there. The best way to observe a meteor shower is lying on your back. That way you can see virtually the entire night sky. If there is some light pollution, orient yourself so that you are facing the darkest part of the night sky.

Prepare to stay up late. Most meteor showers improve dramatically after midnight. This is due to the orientation of the observation site with respect to Earth's orbit around the sun. In the evening, our night sky is facing in the direction opposite to that in which the Earth is moving around the sun. Essentially, we are facing "backward" — looking at where the Earth has been. But in the early morning just before sunrise, our sky is facing "forward" — looking in the direction where Earth is headed in its orbit around the sun. So in the morning sky, we are running into the meteors head-on, whereas in the evening sky a meteor would have to catch up to the Earth from behind; this is far less likely. The reason we see more meteors in the early morning sky than in the evening sky is exactly the same as why more bugs hit the front windshield of your car than the back.

Related to the previous point, meteors will increase when the radiant is highest in the sky. This usually happens in early morning, before sunrise. If the radiant is below the horizon, you will not see many meteors at all. This also means that latitudes for which the radiant reaches a higher point in the sky will experience a better meteor shower than those latitudes where the radiant does not go very high. Meteor showers whose radiant is in the northern region of the sky will not be impressive to viewers in the Southern Hemisphere. Theoretically, a meteor shower is best if the radiant is directly overhead — at zenith.

Meteor showers are rated by their zenith hourly rate (ZHR). The ZHR is the number of meteors per hour that an observer would see at a rural location when the radiant is at zenith. The true number of meteors per hour that you will actually see is always less than the ZHR since the radiant is not exactly overhead. The best annual meteor showers have a ZHR of 60 to 100. A more typical meteor shower would have a ZHR of around 15. On rare occasions, a meteor shower will have an extremely high ZHR — over 1,000, and sometimes as much as 100,000. The sky appears to be "raining" meteors. This is called a "meteor storm" and is *very* rare. One notable example was the Leonid meteor storm of 1833. Meteor storms are *not* annual, and are rarely predictable.

◇The Best Annual Meteor Showers

For Northern Hemisphere observers, the best annual meteor shower is generally the Perseids. This shower occurs every August 12–13, and has a ZHR of around 100. It is consistently good, year after year. And since it occurs in late summer, it is a pleasant time of the year for being out at night. The Perseids tend to produce moderately fast meteors. This shower has a somewhat broad peak. So if skies are cloudy on the 12th–13th, a

day or two before or after will also produce decent displays, though the ZHR will drop a bit. If you plan to watch just one meteor shower in the year, this is the one (unless of course bright moonlight will spoil it).

Rivaling the Perseids is the Geminid meteor shower, which peaks on December 14. It can reach a ZHR of around 100. It has a sharp peak of intensity, but the ZHR is still high for about one day surrounding the peak. So the odds are good that you will be able to catch the meteor shower near its peak. It produces very slow-moving meteors. Since Gemini is high in the sky at 10:00 p.m. in December, you can see substantial meteors well before midnight. However, the rate will generally improve after midnight. Far fewer people bother watching the Geminids than the Perseids for the simple reason that it is cold out in December at mid-northern latitudes. In the Southern Hemisphere, where temperatures are warm in December, the Geminids don't produce as good a display because the constellation Gemini is far to the north. So the radiant is never very high above the horizon. Nonetheless,

Geminids in 2007

Credit & Copyright: Erno Berko

Taken from Kuiper Airborne Observatory, C141 aircraft April 8/9, 1986, New Zealand Expedition, Halley's Comet crossing Milky Way

Southern Hemisphere observers may see up to 20 meteors per hour near the peak activity.

Another interesting fact about the Geminids is that it is the only meteor shower that is known to be associated with an asteroid rather than a comet.[1] The meteoroid stream responsible for the Geminid meteor shower matches the orbit of the asteroid 3200 Phaethon. How an asteroid is able to produce such a debris field is not precisely understood at this time. However, some

astronomers have speculated that Phaethon may be an "extinct" comet — one that has run out of volatile chemicals. The orbit of Phaethon is very elliptical — just like a comet. However, Phaethon never develops a tail, and spectroscopic analysis is consistent with a rocky composition. The Geminid meteor shower seems to be rather recent in origin. Unlike the Perseids, which can be traced back for thousands of years, the Geminids were first noted in the 1860s. The ZHR during the

1870s was estimated to be around 20. So the Geminids have intensified greatly in the past century.

The Quadrantids are the best winter meteor shower. They peak on January 3, producing slow-moving meteors with a ZHR near 100. Unfortunately, their peak is very sharp, lasting only about an hour. If you don't catch the Quadrantids on the hour at which they peak, you will see very few meteors. This meteor shower is named after a no longer used constellation: Quadrans Muralis. On modern star charts, this constellation is now divided into sections of Boötes, Hercules, and Draco. The Quadrantids can be a great shower, but only if conditions are just right and if you observe right around the peak activity. Otherwise, they will be very disappointing.

Moving on to less spectacular meteor showers, we first encounter the Eta Aquarids, which peaks fairly broadly around May 5–6. This is one of two meteor showers associated with Halley's Comet. (Halley's Comet intersects Earth's orbit twice — once on the way in, and once on the way out.) If you look at the Eta Aquarids ZHR, you may see a deceptively high number like 60. But this is misleading, because the radiant of this meteor shower rises only shortly before sunrise, and never gets very high in the sky. As a result, Northern Hemisphere viewers will likely see around 10 (fast-moving) meteors per hour. Southern Hemisphere viewers will see 30 to perhaps 50 meteors per hour in the predawn sky. It's probably the best annual meteor shower for the Southern Hemisphere. About one-third of Eta Aquarid meteors produce persistent trains.

The other shower associated with Halley's Comet is the Orionids. The Orionid meteor shower peaks around October 21, and lasts for a few days. It is comparable in many ways to the Eta Aquarid shower. The ZHR is technically lower, but Orion is higher in the sky for mid-northern latitudes. So the Orionid meteor shower will produce about 20 meteors per hour for Northern Hemisphere viewers, and perhaps twice that many for Southern Hemisphere viewers.

The Lyrids peak on April 22. They have a ZHR of around 20. They are sometimes called the "April Lyrids" to distinguish them from the (less impressive) "June Lyrids" which have a similar radiant. The Delta-Aquarids peak on July 28. They produce moderately slow yellow me-

teors with a ZHR of around 20. The Capricornids peak around July 29–30. They produce slow meteors, and only about 15 per hour at best. But they produce an unusually high number of fireballs.

August is great month for meteors. Several minor meteor showers take place in August. Some of these overlap in dates with the Perseids. But you can always tell which meteor belongs to which shower by the direction it travels. Simply trace it back to its radiant. Beginners will not be happy with meteor showers with a ZHR lower than 20, which is why I haven't listed them. But there are dozens of minor meteor showers that occur throughout the year.

◇The Amazing Leonid Meteor Shower

One meteor shower deserves special attention due to its unusual nature: the Leonids. This annual meteor shower peaks on November 17. It produces the fastest-moving meteors of the annual consistent meteor showers. It is normally fairly unimpressive, with a ZHR of around 20 at best. However, approximately every 33 years (with some exceptions), the Leonids produce a meteor storm with a ZHR in excess of 1,000. During the 1833 storm, the sky of eastern North America appeared to be "raining" meteors during the early morning hours. Many meteors *per second* were observed. When another storm occurred in 1866 producing about 2,000 to 5,000 meteors per hour, the quasiperiodic nature of the Leonid meteor storm became clear. This 33-year period corresponds to the orbital period of the progenitor comet Temple-Tuttle, which was discovered in 1867. Slightly less impressive Leonid meteor storms were also observed in 1867 and 1868 with a ZHR of about 1,000.

The Leonid meteor storm is only *quasi*-periodic, however. It was expected that 1899 would see another meteor storm (particularly in light of the fact that the ZHR of the 1898 shower went up to about 100 from the usual 20). But it didn't happen. In the year 1901 observers were treated to an enhanced Leonid meteor shower with a ZHR of around 300–400. It wasn't quite a meteor storm, but it was still a respectable meteor shower. Likewise, the 1933 date was also a miss; no meteor storm was seen. Though, again, enhanced rates were observed in the surrounding years. The 1932

Leonid meteor shower

Credit & Copyright: Jerry Lodriguss

Leonid shower had a ZHR of around 200. Some astronomers thought perhaps the Leonid meteoroid stream had been perturbed, which would mean no future Leonid meteor storms.

Nonetheless, in 1966, the Leonid meteor storm returned in full glory. Observers in the western United States were treated to a spectacular display with around 40 to 50 meteors per second! As before, the surrounding years produced enhanced meteor showers, but not quite storms. It was with great anticipation that I was waiting for the 1999–2000 Leonid meteor shower. Would another storm occur? Of course, since the timing isn't exact, it made sense to begin observing the Leonids carefully a year or two before the expected peak.

On November 16–17, 1998, while in Boulder, Colorado, I drove to a nearby mountain with a group of my fellow grad students to watch the display. And it was a very good display. Although there were not enough meteors per hour to qualify as a storm, there were nonetheless a lot of meteors. The ZHR was much, much higher than normal. But the really interesting thing was that they were almost all fireballs! I have never seen so many fireballs in one evening. It was a "fireball shower" — the only one I have ever seen. But it was just the appetizer. (Some places on Earth did experience higher

rates than we saw in Colorado, high enough to count as a meteor storm.)

In 2001, I was blessed to observe a true Leonid meteor storm. In the early morning hours, the Leonids streamed in at about 3,000 per hour. It was an amazing experience. They were mostly bright, blue, and fast. A number of them left persistent trains, some lasting for several minutes. The rate continued to improve as Leo rose higher in the sky. It also became obvious that the meteors that happened to occur within Leo were foreshortened; they were coming in at a steep angle and left very short, bright trails. Ones that were farther from Leo were longer. In several instances three or more meteors would occur simultaneously. Enhanced Leonid displays took place several years after that.

The next chance of a Leonid meteor storm will occur around 2030 — or within a few years. Check with your local astronomy news source for detailed predictions as that year approaches.

◇Atmospheric Phenomena

In one sense, events that happen within the Earth's atmosphere might not be classified as "astronomical." On the other hand, astronomers spend a lot more time looking at the sky than most other people, and are more likely to notice unusual atmospheric phenomena. Strictly speaking, meteors belong in this category as well. And yet most people would consider a meteor shower to be a "celestial event." There are a number of different types of atmospheric events that go well beyond the scope of this book. We will here discuss only some of the more common and interesting events that are in some way related to cosmic events.

A rainbow falls in this category. It is caused by a celestial object — the sun and the interaction of its light

with water in the Earth's atmosphere. The reason rainbows are colorful is because the water droplets split the sunlight into its constituent wavelengths, which the brain perceives as color. This happens because water (just like glass) refracts different wavelengths of light by slightly different angles. The water droplets behave like billions of tiny prisms, splitting the sunlight into the familiar color spectrum. The color order is always the same on the primary bow: violet on the inside, and red on the outside. In some cases, a second rainbow is seen, larger than the first and concentric with it. This is a second-order refraction, and so the color scheme is reversed; the outer bow will have red on the inside, and violet on the outside. Rainbows are always centered on a point directly opposite of the sun.

There are other atmospheric events that are similar to but distinct from a rainbow. One example is a solar halo. A solar halo is caused by the reflection and refraction of sunlight off of ice crystals in thin, high cirrus clouds. A solar halo looks like a large illuminated circle surrounding the sun at a separation angle of 22 degrees. For this reason it is sometimes called a "22-degree halo." The refraction causes some separation of the wavelengths of light. So color is often visible in the halo, but the colors are not nearly as vivid as in a rainbow. If colors are visible, red will be on the inside (the

opposite of a rainbow), and blue on the outside. (Violet is not usually visible.)

Lunar halos are also common. It is exactly the same phenomenon, but with the moon as the contributing light source. Lunar halos are best seen when the moon is near full (so as to contribute the most light) and when high thin cirrus clouds are present. They occur at a distance of 22 degrees away from the moon, just like the solar halo. Unlike the solar halo, lunar halos rarely exhibit any evidence of color to the human eye. This is only due to the fact that they are much fainter; the colors are still there.

In some cases, only a fraction of the halo can be seen. And so you will see giant arcs around the sun or around the moon. Occasionally, a second outer halo is also visible at a separation of 46 degrees. The outer halo is almost always fainter and broader than the inner one. For this reason, the 46-degree halo is more common with the sun than the moon.

Another similar phenomenon is known as a parhelion (plural: parhelia), or more commonly known as a "sun dog" or "mock sun." A sun dog is a bright spot (sometimes nearly as bright as the sun itself, though usually significantly less) that occurs next to the sun. Sun dogs are always found directly to the left or right of the sun. They are best seen when the sun is low in the sky. Less commonly, a bright arc will occur directly above the sun and is called an "upper tangent arc." Sometimes you can see all three. They are always separated from the sun by 22 degrees, just like the solar halo. Sometimes sun dogs and solar halos are visible at the same time. In those cases, the sun dogs appear as very bright spots on (or slightly outside) the halo. Sun dogs often show significant color, though usually not as vivid as in a rainbow.

Moon dogs (paraselenae) can also occur, though they are less common than sun dogs simply because the moon is fainter. Moon dogs occur 22 degrees to the left and/or right of the moon, just like sun dogs. An upper tangent arc can also occur 22 degrees above the moon. If a lunar halo is present, moon dogs will appear as bright spots on (or slightly outside) the lunar halo. Moon dogs rarely show evidence of color because they are usually too faint for the cones.

An example of a solar halo

Another very common phenomenon caused by thin clouds is called a "corona" which means "crown." This is when the sun (or moon) will have a glow immediately surrounding it. It is much smaller than the 22-degree halo, and appears to contact the sun or moon, and gets fainter with distance. Solar coronae often form concentric colored rings, though the colors are not very vivid. Lunar cornea may show a trace of color, but less than solar coronae due to their inherent faintness. The atmospheric solar corona should not be confused with the sun's actual corona — a region of plasma surrounding the sun. The latter cannot be seen by eye except during a solar eclipse.

Light pillars are another interesting and fairly common atmospheric phenomenon. Solar pillars occur around the time of sunset or sunrise. They appear as a vertical bright beam extending directly above the sun. Lunar pillars can also form above the moon at the time of moonset or moonrise. This chapter is by no means a complete list of all atmospheric phenomena that can be triggered by celestial light sources. But these are the more common ones.

An example of moon dogs

◇ Solar System Dust

There are two other phenomena that observers might mistake for atmospheric phenomena that are in fact celestial. These are zodiacal light and gegenchein. Both appear as a faint glow, almost like a cloud. However, their source is not atmospheric. Both are caused by sunlight reflecting off of dust in the solar system. Tiny particles (pebbles and grains of dust) orbit the sun, just like the planets do. And like the planets, most of these dust grains orbit in or very close to the ecliptic.

They reflect a tiny fraction of sunlight back to the Earth, which can be seen as a faint band of light along the ecliptic. This band is brightest close to the sun, where it is referred to as zodiacal light. Thus, the best time to see zodiacal light is after sunset (or before sunrise) when the sun is below the horizon, but the brighter region of the zodiacal light is above the horizon. You will need to wait quite some time after sunset, because zodiacal light is much fainter than twilight. So start looking for zodiacal light when twilight ends.

An example of zodiacal light

You will need extremely dark skies to see zodiacal light. The smallest amount of light pollution from a nearby town or any moonlight whatsoever will destroy your chances of seeing it. The best time of the year to see zodiacal light is in early spring after evening twilight (or early autumn before morning twilight for early risers) when the angle of the ecliptic is favorable. It will appear as a fairly broad, faint, glowing band, aligned with the ecliptic. It is nearly always visible from very rural locations on clear moonless nights at such a time.

Gegenschein is similar. It too is sunlight reflecting off dust, and it too is located in the ecliptic. Gegenschein is brightest at a location far away from the sun. In fact, it is located at the solar antipode — the place in the sky exactly opposite the sun. At this location, the dust particles are reflecting sunlight directly back toward the Earth, resulting in a brighter glow. Gegenschein appears as a small, faint, glowing oval, about 10 degrees or so in length and aligned with the ecliptic. As with zodiacal light, gegenschein cannot be seen in the presence of any light pollution or moonlight whatsoever. The best time to see gegenschein is at midnight, when the solar antipode is highest in the sky.

◇ Satellites

It is very common on a clear night to see a faint, slow-moving "star" glide along the night sky. This is likely a satellite. Many of them go over every night. Unlike an airplane, they will have no noticeable size, and no blinking (or red and green) lights! Sometimes when they are at a low angle, it can be hard to tell which is which, and you have to wait until the object is higher in the sky. But with a little practice, you can spot dozens of satellites on a moonless night.

Most of them are faint, around magnitude 4 or 5. But that's still within the limit of human vision, once you are well dark-adapted. Some are fainter than this, and a few are brighter. The international space station rivals the brightest planets. And there is the occasional "iridium flare" which gets much brighter — but more on that later. Satellites travel with a characteristic velocity, which you can gauge by eye with a little practice.

Donnington Castle near Newbury at nighttime as the International Space Station passes overhead. Also the moon and Jupiter are visible. This shot is made up of ten, 15-second shots to capture the movement of the ISS through the sky.

This velocity seems the fastest when the satellite is highest in the sky, since it is closest to the observer at that time. A typical satellite takes about 7 minutes to go from one horizon to the other. It takes 90 minutes to orbit the Earth — but that doesn't mean that you will necessarily see it again in 90 minutes. The Earth is rotating, and so the satellite may not go over your location on its next pass.

Two conditions must be met if you are going to see a given satellite. First, it must pass over your location on Earth, or at least relatively close to that location. Second, the satellite must be sufficiently illuminated by sunlight. It may seem surprising at first that the second condition would ever be satisfied. After all, it must be nighttime if you are going to see the satellite, so how can it be illuminated by sunlight? The answer comes from the fact that typical satellites orbit at about 200 miles above Earth's surface. And it is still daylight "up there" even though the sun has set for those on Earth's

surface. It is the same reason that someone on a mountaintop can watch a sunset after the sun has already set for those people at the mountain's base. For this reason, there are certain times and seasons where it is easier to see satellites than at other times and seasons, due to the relative position of the Earth and sun.

The best time of the year for satellite viewing is early summer or late spring. (Winter is the worst.) The best time of night is just after evening twilight or just before morning twilight. At such a time, the angle of the sun is such that most satellites passing overhead will be illuminated by sunlight, even though the sky appears nice and dark to the observer. This maximizes the contrast and allows you to see the faintest satellites.

Just after evening twilight, the portion of the sky where satellites will appear illuminated by sunlight is maximized. As the night progresses, the Earth's shadow will creep up like a blanket in the eastern sky. You may notice that satellites moving eastward will slowly fade and disappear at a certain point in the sky, as they creep into Earth's shadow. You are essentially watching a "lunar" eclipse of a satellite. You will notice that the area where satellites go into eclipse gradually moves westward as the evening progresses, until eventually, you won't see any satellites at all because they are all eclipsed in Earth's shadow. Then as morning twilight approaches, satellites will once again be visible in the eastern sky, as the blanket of invisibility drops lower and lower in the west.

It is possible to use computer software to predict exactly when and where satellites can be seen on any given evening. As of the writing of this book, there is a website, www.heavens-above.com, which will compute the passing times and positions of brighter satellites for your location on Earth. (The international space station is a very popular observing target, and well worth seeing.) There are cell phone apps which can also do this. Some programs only compute the positions of satellites, whereas others also calculate whether the satellite is illuminated by sunlight. Remember that this second condition must be met if the satellite is to be visible; otherwise it might pass directly overhead, but you will see nothing.

At mid-northern latitudes, most satellites you observe will be traveling at a high inclination — nearly north-to-south, or south-to-north. Some will be moving west-to-east. For those people living closer to the equator, more of the west-to-east satellites will be visible. You will only very rarely see a satellite traveling east-to-west. Such a direction is opposite to Earth's rotation, and it requires extra fuel to launch a satellite into such an orbit. So it's never done unless there is a really compelling reason.

Most satellites maintain a fairly steady brightness, but occasionally satellites will appear to "pulse," often with a period of half a second to a few seconds. If the pulses are quasi-regular, the satellite is a tumbler; it is slowly rotating and catching the sunlight at various angles. These are often spent rocket cases. Some satellites

have unusual shapes and can appear to brighten and fade erratically as their various surfaces catch the sunlight at different angles.

The best example of the temporary brightening of a satellite by specular reflection of sunlight is the so-called "iridium flare." The company Iridium Communications Inc. has launched and maintains 66 Earth-orbiting satellites. These satellites are used for communication and data transfer with satellite phones. They can be seen with the unaided eye (barely), and shine around magnitude 6. The satellites themselves have an unusual shape — they have antennae which are highly reflective. When sunlight strikes these antennae at just the right angle, an observer on Earth will see the satellite become incredibly bright. They can reach magnitude -8, much brighter than Venus. This event is called an "iridium flare." It lasts only a few seconds. The satellite gradually brightens, and then gradually fades back down to magnitude 6.

The maximum intensity of the iridium flare depends on a number of factors, such as the position and distance to the satellite, and the sun angle relative to the observer. However, these factors are predictable, so it is possible to calculate in advance exactly when and where an iridium flare will occur, and how bright it will appear. They are fun events to watch. You can consult an internet site such as www.heavens-above.com and enter your location to find when the next iridium flares will occur. They are quite common, with several happening on a typical week. The same website also has calculations for passes by the international space station, and other interesting satellites and current spacecraft.

Chapter 6

Telescope Basics

A telescope can open up amazing views of creation that simply cannot be seen without one. It is certainly an investment worth consideration. But what kind of telescope should you get? What are the advantages and disadvantages of different kinds of telescopes? What will best serve your needs for the amount of money? In this chapter we explore these questions and investigate the kinds of telescopes that are best for a given purpose.

◇The Functions of a Telescope

Basically a telescope does three things: (1) a telescope *magnifies* — it makes little things look big; (2) a telescope *resolves* — it makes fuzzy things look sharp and clearer; (3) a telescope *gathers light* — it makes faint things look bright. These three abilities are what make a telescope so useful: magnifying power, resolving power, and light-gathering power. Many people new to astronomy assume that the first (magnifying power) is the most important. But, in fact, the third is probably the most important. Many objects in the universe are quite large, and would easily be seen with the naked eye, except they are too faint.

So one of the telescope's most important functions is to make faint things bright enough to be seen. Effectively, a telescope is a "light bucket." It captures light from a large area, and "squeezes it down" so that it will fit into your eyeball. The larger the telescope, the more light it can collect, and the brighter the universe will appear. Many things that cannot be seen at all with the naked-eye will be bright and obvious as viewed through a telescope. A larger (greater in diameter) telescope will allow you to see more things than a smaller telescope, since the larger telescope has more light-gathering power.

Resolving power is the ability to "separate" things that are close together. For example, two stars that are very close together will appear as one star to the naked eye. But a telescope will allow you to see that there are two stars there. Basically, the higher the resolving power, the better view you will get. A view of Jupiter through a telescope with high resolving power will look sharp and crisp and enable you to see many fine details that you could not see with a lesser telescope. As with light-gathering power, a larger diameter telescope will have greater resolving power than a smaller one. Telescopes also magnify — they increase the apparent size of the section of the sky at which they are aimed. This allows you to see details that you cannot see with the unaided eye — craters on the moon, the rings of Saturn, the belts and zones on Jupiter. The magnifying power of a telescope does *not* depend (directly) on its size. In fact, you can choose how much you want your

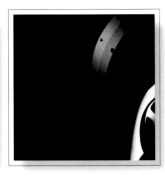   

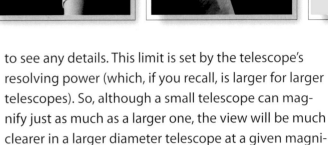

telescope to magnify by selecting the appropriate eyepiece. This will be discussed later. The point here is that *any* telescope can magnify by *any* amount! In fact, there is a common "scam" in telescope advertising that makes use of this fact. Some telescopes are advertised by their magnification: "This telescope can magnify 500 times!" Don't be fooled. This advertisement is technically true but is misleading since *any* telescope can magnify 500 times or by any other amount as well!

Although you can magnify by any amount you want, there is a tradeoff. The larger things appear, the fuzzier/blurrier they appear. If Jupiter looks sharp and crisp at low magnification, it may look fuzzy and unclear at high magnification. So although there is no theoretical limit on magnification, there is a practical limit — at some point the image will be too fuzzy and unclear

to see any details. This limit is set by the telescope's resolving power (which, if you recall, is larger for larger telescopes). So, although a small telescope can magnify just as much as a larger one, the view will be much clearer in a larger diameter telescope at a given magnification.

◇The Size of the Telescope

The overall ability of a telescope is determined by the diameter of the primary lens or primary mirror — the "aperture." A "fatter" telescope is able to gather more light from the sky than a thinner one. The light-gathering power is proportional to the area of the telescope which is proportional to the *square* of the aperture. The resolution goes linearly with the aperture. Let's use a practical example to illustrate this. Suppose we wanted to look at a globular star cluster. We first look through a

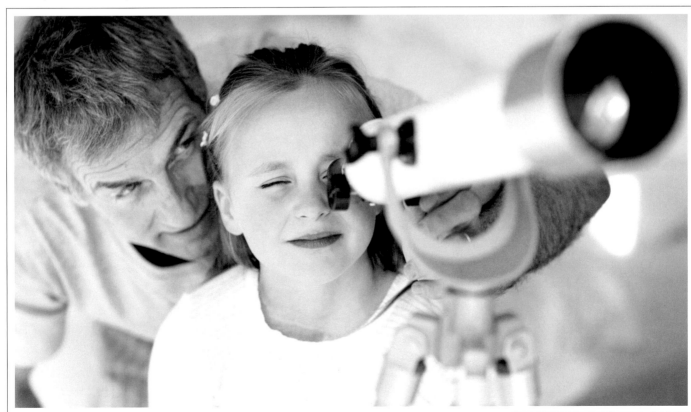

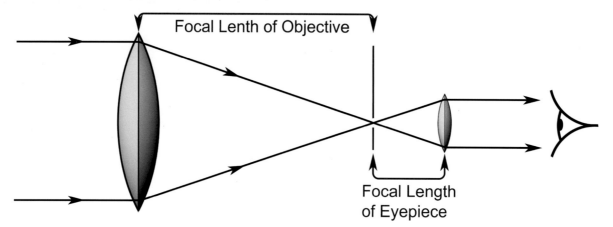

6.1 The light path from a distant source through a refracting telescope. The magnification is the focal length of the objective lens divided by the focal length of the eyepiece.

4-inch aperture telescope, and then through an 8-inch aperture telescope.

Since the 8-inch telescope has twice the diameter of the 4-inch, it has twice the resolving power. Therefore, the stars will appear sharp and crisp as seen through the 8-inch telescope, but they will blend together in the 4-inch telescope. Instead of seeing thousands of stars, we will see only a single blur through the 4-inch. Furthermore, since the 8-inch has twice the diameter of the 4-inch, it has *four* times the light-gathering power (since the square of two is four). The globular cluster will appear four times brighter in the 8-inch than it does in the 4-inch. Light gathering power is very important for observing things that are faint.

◇Kinds of Telescopes

At the most basic level, there are two kinds of telescopes: refractors and reflectors. Reflectors use curved mirrors to reflect and focus incoming light and pass it through a final lens (an eyepiece) to make it suitable for viewing. Refractors use lenses only — no mirrors. Most people think of refractors when they think of a telescope, even though refractors are less used by professional astronomers than reflectors. Let us now take a look at refractors in detail, and discuss their advantages and disadvantages over reflectors.

◇Refractors

Refractors are the simplest type of telescope and the first to be invented. A basic refractor consists of only

two lenses. Light is bent and focused by the larger primary lens at one end of the telescope, and then re-collimated (the beams are made parallel to each other) by the small lens at the other end FIGURE 6.1. The small lens is what a person looks into to see the image, so that lens is called the "eyepiece." The image will appear inverted; everything will be upside-down and backward (you'll get used to it).

The magnification of a distant object is simply the focal length (the distance it takes for light to come to a focus) of the primary lens divided by the focal length of the eyepiece. Telescopes are designed so that the eyepiece is exchangeable. By removing one eyepiece and inserting a different one with a smaller focal length, you increase the magnification. The focal length (in millimeters) is almost always printed on the side of the eyepiece. Sometimes the telescope itself will have the focal length printed on it, or it will be in the manual that comes with the telescope. As a rough estimate, the length of a telescope is usually a good indication of its focal length at least for refractors and Newtonians. You should have at least one low-power eyepiece (~75x) and one high magnification eyepiece (~300x).

Refractors are easy to recognize because they are usually very long and thin FIGURE 6.2. A refractor tends to give very high quality images for a given size of lens. This is in part because it has an unobstructed aperture; there is nothing "blocking" the lens (not the case with most reflectors). Generally speaking, a refractor with a

6-inch lens will give a much better image than a reflector with a 6-inch mirror. My experience is that this is especially the case with planets and the moon; refractors produce much sharper images.

However, a refractor has a few disadvantages from the reflector. Refractors are inconveniently long for a given aperture (the width of the lens). If you buy a refractor that is small enough to be portable, the lens will probably be less than three inches — you'd be better off to get a good set of binoculars. (Many of the telescopes offered at Walmart, Target, etc., are small refractors — I don't recommend these.) The high-quality refractors (five to ten feet long or more) are generally very expensive. A good-quality refractor will be more than $10,000. In general, I would *not* suggest buying a small, cheap refractor.

Refractors also suffer from "chromatic aberration." Any bright object you view through a refractor will be surrounded by a little purple halo. The reason for this is that refractors work by bending light; but glass does not bend all wavelengths of light (which the mind perceives as "colors") equally. In the same way that a prism (by design) splits white light into its constituent colors, the lens of a refracting telescope (unfortunately) does the same thing. Some of the more expensive refractors can nearly eliminate chromatic aberration by using a combination of lenses.

Isaac Newton was the first to understand why chromatic aberration occurs. He was also the first to devise and implement a solution to the problem. Newton realized that although glass does not bend all light wavelengths equally, a mirror does *reflect* all wavelengths equally. A telescope that uses a mirror instead of a primary lens will not suffer from chromatic aberration. Newton was the first person to construct a reflecting telescope.

6.2　A 5.5-inch diameter refracting telescope on an equatorial tripod

◇ Reflectors

Reflectors use a curved mirror (instead of a primary lens) to bring light to a focus; they use an eyepiece (lens) just like a refractor to re-collimate the light for viewing. Reflectors have two main advantages over a refractor. They do not suffer from chromatic aberration, and they are much shorter (and therefore cheaper, easier to make, and more portable) than refractors for a given diameter. (Recall that the diameter sets the light-gathering power and resolution.)

Reflectors inevitably have a more complicated design than refractors for one simple reason: a mirror reflects light back in the direction from which it came. This means that in the simplest kind of reflector, the eyepiece (and the person looking through the telescope) would be blocking the target object. To get around this problem, almost all reflectors use a secondary mirror to redirect the light to the eyepiece. The position and orientation of the secondary mirror depends on the

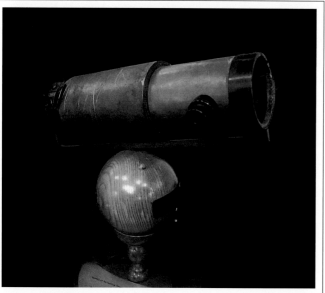

Photograph © Andrew Dunn, 5 November 2004.

A replica of Isaac Newton's second reflecting telescope of 1672. This replica of that second Royal Society reflector is in the Whipple Museum of the History of Science in Cambridge.

type of reflector. There are many, many different kinds of reflectors, so we'll just address the most common kinds.

◇ Newtonians

Since the first reflecting telescope was designed and built by Isaac Newton it bears his name: the Newtonian reflector. Newton's solution was to put the secondary mirror near the focal point of the primary, and orient it at a 45-degree angle so that light is directed out the side of the telescope at a 90-degree angle. Newtonian telescopes are easy to recognize; they have a long barrel (though not as long as a refractor) and the eyepiece is on the side of the telescope near the open end **FIGURE 6.3**. The Newtonian telescope is a good design. It is relatively simple, and inexpensive to make.

It surprises many newcomers to astronomy that the shadow of the secondary mirror cannot be seen when looking through a Newtonian telescope. It is, after all, blocking a small section of the sky from falling onto the primary mirror. But the secondary mirror is much closer than the distant star on which the eyepiece is focused. The secondary mirror is therefore extremely "out of focus" as far as the observer is concerned. So in practice it is as if the secondary mirror is not even there. However, in principle, the secondary mirror does block a small amount of light and makes the view slightly less bright than it would be in a refractor of equal diameter.

◇ Cassegrains

Cassegrain telescopes are much shorter than New-tonians (for a given diameter) because the secondary mirror is placed much closer to the primary and not near the focal point. With a Cassegrain style, the secondary mirror is not oriented at 45 degrees, but instead is aimed directly back at the primary mirror. The primary mirror in a Cassegrain has a hole at its center. The secondary mirror directs the light through this hole and then onto the eyepiece. Large diameter telescopes (such as those used in many observatories) are often Cassegrains (or a similar style) because an equivalent Newtonian would be too long, and it would be inconvenient to look through the eyepiece (which might be several stories above the ground for a big telescope). One disadvantage of the Cassegrain is that its secondary mirror is larger than that of an equivalent Newtonian, and thus blocks more light and decreases contrast.

◇Catadioptrics

Generally considered to be the best all-around general use telescope for amateur astronomers is the Schmidt-Cassegrain FIGURE 6.4. This telescope is the same basic design as a Cassegrain, except that it has a "corrector plate" on its open end. This piece of glass appears flat, but it isn't. Its thickness varies across the surface so that it is a "lens" of sorts, but much less powerful than the strong lens of a refractor. The Schmidt-Cassegrain is classified as a catadioptric

telescope — meaning it uses both a (primary) lens and a mirror. Most of the light bending is still done by the primary mirror, and so it is more like a reflector than a refractor, and does not suffer from any significant chromatic aberration.

The Schmidt-Cassegrain has a number of advantages over other styles. For mathematical reasons we won't go into, the primary mirror of a telescope is not able to bring every object in the field of view into perfect focus. The corrector plate of the Schmidt-Cassegrain partially compensates for this, and improves the view.

6.3   A 10-inch diameter Newtonian telescope on an equatorial tripod

Schmidt-Cassegrain telescopes are also very compact and portable for a given aperture.

The Maksutov-Cassegrain is very similar to the Schmidt-Cassegrain. It too has a corrector plate on the front end. The difference is that the corrector plate for the Maksutov-Cassegrain is very thick and is noticeably curved inward. The secondary mirror is simply a silvered region on the inside of the corrector plate. This design is easier to make than a Schmidt-Cassegrain, though it requires more glass. Maksutov-Cassegrains are heavier than Schmidt-Cassegrains because of the thick corrector plate. They take longer to reach thermal equilibrium (discussed in chapter 7) than a Schmidt-Cassegrain, but are otherwise very similar. The

6.4 An 8-inch diameter Schmidt-Cassegrain telescope on an equatorial tripod

From simple to the more complex,
telescopes are available in a variety
of price and capability ranges

Schmidt-Cassegrain is generally better if you have a choice between the two.

◇ Which Telescope Style Is Best for Amateur Astronomy?

Overall, two styles of telescope stand out above the rest for general use in amateur astronomy circles: the Newtonian reflector, and the Schmidt-Cassegrain. These styles of telescope will give you the most observing ability per dollar. Either one would be a good choice. Which one is best depends on exactly what you want to do with them.

The Schmidt-Cassegrain is usually a bit more expensive than the Newtonian for a given aperture. But, it is about half the length, and therefore far more portable. It is easier to use as well. Once the Schmidt-Cassegrain is set up, it is always at a convenient height to view virtually any object. Since the Schmidt-Cassegrain is a closed tube, it is less prone to dust and other contaminants than a Newtonian.

The Schmidt-Cassegrain has a few minor disadvantages over the Newtonian. Since the Schmidt-Cassegrain has a larger secondary mirror, the light-gathering power will be slightly less, and the contrast slightly less than a Newtonian of equal aperture. Images tend to appear sharper in Newtonians.

The Schmidt-Cassegrain has one major (and very annoying) disadvantage over the Newtonian: It suffers from "dewing." As the evening progresses, dew tends to collect on the corrector plate, and you find that you can no longer see anything. This won't necessarily happen every night (and is worse in some climates than others), but it happens often enough to be annoying. The reason is because the corrector plate is able to radiate heat into space, and so its temperature drops below the air temperature, allowing water to condense.

There are various ways to heat up the plate slightly once this happens. Also, there are various extras you can buy to prevent it from happening such as a "dew shield" or an electronic heating unit. But with a Newtonian, you don't have to worry about these things. Newtonians do not suffer from "dewing" because they have no corrector plate. (Dew will not collect on the mirror because it is partially thermally "insulated" from space by the tube of the telescope — which acts just like a dew shield.)

The main advantage of the Newtonian is that it is generally cheaper for a given aperture. The Newtonian has a longer tube and is less easily transported than its equal-aperture Schmidt-Cassegrain. Also, since the observer looks into the side of the Newtonian tube, he or she may be in an uncomfortable position, depending on where the telescope is pointed; this also depends on the mount (discussed below). However, in some cases the telescope tube can be rotated on the mount so that the eyepiece is at a reasonable height. (This may sound like a minor point. But when you observe for hours it really isn't — trust me.) Since Newtonians have a smaller secondary mirror than Schmidt-Cassegrains, the contrast is slightly better. I have found that views of the planets and the moon are generally a bit better in a Newtonian than a Schmidt-Cassegrain.

Bottom line: the Newtonian is slightly cheaper. The Schmidt-Cassegrain is slightly more convenient and portable. Either is a good choice.

A Schmidt-Cassegrain telescope with a spotting scope and a telrad

◇What Size Telescope Is Best for Amateur Astronomy?

The size of a telescope is one of its most important aspects. Make sure to get at least a *6-inch* aperture telescope. (This rules out the "toy" refractors that you'll find in many department stores.) A 6-inch aperture is the smallest telescope that allows you to see details in hundreds of faint astronomical objects like nebulae, galaxies, and globular star clusters. This number (6 inches) is subjective, of course, and it depends on how dark your skies are. A 5-inch telescope under dark skies could easily beat a 10-inch under light-polluted skies.

A *10-inch* telescope is probably my favorite size if you want to move the telescope. I find that a 10-inch telescope is usually the right trade-off between size and portability. Obviously, with greater size you can see more, but it becomes increasingly difficult to transport the telescope once you get much larger than 10 inches. Of course, if you're going to have your telescope permanently mounted, this isn't an issue. But most amateur astronomers do move their telescope — if only to take it inside after viewing. I also find that you can *clearly* see the individual stars in a globular star cluster, whereas this is more difficult in a 6-inch telescope. Globular star clusters are stunningly beautiful, but you won't get the full experience with less than about 8 inches of aperture.

If you *already* have a telescope smaller than 6 inches, don't throw it out; you'll still be able to enjoy a number of things with it. But for those people considering getting a very small telescope, I would recommend instead getting a nice set of binoculars. A powerful set of binoculars will allow you to see anything a small (less than 6 inches) telescope can see, but with both eyes — and right-side up. Binoculars (or the small telescope you already own) will allow you to observe the moon (which is truly beautiful in first and third quarter phases), bright stars, open star clusters, the Androm- eda Galaxy, and the oc-

casional bright comet. Additionally, they have a large field of view and are very useful for finding the general vicinity in which an object is located. However, most of the more spectacular objects (nebulae, star clusters, galaxies, and detailed images of planets) will not be visible, or will be very disappointing through binoculars or a telescope smaller than 6 inches. Again, the 6-inch cutoff is not a "hard" limit, but my experience is that you won't want to go smaller than this.

◇What Kind of Mount Is Best?

Any telescope requires a mount: a tripod or some other device on which the telescope rests. A mount allows the telescope to pivot in at least two directions, thereby allowing the user to point the telescope (in principle) in any direction in the sky. Another function of a mount is to "track" an object in the sky using a "clock drive." A clock drive is a motor that slowly rotates the telescope in the opposite direction the Earth rotates — thereby compensating for the Earth's rotation. Some mounts come with a clock drive; others don't. Often the clock drive is attached to the telescope rather than the mount.

Without a clock drive, an object you are viewing will slowly drift out of the field of view since the telescope is positioned on the rotating Earth. So if you don't get a clock drive, you'll have to slightly adjust the telescope every few minutes and manually re-center the object you're looking at. The effect is more severe at higher magnification. It's not a big deal, and you will

quickly learn to readjust the telescope very efficiently. However, if you wish to do *photography* through your telescope, it is absolutely essential to get a clock drive. Even if you don't want to do photography, a clock drive is a very nice feature to have, particularly if you want to have other people looking through the telescope as well.

Telescope mounts come in two varieties: equatorial mounts, and horizon or "alt-azimuth" (altitude-azimuth) mounts. The difference is where the two (perpendicular) axes point. With an alt-azimuth mount, one axis allows you to move the telescope in an up-down fashion (altitude); the other (primary) axis rotates the telescope in the horizontal direction (azimuth). With an equatorial mount (once adjusted and aligned), one axis allows the telescope to be pointed toward or away from the North Celestial Pole. The other (primary) axis rotates the telescope along the celestial equator. The telescope is therefore attached to an equatorial mount in a "tilted" fashion. The tilt is adjustable, and should be set to match the latitude of the observing site; of course this only needs to be done once, unless you move to a different latitude. Some alt-azimuth mounts can be converted into equatorial mounts by the addition of an equatorial "wedge."

When setting up an equatorial mount, you must align it so that its central axis points toward the North Celestial Pole (essentially at the North Star). For casual observing, the alignment does not need to be very precise, and can be done in seconds. For astrophotography, the alignment needs to be more precise and this can take some time to set up. Many equatorial mounts have setting circles which allow the user to find objects using coordinates. This isn't possible with an alt-azimuth mount unless it is computer controlled.

One major advantage of an equatorial mount is that they usually come with a clock drive either on the mount itself or on the telescope. Since an equatorial mount is aligned with the Earth's rotation, only a single motor running at a constant speed is necessary to compensate for Earth's rotation. Alt-azimuth mounts cannot use a clock drive unless the pointing is computer-controlled. An equatorial mount is the best for astrophotography. A computer-controlled alt-azimuth mount works very well for short exposures, but cannot be used for longer ones because the field of view rotates (though in some cases depending on how it's done, the CCD software can compensate for this).

Another consideration when considering which type of mount to get is that it is often difficult to point a telescope in a direction that is very close to the alignment of its primary rotation axis. For an equatorial telescope, this means it is difficult (and in some cases impossible) to look at something very close to the North Star. For an alt-azimuth telescope, it may be difficult to look at something that is directly overhead.

Overall, an equatorial mount (with clock drive) is probably best once it is set up, though it is a bit more awkward than a simple alt-azimuth mount.

Small refracting telescope on alt-azimuthal mount.
Photo by Kosebamse

Dobsonian mount

I have found that a computer-driven alt-azimuth mount also works very well, though it takes longer to set up. And many of these can be converted into an equatorial with the addition of a wedge. An alt-azimuth mount is probably the least expensive and most easily transported. A particularly common alt-azimuth mount is the "Dobsonian." This mount is inexpensive because it is very easy to make. It is also very portable and easy to use, and is therefore a popular choice — if you don't need a clock drive. Only Newtonian telescopes (or similar variations) use this mount. A disadvantage of a Dobsonian mount is that the telescope is sometimes inconveniently positioned — especially when pointed at objects near the horizon. If you want to do astrophotography, get an equatorial mount or a computer-controlled telescope with an alt-azimuth mount. Computer-controlled systems make astrophotography much easier. In fact, I have found that astrophotography is very challenging without a computer-controlled telescope. The computer control is able to compensate for Earth's rotation much more precisely than can be done with a quick equatorial set up.

◇Computer Control Systems

Many of the newer telescopes come with computer systems that allow you to input coordinates and then the telescope automatically goes to the target. This is certainly a useful feature, though it is not essential. It can be helpful when trying to find a new object — especially a faint one. Simply input the coordinates and the telescope slews to the object. I have found that most such systems are not quite as precise as people might hope. They will certainly get you very close to your target object, but you may have to adjust a bit to get it centered.

Believe it or not, there are drawbacks to computer-controlled telescopes. One is that they take longer to get started. After setting up the tripod, a GPS computer-controlled system might take 10 to 15 minutes to find a satellite and go through its initialization routine. A simple equatorial clock drive is ready to go with the

flip of a switch — about one second. If a computer-controlled system is bumped, you have to go through (at least part of) the initialization routine all over again. But a simple equatorial clock drive system just needs to be pointed at Polaris again.

There is a subjective drawback to computer control software. I've noticed that people who rely on such systems often do not know how to find deep-sky objects any other way. Simply typing in two coordinates (or an object name) and watching the telescope move to its target does not give the user a "feel" for where objects really are. I find that it is very enjoyable to learn where a deep-sky object is in the sky and move the telescope myself to the target. It's a pleasant challenge, and it gives me an appreciation for the night sky that coordinate-users may lack. Also, I can tell from a quick glance what objects are going to be visible at a given time and which are below the horizon. Of course, computer guiding software is a nice bonus; you don't have to use it, but you may want to in a pinch. If you do get a computer-controlled system, I recommend that you turn it off at least every now and then and hone your star-hopping skills.

Computerized mount

◇The Spotting Scope

Most telescopes come with a second small refractor telescope attached to them. This is a spotting telescope (or "spotter"). Its purpose is to allow you to find and center a target object. Without a spotter, pointing the telescope (without computer aid) at even an obvious, bright object like the moon can be surprisingly challenging to newcomers. This is because a telescope zooms in on such a small section of the sky that trying to find that tiny spot by "eye-balling" down the telescope can be very difficult. The spotter scope has a much wider field of view than the main telescope. Thus, it is much easier to find something in the spotter scope. Centering the object in the spotter causes it to be centered in the main telescope as well. The spotting scope needs to be aligned with the main telescope the first time it is used — or any time it gets bumped out of alignment. A spotter scope usually has cross hairs which identify the exact center. In some cases, these can be illuminated by varying amounts. Since the spotting scope is a telescope, objects appear inverted.

It is becoming more common these days to have a telrad instead of (or in addition to) a spotting scope. A telrad is a bit like a "heads-up-display"; it looks like nothing but a piece of glass through which you can see the stars beyond. But the telrad adds a laser-produced arti-ficial spot, concentric circles, or cross hairs that indicate exactly where the telescope is pointed. The intensity of the laser is usually adjustable. Like the spotting scope, the telrad must be aligned with the main telescope the first time it is used. It makes pointing the telescope at the desired object extremely easy. Beginners will find telrads a lot easier to use than a spotting scope.

◇What's the Best Combination?

If you want to spend as little money as possible and you don't want to do astrophotography, a 6-inch to 12-inch Newtonian reflector with a Dobsonian mount may be the best choice. For slightly more, you can get either a bigger telescope, or a higher quality telescope/mount design. My first choice would be a 12-inch Schmidt-Cassegrain with an equatorial mount and clock drive. This design is compact, and therefore easily transported; yet it is large enough to see many of the wonders of the universe. If you want to do astrophotography, get a computer-controlled system; these generally track much better than the alternative. It is my hope that using the principles outlined above, people will be able to select a telescope that will best fit their interest and finances and allow them to enjoy the wonder of the night sky.

◇Telescope First-Time Setup and Use

The most important tip I can offer regarding setting up your new telescope for the first time is this: do it during the day. You can even do it inside. You don't want to be trying to figure out some aspect of the telescope on the night you are trying to use it. Spend some time learning how to assemble and disassemble the telescope and mount. Use the daylight to make sure the spotter scope or telrad is aligned.

↘ Telescope Setup

1   If you have a Newtonian telescope, the first thing you will want to do is to make sure the telescope is approximately collimated — that its mirrors are at the proper angle. This is easy to do.

2   Remove any eyepiece that may be in the eyepiece holder.

3   Then look into the eyepiece holder. You should see a reflection of your own eyeball.

4   This reflection should be dead center in the field of view.

   If it isn't, use the three screws on the bottom of the primary mirror to adjust the angle of the mirror. It is useful to have a friend help with this so that one person can be looking through the eyepiece holder while the other one makes the adjustment.

5   The secondary mirror itself can be adjusted up and down as well. (At night, you can check the collimation by defocusing the telescope on a bright star. The out-of-focus star should appear as a ring with the hole in the middle. If the hole is not centered in the ring, the telescope needs to be collimated.)

Next comes the mount set up. Since there are many different types of mounts, I cannot give a generalization of how to do this, other than to simply say follow the instructions that came with the telescope.

Telescope Mount Setup

1 A Dobsonian mount will be simple, and consists of not much more than setting the telescope in its groove.

2 A horizon-based tripod mount is not much harder. The only difficulty will be in guessing how long to adjust the legs, and making sure they are tight.

3 Equatorial mounts are the most complex, and may involve counterweights and take several steps. An important tip here is to make sure the mount is set up completely — including counterweights — before putting the telescope on it.

Additional Tips: After the telescope is securely on its mount, get a feel for how the telescope moves. Try pointing it in various directions, and learn how to lock down each rotation axis. After you get a feel for it, try pointing at a distant object, like a tree or streetlamp. If you are practicing inside, you can point the telescope through a window at something outside. (The view will not be great because the window-glass will cause some distortion. But that's okay; it's just practice.)

Next, line up the spotter scope and/or telrad. To do this, first point the telescope at some obvious distant object, like the tallest tree or the top of a house, and make sure the selected target is dead center in the field of view. Then lock down both axes of the telescope so that it cannot move. If the target is terrestrial (which I highly recommend), make sure the clock drive is turned off so that it will not drift. If you're doing this at night and can only find a bright celestial target, then of course you'll want the clock drive on. Now adjust the spotter scope or telrad so that the target is centered in the cross hairs. Often spotter scopes are held in place by six screws: three on one end forming an equilateral triangle, and three on the other end as well. If this is the case, then you can adjust the position of the spotter by loosening one of the three screws in the triangle,

and then tightening another one. When you're done, the spotter scope should have the target in the cross hairs, and all the screws should be snug. Double check by looking through the main telescope to make sure the target is still centered.

If the telescope has a clock drive, turn it on just to make sure that it works. Some telescopes have an internal rechargeable battery, others use internal disposable batteries, and some use external power. If your telescope does not have internal batteries, but has a jack for external power, such as a 12-volt input, I highly recommend buying an external rechargeable battery to use for that port. You can place the battery under the telescope's tripod where it is out of the way. For obvious reasons, it's best to avoid using electrical cords outside at night. Make sure the batteries are charged and ready to use for night viewing.

About an hour before you are ready to start your nighttime observing session, take the telescope outside and set it up. This will give the telescope time to reach thermal equilibrium so you will have the best viewing. Leave all lens caps on until the moment you are ready to start viewing, to prevent dew from collecting.

Telescope Alignment

You can begin the alignment of the telescope as soon as it is dark enough to see the North Star (or any stars if the telescope is computer controlled). Place the telescope tripod on a non-tilted surface — as flat as you can find. If your telescope does not use a clock drive (such as with a Dobsonian mount) then you don't need to do any kind of alignment; just start observing. Otherwise, you'll want to orient the telescope so that the clock drive correctly compensates for Earth's rotation.

If the telescope is computer controlled, turn it on, and begin the auto-alignment program. The initialization procedure varies from telescope to telescope, but will usually be some variation of the following: The telescope will use internal instruments to compute its approximate orientation. If it has a GPS system, it will use satellites to determine its current latitude and longi-

Pointing out the North Star

tude. Otherwise, you may have to manually enter your latitude and longitude. Then the telescope will select a star and try to point to it. It will usually not be very close. You will have to manually adjust the telescope so that it is centered on the star and then enter. If you don't know the star, some programs will let you select another star. Then the telescope will select one additional star, and you will do this again. After this, the telescope is properly oriented and will track automatically. This process usually takes a few minutes.

If the telescope is not computer controlled but does have a clock drive, you will use the North Star to orient it. On an equatorial mount, there is a latitude setting. Adjust this to your latitude, and lock it down. You should never have to adjust that setting again unless you move to another state. Now, turn the telescope so that the primary axis is pointing directly toward the North Star. Some telescopes have a small spotter scope built into the mount, which makes it easy to center right at the North Star. If not, just eyeball it. The closer you get to being lined up with the North Star, the better the telescope will track. If you are not doing astrophotography, it really doesn't need to be all that precise. It shouldn't take more than a few seconds to do this. Turn on the clock drive and you are ready to go.

If you need more precise polar alignment for astrophotography, you can set the declination of the telescope to 90 degrees, and then adjust the tripod until the North Star is centered. Then rotate the right-ascension axis by 90 degrees. If Polaris remains stationary, the telescope is well aligned. If Polaris moves, adjust the tripod slightly and try again.

◇Observation for Beginners

Once the telescope is aligned, you can begin observations. The first time you use a telescope, I recommend getting some practice using the spotter scope, or telrad, if you have one. Even if the telescope is computer controlled, I suggest using the controls to *manually* find a few bright objects, just to get a feel for the spotter scope. I have found that telrads are very intuitive, and beginners can use them right away. However, beginners sometimes have trouble with spotter scopes. This is because spotter scopes (1) invert, (2) magnify, and (3) brighten. So what you see through the spotter scope will not look the same as what you see with the unaided eye. It takes some practice to get used to this.

I highly suggest beginning with the moon — it's the easiest object to target. People who have never used a telescope before are often surprised at how tricky it can be to target an object, which is why it is helpful to start with something bright and easy to find. If the moon is not above the horizon, try a bright star or planet instead. Sight down the barrel of the telescope; imagine that it has "gunsights" on the top of the barrel, and line up your head with those. This will indicate where the telescope is currently pointed. Remember to sight down the telescope to where it is pointed — not where you *want* it to be pointed. Beginners have a tough time with this. Then move the telescope, keeping your head lined up with it until it is pointed at the desired target. If you are successful, the target should now be in the field of view of the spotter scope.

If it's not, and the target object is the moon, you can often use the glare surrounding the moon to tell which way you need to go. If the target is a bright star and does not appear in the spotter, try moving the telescope slightly in a spiral fashion while looking through

the spotter. Often the target is very close and will appear. If you have low magnification on the spotter scope (which is the way most are set up), then you don't need to be as precise with your initial attempt since the field of view will be larger. Once the target is visible in the spotter, move the telescope slowly until the target is centered in the cross hairs. If the spotter scope is well aligned, the target will now be visible in the main telescope.

◇Spotter Scope Tips

Remember that what you see in a spotter scope is not what you see with the naked eye. First of all, the image will be inverted. If your naked eye sees a blue star above and to the right of a red star, then in the spotter scope you should expect to see the blue star below and to the left of the red one. Basically, you'll want to turn your mental map upside-down and backward

Spotter scope

when you go to look through the spotter scope. This also means that you will push the telescope in the opposite direction from what you might expect when looking through the spotter. For example, if the target object is below center, your intuition might lead you to think you are pointed too high, and so you should push the telescope down. But since the image is inverted, you are in fact too low and you should push the telescope up. The image of the target will then move up in the spotter. It's a strange experience for beginners, but you will very quickly adapt to this.

Second, remember that the spotter scope magnifies a bit, but usually only by a few times, depending on the design. So in our previous example not only will the blue and red stars have switched positions, but they will now be several times farther apart. Keep this in mind when "star hopping" (described in chapter 7). Unless objects are very close together in the sky, they will probably not be in the same field of view in the spotter scope.

Third, the spotter scope has a small but perceptible amount of light-gathering power. It will make things look a bit brighter than they do to the naked eye. Beginners often don't mentally compensate for this. As a result, they think they are centered on the target star, when in fact they are not. The star in the spotter is actually a *fainter* star than the target, but which appears brighter due to the amplification. Remember, if it looks identical to what your naked eye sees, it's not the right star; it should appear slightly *brighter* in the spotter.

The real difficulty in this third point is not so much the change in brightness (which is noticeable, but not overwhelming). Rather, it is the sudden appearance of extra stars which were too faint to be seen at all with the unaided eye. Suppose you see with the unaided eye a very small equilateral triangle of stars, with a reddish star on the top vertex. You would expect to see in the spotter a much larger triangle, upside-down with the reddish star at the bottom. But in fact, you see five stars, forming an irregular pentagon. Are you at the right location? Perhaps so. If you notice that the two extra stars are fainter than the rest, and mentally subtract them, you get the upside-down triangle you were expecting.

It doesn't take long at all to learn to adjust for these effects. It's just something that beginners often haven't considered. Basically, if you want to know what to expect when looking through the spotter scope do the following. Take the mental picture of what your naked eye perceives, rotate it 180 degrees, zoom in a few times, brighten slightly, and add a few extra faint stars. That's about what you will see in the spotter if you are pointed in the right location.

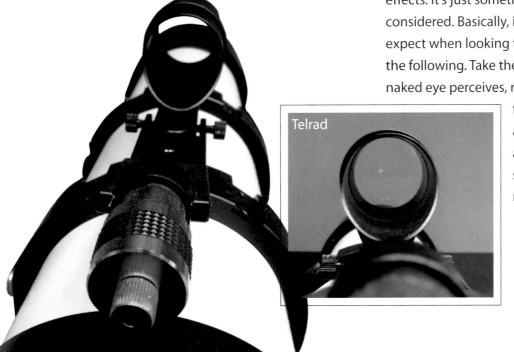

Telrad

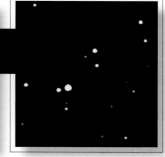

Chapter 7

Telescope Observing Sessions

In this chapter we discuss a number of strategies to get the most out of an observing session. There are some simple tricks like observing in a west-to-east fashion, using low magnification, and so on that will help you get the best views of anything you observe. I will presume that the reader is familiar with basic telescope setup (covered in the previous chapter), and will now move on to some more advanced strategies for improving your telescope experience.

◇ Appropriate Attire and Preparation

Simple preparation can make a telescope session a lot more enjoyable than it would be otherwise. Consider what the temperature will be like at night, and dress appropriately. Remember that the temperature drops a bit at night, and continues to fall throughout the night. So while you may not have needed a jacket during the day this may change at night. This is particularly the case on good observing nights. Clouds trap heat and cause nighttime temperatures to be warmer than they would be otherwise. So the clearest nights will generally be the coldest nights.

The amount by which the temperature drops will depend on where you live, of course, and the time of year. Humid, coastal regions tend to experience less of a temperature drop at night than arid landlocked

regions. Obviously, dressing warm won't be an issue if you are observing from Florida in the middle of summer. But at other locations in other times of the year, give some thought to what the temperature will be like at night.

Also, remember that standing outside in the cold is not the same as a quick dash to the car. We may need only a light jacket for the 15-second walk to the car. However, to stand outside in that same chilly air for an hour or more is quite a different matter. A good guideline is: dress a bit warmer than you think you should, and dress in layers. Then you can always remove a layer if you get too warm. A wool hat is particularly good for keeping warm since much heat is lost through the head. Telescope observing is a lot more fun if you are comfortable. I would say that more than 90 percent of telescope observers do not dress warm enough on their first session, and they are uncomfortable. If this happens to you — I told you so!

Bring a flashlight — a red flashlight is best. Red flashlights will not spoil dark adaptation. They will allow you to read a star chart without entirely ruining your night vision. See chapter 3 on the design of the eye for more details about this. Also, consider bringing binoculars. Many telescope objects can be seen faintly with binoculars, so this can help you locate an object quickly.

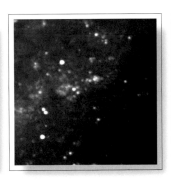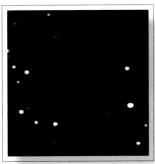

For that matter, there are a number of celestial gems that look just lovely in binoculars. Consider bringing a lawn chair with you unless you don't mind standing for hours. A stool or stepladder may be helpful if you have a larger telescope, or if you have children with you who may need a step or two.

A green laser pointer is useful for pointing out celestial objects to other people. The beam will be visible at night if you use at least a 5 milliwatt green laser pointer. For arid climates, the beam does not show up as well, and you may wish to use a more powerful pointer. Also, some green laser pointers do not work well in the cold, and will not shine at full intensity if at all. Note that pointers more powerful than 5 milliwatts are classified differently by the FDA, and different laws may apply to them. Never point the laser at an airplane, or at another person. Make sure that such laser pointers are legal in your country (they are legal in the United States as of the writing of this book) and that you use them in a safe and legal fashion.

Remember to set up your telescope (or at least have it outside) long before you are going to use it. An hour will usually suffice. This will give the telescope time to cool down to the ambient air temperature, which will improve your views. If the telescope temperature does not match the air temperature, all objects will appear fuzzy and "wavy" due to convection within the telescope.

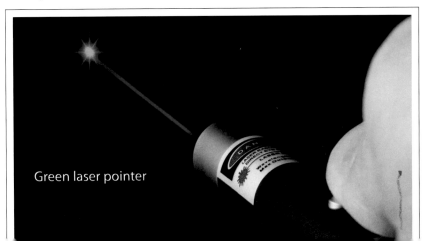
Green laser pointer

◇ Dark Adaptation

Give some thought to maintaining your night vision. When you are in a dark environment, your eyes will immediately begin to adjust. Within a few minutes you will be able to see things you couldn't just moments earlier. Allow yourself about 10 to 15 minutes to get reasonably dark-adapted, and expect about a half hour to become more or less fully dark-adapted. See chapter 3 for more details on this.

The most important thing to remember about dark adaptation is to avoid bright light. Bright light can spoil your dark adaptation in seconds. Avoid going inside. If you are observing with other people, ask them to keep their flashlights off. If you absolutely must turn on a light, consider keeping your dominant eye closed to maintain its night vision. Some astronomers use an eyepatch for this reason. Use red light (especially red LEDs) for checking star charts, but even then it is a good idea to use only your nondominant eye for reading.

◇ Dewing

If your telescope has a corrector plate on the open end, you will likely have to deal with the problem of "dewing." Dew has a tendency to collect on the corrector plate, particularly if you live in a humid climate. The best way to reduce dewing is to use a dew shield. You can buy these pretty cheap, or you can even make one yourself. A dew shield is simply a cylinder that attaches to the end of the telescope. It drastically reduces the amount of heat the corrector plate can radiate to space by blocking all angles except the one directly in front of the telescope (which is the only angle you need for viewing anyway).

Alternatively, you can buy an electronic "dew-zapper" that slightly heats the corrector plate, preventing dew from collecting. Some telescopes have this built in (though this is not common). I have used both, and in my experience the dew shield is far superior. It's more bulky and more awkward than a zapper, but it works better.

Even a dew shield will not always prevent dew from collecting. Therefore, once dew has collected, you need to know how to get rid of it. The worst thing you can possibly do is to wipe it off. This can leave micro-sized scratches on the plate which will eventually degrade viewing. Don't do it. The best way to get rid of dew on a plate is with a hair dryer on the warm setting. This will gently heat the corrector plate and the moving air will cause the dew to evaporate very rapidly. It's a great solution and works in seconds. Of course, most hair dryers require an electrical outlet, which is not always available depending on where you set up the telescope. So there are alternative ways to heat the plate.

First, if dew collects on the plate, point the telescope directly at the ground. This will prevent the plate from radiating heat into space. Often, this by itself will solve the problem.

The dew will eventually evaporate if the telescope is pointed down. However, it takes time. You can speed up the process by giving your telescope a "hug." Put your hands around the front part of the barrel, where the corrector plate attaches to the telescope. Do not touch the plate itself, but hold onto the exterior of the telescope as close to the plate as possible. Body heat from your hands will flow into the corrector plate and warm it enough to make the dew evaporate. It usually takes about five minutes for the dew to clear up.

Earlier, we pointed out that you should have the telescope outside early, so that it has a chance to reach the ambient air temperature. However, if you don't have a dew shield, and dewing is a problem, you may want to modify this rule a bit. Instead of having the telescope outside an hour before viewing, perhaps 15 minutes will suffice. To have the telescope a bit warmer than the ambient air temperature will prevent dewing. There is a tradeoff here because if the telescope is too much warmer than the ambient temperature, it will distort viewing. Remember, if you use a Newtonian telescope, you will never have to worry about dewing anyway (at least on the main telescope).

◇Location, Location, Location

Pick a good spot to do your astronomy. One important consideration is to have an unobstructed horizon. Avoid tall trees for example. A nice flat yard with no trees or nearby buildings is ideal. If you can't completely get away from all obstructions, at least consider what part of the sky you are primarily going to be looking at, and make sure there are no obstructions in that area. For Northern Hemisphere observers, make sure your southern horizon is unobstructed. There aren't as many things to look at near the Celestial North Pole, so it is not quite as much of a problem to have a tall tree to the north as it is to have one to the south.

Dew shield

◇Avoid Light Pollution

Perhaps the most irritating problem faced by the astronomer is light pollution. Light pollution is the brightening of the nighttime sky caused by artificial lights. If you live in or close to a city, you will notice that the night sky is not as dark as it is in the country. Stray light from streetlights, buildings, and so on is scattered in the atmosphere, and makes the sky glow, often with a reddish hue. Light pollution will make your views of deep-sky objects *much* worse than they would be otherwise.

Light pollution will have virtually no effect on bright targets. The moon, Jupiter, Venus, and bright stars will not suffer any noticeable degradation in light-polluted skies. But light pollution has a strong effect on globular clusters, and an even stronger effect on nebulae and galaxies. A moderate amount of light pollution can wipe out all but the brightest galaxies. Galaxies that are easily seen in binoculars under dark skies may be impossible to see in a telescope under light-polluted skies.

The best way to deal with light pollution is to get away from it. Get as far away from the city as you can, and your views of the universe will improve drastically. Again, it will make no difference for the brightest objects: the moon or Jupiter. These can be seen just fine from the city. But really, there are only a few bright objects like this. Most of the objects you will want to see will be deep-sky objects, which are faint and are strongly affected by modest amounts of light pollution. It is well worth taking a 15-minute drive away from your town into a rural location to get the best views of the night sky. This is true not only for telescope observing, but for binocular and naked-eye observations as well. People who live in a city are often amazed at how beautiful the Milky Way looks when they see it for the first time from a dark rural location.

A mountain top is a great place to do astronomy, because you can get "above" a substantial percentage of light pollution. Alternatively, having a mountain in between your location and the nearest city is also helpful. But the most important factor is to get as much distance as possible between you and the nearest city.

Of course, if you live in or near a source of light pollution, there are times when you may not feel like making the trip; you may just want to observe from your backyard. There are ways to mitigate light pollution in that situation. Obviously, be sure to turn off any lights on your property that you can; and you might want to ask your neighbors to do the same. There are special filters that can be attached to telescope eye pieces to reduce the effects of light pollution. Narrow band filters such as an Oxygen III filter work spectacularly well, but only for certain types of objects (certain nebulae). Alternatively, you may enjoy some improvement using broad band "light pollution" filters which work for a large range of objects. However, nothing beats getting away from the city and observing in a dark rural location.

Many people don't realize that light pollution is largely preventable. Many city lights are poorly designed; a good portion of their light is upward-directed which

Example of light pollution

An example of a computerized telescope

serves no useful purpose. Such lights not only waste energy, but they are contributing to the destruction of a natural resource: our night sky. In some cities, people are aware of this problem and have taken steps to correct it, such as the construction of lights that are designed to shine downward only. Such lights illuminate the streets, without causing as much light pollution. This not only helps us enjoy the night sky, but it saves energy, too. Some organizations like the Dark Sky Society work hard to reduce the amount of light pollution in cities around the United States, and I commend them for their efforts.

◇New Moon

The moon itself produces some light pollution — when it is out. Therefore, if you are going to be observing faint deep-sky objects, it is crucial that you pick a moonless night, or at least a night when the moon is in a crescent phase. It will do very little good to get away from city lights when the moon is full. Ideally, pick the date of the new moon or the surrounding few days. If you are not planning on staying up very late, you can also pick dates when the moon is in its waning phases; anything after 3rd quarter usually suffices because the moon won't rise until around midnight.

Of course the moon itself is enjoyable to observe, particularly around the 1st quarter phase. So there is a tradeoff here. But remember that the first quarter moon is not all that bright compared to full. The full moon is about *nine times brighter* than first quarter due to the way the sunlight is reflected. I find that I can see most deep-sky objects of interest when the moon is at 1st quarter or less. In fact, I actually prefer to do telescope sessions around 1st quarter moon, so that I can enjoy a stunning view of the moon itself, as well as most deep-sky objects. It's possible to get the best of everything on such nights.

Unless you are planning on looking at very faint objects, or doing a Messier marathon (see chapter 11), a crescent or first quarter moon is not likely to spoil your view. It's only when the moon reaches the gibbous phase that it becomes a real problem. Avoid the gibbous and full moon phases like the plague. The only exceptions are if you intend to view only bright planets or the moon itself. Bright moonlight or artificial light pollution will have very little effect on planets. But keep in mind that you might not see some of Saturn's fainter moons under bright moonlight.

◇Atmospheric Effects

The atmosphere is great for breathing, but it's terrible for astronomy. Have you ever looked far down a road on a hot summer day? You can see "ripples" as the air moves in response to temperature differences. Well, telescopes magnify this effect tremendously. Even the slight temperature differences in the air cause motion which can be seen in a telescope, causing ripples to blur and confuse the image of any object you are viewing. This effect is called "seeing." Some atmospheric effects are unavoidable, but others can be prevented with a little forethought. For the best telescopic views, you must seek conditions of "good seeing."

If it is a windy night, you are probably going to have bad seeing. There's not much that can be done. But of course you can plan which night to do your viewing, taking the weather into consideration. From experience, I have found that the best seeing occurs when there has not been any significant weather (rain, storms, temperature changes, etc.) for several days, and when there is not any expected for the next several days. You are looking for calm nights with as little change in temperature as possible. You may notice that stars twinkle a lot more on windy nights than on calm nights. Twinkling is just a severe form of bad seeing. If the stars are twinkling, you know you are not going to get a very good view that evening.

Some locations are much better than others. Higher elevations are generally better than lower elevations; you're looking through less atmosphere. So a mountain top is better than a valley (this helps with light

A thin waxing crescent moon

Stars of the Milky Way with the Andromeda Galaxy shown to the left

pollution, too, as discussed earlier). It is better to be upwind of mountains or on the first range, than downwind. Mountains generate atmospheric turbulence, which causes bad seeing. So if you are on the first ridge (in terms of the direction that weather moves) then you will not experience that turbulence.

But aside from the occasional vacation, you are probably not going to want to travel far to do astronomy. You are stuck with the surroundings you have. That's fine. But there are still ways to minimize bad seeing. Think of where the local sources of heat will be, and avoid them. For example, avoid looking over a heated building. If you know you are going to do a lot of observations in the southern region of the sky, don't set up on the north side of your house. You would then have to look over your heated house to see your target objects, and the heat from your house will make them blurry. Ideally, it would be best to get far away from any heat source. But it's not so bad to have a house to the north if your primary viewing will be to the south. If you cannot avoid viewing over heated structures, try to at least get as far away as possible; distance will help.

Often, much of the bad seeing occurs within the

telescope itself. This is why it is so important to let the telescope reach thermal equilibrium before starting any serious viewing. Some astronomers have reported improved seeing by attaching a low-power fan to the back of the primary mirror, thereby quickly bringing the mirror to the ambient temperature.

◇Observe West to East

Seeing is the result of motion in the atmosphere. The more atmosphere you have to look through, the worse the seeing will be. When the telescope is pointed close to the horizon, you are looking through a lot of air because you are at a low angle. Therefore, seeing will generally be better for objects that are nearly overhead than objects that are near the horizon. This is sometimes even noticeable to the unaided eye. You may notice that stars twinkle ("twinkling" is just bad seeing) more severely if they are close to the horizon than those that are high in the sky. Just like looking down a road on a hot summer day, objects that are low in the sky are much more strongly affected by atmospheric turbulence than those that are higher.

You might at first think that you don't have any control

over where an object in the sky is located. But in fact, you do! From our perspective, as stars revolve around the celestial pole, their position in the sky changes throughout the night. And you can always pick the time to observe the object. Ideally, the smart thing to do is to pick the time when the object will be at its highest point in the sky. Of course, you may not want to wait until 3:00 a.m., so there is a tradeoff here. But in general, *you will get the best views of all your targets if you observe them in the order of west to east.*

Think about it: objects in the western sky are in the process of setting. They are getting lower every minute, and so you have to look through increasing amounts of atmosphere to see them. It makes sense to look at these western objects early in the evening when they are as high as they will be, and will look as sharp as they can. Meanwhile, objects in the eastern sky are rising. They are getting higher every minute, which means your view of them will improve throughout the night. You will get a better view of these objects if you wait until later in the night. Therefore, when you plan out what objects you want to look at, start with those that are in the western sky, and end with those that are in the eastern sky. You will get a much better view of them than you would if you did the reverse.

◇Observe Bright to Faint

Another guideline to consider (and which may conflict at times with the previous one) is to observe the brighter objects first, and then the fainter objects later on. There are two reasons for this. First of all, your eyes will not be fully dark-adapted when you first start viewing. Remember that your night vision gradually improves as the night goes forward. So you might as well take advantage of that and save your best night vision for the faintest objects toward the end of your observing session. Second, the sky will be darker later in the evening, which will also help when viewing faint objects. In fact, if you start with the moon, you can begin your observing while the sky is still quite bright. Jupiter

and Venus look lovely even in twilight. Save the faint deep-sky objects for the darker portion of the night.

Of course, this guideline might at times be contrary to the previous guideline of observing west to east. In this case you will have to give some consideration as to which of the two effects is more important. If you are going to observe a faint galaxy, it is crucial to be as

Try to observe the brighter objects first, and then the fainter objects later.

dark-adapted as you can be and to have a very dark sky. So save that galaxy for later in the night, even if it is in the west — unless, of course, it is so low in the west that it will set shortly. On the other hand, a very close, yet bright double star requires the best seeing conditions. So the west-to-east rule is more important here, even though the star is bright enough to be seen early on. Certainly, don't even bother looking at galaxies or faint nebulae if it is still twilight. You will not have much success.

◇Use Low Magnification

For almost all telescopic objects, I recommend using the lowest magnification possible for the telescope. This amounts to using the eyepiece with the longest focal length. Do not exceed the field of view of the telescope though. In other words, if you go lower than the lowest recommended magnification for a given telescope, it will not increase the field of view. It will just produce a sort of "tunnel vision." Usually, the best eyepiece is the highest focal length eyepiece that came with the telescope.

There are several reasons for preferring low magnification. First of all, the higher the magnification, the blurrier the target will appear. So you will get the sharpest, most crisp views with the lowest magnification. This is particularly helpful in nights where the seeing is poor. Generally, the most aesthetically pleasing view will be the lowest magnification. Second, lower magnification gives a larger field of view. Many telescope objects are quite large anyway, and you won't see the entire target at high magnification. This is often the case with open star clusters.

Third, as a result of having a larger field of view, lower magnification makes it easier to find the target object. You don't have to be as precise to get the object in the field of view. This is particularly important in finding objects manually (my preferred method). But it is also relevant when using a computer-controlled system. I have found that many computer-controlled systems are not terribly precise. They get close to the target, but the target is not exactly centered. This can be due to a number of issues, such as slack in the motors, flexing of the telescope, and so on. It's not as much of a problem at low magnification though because you don't need to be as precise.

Fourth, lower magnification reduces the problem of tracking errors. Most telescopes do not track perfectly. It's not as noticeable at low magnification. But re-member that magnification increases not only the apparent size of the target, but its apparent angular velocity as well. This is really noticeable if you are using a telescope that does not have a clock drive, such as a standard dobsonian. With no clock drive, you will have to adjust the telescope every couple of minutes to stay on the target at low magnification. But at higher magnification, you may have to adjust it every 20 seconds or so. It is also a lot easier to accidentally bump the telescope and lose the target completely at higher magnification, since the field of view is so small.

Fifth, lower magnification increases the surface brightness of faint objects. This will make it a lot easier to see that faint nebula or galaxy. Changing magnification does not change the overall brightness at all (the same amount of light is coming into the telescope after all), but it does change the surface area of the image. So a faint nebula is "spread out" over a large area at high magnification, whereas the same amount of light is concentrated into a smaller area at low magnification, increasing the brightness per unit area (surface brightness). The receptors in the eye are better able to detect something with high surface brightness than something with lower surface brightness. So lower magnification increases contrast and almost always makes it easier to see faint objects.

One possible exception to this fifth guideline is the observation of very faint stars or moons under light-polluted skies. Since the targets in this scenario are essentially point sources, higher magnification will reduce the surface brightness of the light pollution, while not significantly reducing the surface brightness of the target. Higher magnification may result in higher contrast in this situation. When in doubt, try it both ways and see which one gives the better result.

In summary, low magnification is almost always better for almost all objects. There are a few exceptions to this guideline. First, planets sometimes look better at medium to higher magnification. Saturn, Jupiter, Venus, and Mars often look pretty good at moderate magnification. These objects are plenty bright, so there

When and where you choose to view specific objects can determine the success of your stargazing adventure

high magnification. Other than that, about the only other thing I bother to zoom in on is a good globular cluster — and only if it is on a night of good seeing. Apart from those few exceptions, try sticking mainly with a low power eyepiece. Overall, it will give you the best views and is the easiest to use.

◇Focusing

There is no magic trick in learning to focus a telescope. It just takes patience and practice. I prefer manually turning a knob so that I can get a "feel" for where the best focus is. But some systems require you to use electronic focusing. Either way, remember that there is usually some slack in the focus. In other words, if you have been moving the eyepiece outward, and you change direction and go inward, you may have to turn a little bit before the inward motion takes effect. This is also often the case with electronic systems. Electronic focus systems often have a numerical readout indicating where the focus is. But due to slack in the system, reaching "12" going in may not be the same as "12" going out. So make sure you approach the target number from the same side each time.

is no need to worry about the loss of surface brightness. In fact, reduced surface brightness may be an advantage in these cases. Again, there will be a loss in crispness as we zoom in. But sometimes higher magnification makes it easier to see certain surface features. Try experimenting with different magnifications to see which produces the best result. Keep in mind that the best eyepiece may be different from one night to the next, depending on the seeing.

Certain close binary stars also often look good under

Out-of-focus stars look like little donuts. Your goal in focusing the telescope is to make those donuts shrink down to sharp points. If you go too far, the stars will turn back into donuts again. I find it helpful to intentionally go back and forth past the sharpest focus several times so that I have a feel for where the best focus is. I find it easiest to adjust the focus by selecting a few moderately faint stars and trying to get them as crisp as possible. It can be harder to focus on a bright star or an extended object like a planet.

If the stars cannot be brought down to a sharp point, there may be other difficulties. If the stars can be focused to a horizontal or vertical line, this is an indication that the primary mirror has *astigmatism*: its curvature is different on one axis than the other. Unfortunately, there is no simple way to fix this problem. If the stars will not focus to a point, but rather become like little "comets" with a tail pointing in one direction, this is a symptom that the telescope needs to be collimated (see below). If the stars cannot be focused because they exhibit motion ("dancing" and fluttering around), this is an indication of bad seeing. It could be the atmosphere, or it could be that the telescope has not yet reached thermal equilibrium. If it is the latter, the problem will go away with time. In the meantime, just remember to use the lowest magnification eyepiece to reduce the appearance of bad seeing.

◇Glasses

Many people ask, "Should I leave on my glasses when looking through a telescope?" The answer: it depends on the situation. If you have astigmatism, then *yes you should always wear your glasses* when doing astronomy. Astigmatism means that the cornea/lens of your eye has a different curvature in the horizontal direction than in the vertical direction. Glasses are designed to compensate for this. You can tell if you have astigmatism by the following: take your glasses off, turn them around and look through one of the lenses. Then rotate the glasses by 90 degrees. If the view does not change, there is no astigmatism. If the glasses are compensating for astigmatism, then when you rotate the glasses by 90 degrees, things will stretch or shrink horizontally while the opposite happens vertically. Try this with both lenses; some people have astigmatism in one eye but not the other.

If you don't have astigmatism, then you don't necessarily have to wear glasses when looking through a telescope. It is always possible to focus the telescope for your eyes. There are pros and cons either way. If you are observing by yourself, and you do not have any astigmatism, I recommend leaving the glasses off.

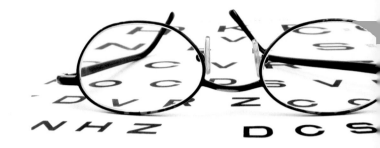

Glasses block a small fraction of light, slightly dimming and distorting every target object. Granted, it's a small amount, but when you are looking at a faint galaxy, you can use every photon you can get! Also, if you are far-sighted (you put glasses on only to read) then you might be able to get away with leaving your glasses off even when observing with others. What seems in focus for your eyes should approximately match what seems the proper focus for others who don't wear glasses at all.

If you are nearsighted (you take your glasses off to read), then you can always leave your glasses off and focus the telescope for your eyes; *however,* it will be out of focus for people who don't wear glasses. In other words, if you are nearsighted and observing with a group of people, it may be the "polite" thing to do (and certainly faster) to leave your glasses on. Otherwise, you will have to refocus the telescope for your eyes, and then the person going after you will have to refocus again for his or hers. And this must be done for every object. It may not be a big deal if the other observers have some telescope experience, and can focus quickly. But sometimes people new to astronomy have difficulty getting the focus exactly right. And so it is best to focus the telescope once and then not mess with it.

◇Collimation

When focusing a reflecting telescope, you can also check for collimation. "Collimation" is the process of aligning the mirrors. To check this, pick a bright star, center it, and then adjust the focus so that the star is *not* at all in focus. The star should look like a large donut. If the hole is exactly centered in the ring, then the telescope is properly collimated. Otherwise, you will need to adjust the angle of the mirror. This is often done by adjusting three screws at the base of the telescope, although some systems allow you to collimate electronically. Your goal is to get the hole centered in the donut. Note that you will probably have to re-center the star each time you make an adjustment.

◇Use Averted Vision

When looking at faint objects (which is basically everything other than planets, bright stars, and the moon), remember to use averted vision. Don't look directly at that faint galaxy, or you won't see it. This is because there are no rods in the center of your field of vision (the fovea). See chapter 3 on the design of the eye for more details on this. Look a little to the left or right of a faint object to see it most clearly. If you look too far away, you won't get a sharp image, and if you look too close you probably won't see it at all. Experiment a bit to find the best angle for your eyes. This tip is really important — please take it seriously. Using averted vision can make the difference between enjoying a view of a spiral galaxy versus seeing nothing at all.

You don't need to use averted vision when looking at extremely bright sources, like planets or the moon. However, with planets, you might want to try it both ways. Rods are able to pick out certain features like horizontal and vertical lines that cones sometimes miss.

Remember that *some* rods are connected in such a way as to be sensitive to motion. They can "see" a moving object, but not a stationary one. You can take advantage of this by slowly moving the telescope back and forth while viewing a very faint object. The motion might actually help you to see it. I have found this trick to be very helpful in spotting faint galaxies.

Use your dominant eye (see the chapter on the eye) for observing all deep-sky objects. Consider using your nondominant eye for very bright objects, such as the moon. This will allow you to maintain your dark-adaptation in your dominant eye. You can also use your nondominant eye for reading star charts, and so on without light-adapting your dominant eye.

◇A Moment of Good Seeing

The real trick to getting a spectacular view of a celestial object, particularly a bright one like Jupiter, Saturn, or the moon, is to wait for a "moment of good seeing." Earlier we discussed how differences in air temperature create turbulence, which cause target objects to appear fuzzy. This condition is called "seeing." Some nights are better than others; you will get your best views on nights of good seeing. But another important tip is to recognize that seeing can also fluctuate from moment to moment. You will find, for example, that if you look at Jupiter for one minute, most of the time it will "dance" and be a bit fuzzy. However, for a few seconds it will become still and exceptionally clear. This is called a moment of good seeing.

When looking at any celestial object, take your time and wait for those moments of good seeing. With a little patience, you will be rewarded with a spectacular view. It may last only a few seconds. But if you wait another minute, chances are you will get another really sharp view. Of course if you are observing with a group of people who also want a turn, you may have to compromise a little bit. But if you are observing by yourself, take a good five minutes and just stare at Jupiter. You may find that you can spot storms, moon shadows, and thin belts during moments of good seeing.

◇The Six-Inch Rule

When it comes to seeing, there is a characteristic length which corresponds to a column of air: about six inches. In other words, you can think of the atmosphere as a bunch of columns that are constantly moving and dancing about due to turbulence, and the diameter of each of these columns is about six inches. For this reason, if you are using a six-inch telescope (or smaller), you are looking through only one column of air. However, if you are using a telescope larger than six inches, your telescope is looking through several columns of air. Let's consider how this will affect a view of the planet Jupiter.

On nights of poor seeing, a six-inch or smaller telescope will be looking through a single column of air, and will see a single image of Jupiter which is dancing and jumping around a bit in response to the motion of that air column. However, a larger telescope is looking through several air columns; a view through this telescope will reveal several overlapping images of Jupiter

which "average" together to make a single stable, but blurry image.

For this reason, on nights of poor seeing, some astronomers believe it is better to use a six-inch or smaller telescope for views of bright objects like Jupiter, because you get a single, fairly sharp though animated image of Jupiter, whereas a larger telescope gives a stable but fuzzy image. It's one of those rare situations where a smaller telescope might actually give the better view.

You can always make a larger telescope effectively into a smaller one by stopping down the aperture as follows. Take a piece of cardboard (or any opaque material) and cut a six-inch diameter hole into it. Then place the cardboard over the open end of the telescope. Now, the telescope will only be looking through a single column of air. It will have an effective diameter of only six inches, and will generate the same type of image as a six-inch or smaller telescope. Some astronomers suggest that an even smaller opening will further improve the view. But recall that there is a trade-off here. A smaller aperture means the resolution drops (making the image more fuzzy), and the brightness drops. (The latter may not be a problem for Jupiter.) In my experience, stopping down the aperture rarely improves the view significantly. But you may find some improvement on certain nights.

◇Star Hopping

Bright naked-eye objects like the moon, planets, and bright stars are pretty easy (with a little practice) to center in the telescope because they are easily visible to the naked eye. Locating objects that are not visible to the unaided eye ("deep-sky objects") can be more challenging. And there are several ways to do it. If you have a computer-controlled system, this might be the easiest way. Many newer telescopes have built-in computer tracking which allows you to type in the name of any number of thousands of catalogued celestial gems, and with the press of a key the telescope will slew to the target.

But there are some drawbacks to using computer-control exclusively to locate deep-sky objects. First of all, you haven't really learned how to find the object in the sky. In fact, you can't really say that you have found the object, because you didn't. The computer did. There is no challenge in letting the telescope do the work. But beyond that, you don't gain an appreciation for where the object is located. Had you learned how to locate the object manually in terms of its relation to other visible stars, you would in the future know where it is located. You can tell if it is above the horizon just by looking at the surrounding stars. People who rely on computer-controlled tracking generally have very little knowledge of the night sky. They cannot easily plan their west-to-east observing strategy, because they really don't know where the objects are located in the sky. It's better to learn how to find deep-sky objects, and then you can know just by glancing out the window which ones are able to be viewed at the moment.

Also, people who rely exclusively on computer tracking find that they cannot function without it. So if they are using someone else's telescope which lacks such controls, they will not be able to find any deep-sky objects. Alternatively, there will come some night where the telescope computer controls will not work for some reason. Maybe the battery died, or a motor went bad, or you forgot the hand-paddle. If you are dependent on computer-control, your evening is ruined. But if you know how to find the objects manually, it's not a problem at all. Therefore, if your telescope does have computer-control, do yourself a favor and don't always use it. Learn to find at least some deep-sky objects manually. Frankly, it's a lot more fun to find them manually anyway.

You can also use setting circles to find a deep-sky object. In this case, you would look up the coordinates in a book or in a computer program. You then turn the telescope until the setting circles match the right ascension and declination of your target. In order to do this, you will first have to align the right ascension circle; you do this by adjusting it to match the right ascension of a bright star. Finding objects this way is not terribly precise, and it's not a method I normally use. Using setting circles has the same drawback as using computer-control: you don't actually know where the object is with respect to the visible stars. And it's slower than computer-control. So I consider this method a last resort. I would only use it if the only information I had on an object was its coordinates. Even then, I would try to find that location on a star chart or computer program to visually see where the object is located.

By far, the best way to find deep-sky objects is with a technique called "star hopping." This is far more enjoyable than any other method. It helps you learn where the objects really are in the night sky. And eventually (with some practice) it will be the fastest way to locate your target. (Yes, I can usually beat the computer.) Star hopping is a technique whereby you learn to visualize where the deep-sky object is in relation to visible stars and constellations. It is easy to do, but rather difficult to describe.

Follow these steps, based on what kind of telescope you may be using.

⬎ Star Hopping

1   Use a star chart or a computer program to locate the target deep-sky object in relation to the surrounding stars.

2   Locate the star or stars closest to the target object.

3   Now find this location in the real sky with your unaided eye. Try to find a small group of two or more stars and memorize their shape.

4   Then point the telescope to this location.

↳   If you are using a spotter scope, point it to the small group of stars you just memorized.

↳   Remember that the shape will be (1) larger, (2) upside-down and reversed, and (3) brighter than the shape as it appears to the unaided eye (see the previous chapter for details on the spotter scope).

5   Then, while looking through the spotter scope, move the telescope to the location of the deep-sky object, remembering its location relative to the shape. Many deep-sky objects are visible as a faint smudge in the spotter scope.

6   Center the spotter on this smudge and the target will be centered in the main telescope and ready for viewing.

Chapter 8

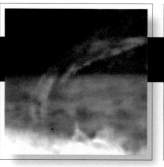
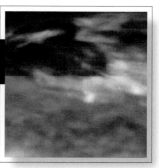

The Moon and the Sun

For our introduction to telescope objects, it makes sense to begin with the two brightest celestial objects: the sun and the moon. Both are amazing telescope objects, though of course you will need to use a solar filter to the view the sun safely (or use the projection method). These objects are large, bright, and detailed — in sharp contrast to most other astronomical objects. And they never look exactly the same twice. The different phases of the moon and the slight latitudinal and longitudinal libration will give you a slightly different perspective on the moon night after night, and year after year. The sun always has a slightly different pattern of sunspots and other features every time you view it. This makes them excellent celestial objects for beginners and experts alike.

◇ The Moon

I never tire of viewing the moon through a telescope. It is stunningly beautiful, and yet its beauty is very different from that of the Earth. The moon is a "magnificent desolation" of craters, maria, mountains, and ridges. As the moon goes through its various phases, the sunlight catches its rugged terrain at various angles, casting dark shadows and giving the moon an extremely high contrast. Compared to the many other astronomical objects where you are straining to see any detail on a tiny, faint smudge, the moon is a refreshing alternative.

The moon looks best in a telescope when it is in or near first quarter or third quarter. (In the chapters on celestial motions, we covered lunar phases and how these relate to moonrise and moonset times.) If (like me) you are not a morning person, then first quarter will be your favorite phase. The first quarter moon is highest in the sky around sunset. For early risers, the third quarter moon is high in the sky and best viewed a bit before sunrise. During these phases the angle of sunlight is steepest, and so we get the best views of lunar shadows of mountains, ridges, and craters. Ideally, the first quarter moon is best viewed in the evening sky in early spring. At such time the moon is very high in the sky due to the angle of the ecliptic. However, the first quarter moon really looks pretty good any time of the year FIGURE 8.1.

The dividing arc between day and night on the moon is called the "terminator," since this is where sunlight stops. The terminator appears as a vertical line right down the center of the moon in first or third quarter phases. The terminator is where you will see the longest shadows, and you get some of the prettiest views of the lunar surface. The human mind is an amazing thing; it is able to reconstruct the three-dimensional shape of the lunar surface from the angle of lunar shadows. You will be able to discern mountains from valleys near the terminator. It is during first and third

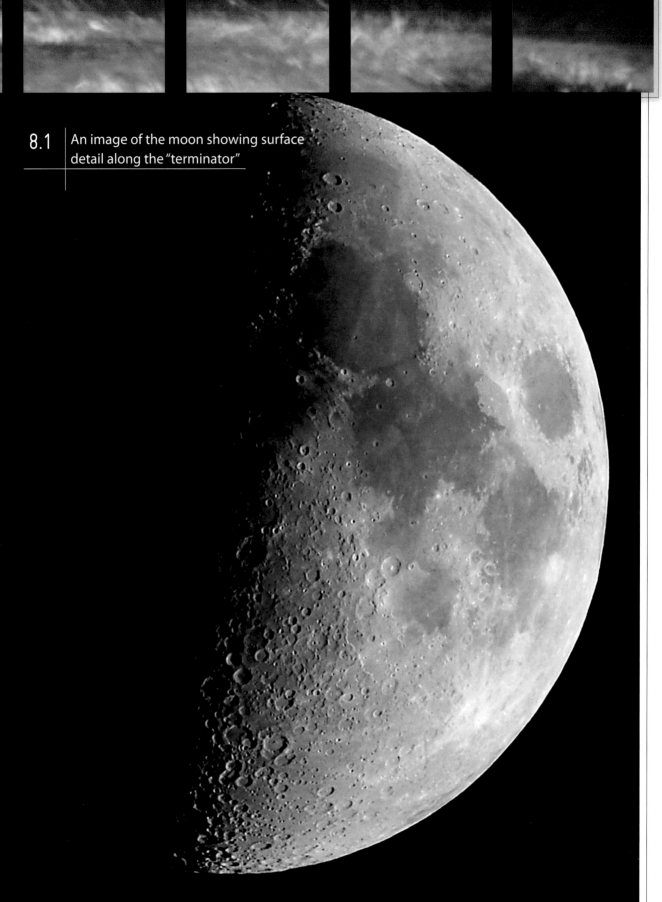

8.1 | An image of the moon showing surface detail along the "terminator"

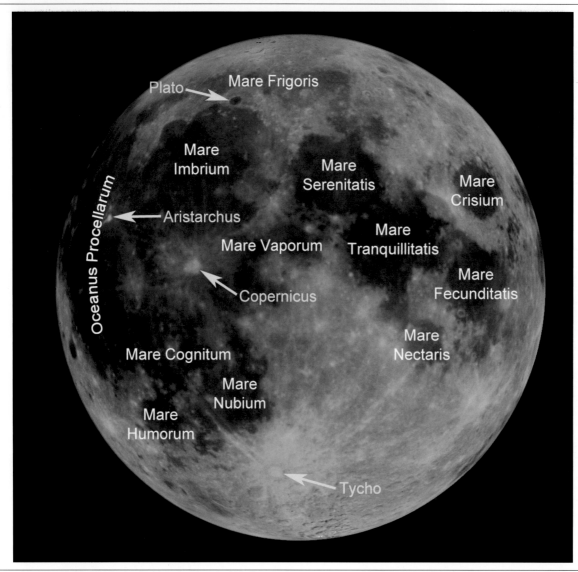

Plato — Mare Frigoris
Mare Imbrium
Mare Serenitatis
Mare Crisium
Oceanus Procellarum
Aristarchus
Mare Vaporum
Mare Tranquillitatis
Copernicus
Mare Fecunditatis
Mare Cognitum
Mare Nectaris
Mare Nubium
Mare Humorum
Tycho

8.2
A map of the most prominent lunar features. Maria are indicated with white labels. Craters are indicated with yellow labels.

During the full moon there is no shadow

quarter phases that the moon will look like a true sphere, as opposed to the full moon which looks flat as a dime. During full moon you will see no shadows whatsoever since the sun is at about the same angle as the Earth. Without any shadows for reference, the mind cannot reconstruct the three-dimensional structure, and information on lunar relief is missing.

A day or two before or after first (or third) quarter will also provide stunning views, and will reveal the three-dimensional nature of the moon. The terminator as seen before or after first or third quarter phase will be a noticeably curved arc, rather than a vertical line. This, too, is indicative of the spherical nature of the moon, and the human mind will interpret it that way. It really is astonishing how three-dimensional the moon ap-

pears when viewed in a telescope and when near first or third quarter.

◇Lunar Features

Several types of lunar features are visible in a small telescope at modest magnification. Craters are perhaps the most obvious. They tend to be circular, and they appear that way when viewed near the center of the lunar disk. However, when craters are near the limb, they appear elliptical due to foreshortening. There are several different types of lunar craters. Many will have a hemispherical appearance; they have a rounded center and usually have an elevated ridge at the rim. Occasionally the craters are rimless, lacking the surrounding ridge.

Sometimes craters have a flattened floor, rather than a rounded one. It is also common for the larger craters to have a central peak. This is the "splash" that occurred when the impact event that caused the crater happened. Craters are often overlapping. In addition, you will see hills or mountains on the moon. Sometimes these occur as extended ridges. It is also common to see faults, where one surface is elevated relative to an adjacent one. These are all relief features, so they are best viewed near the terminator where their shadows are longest.

The moon also has features that are not due to relief, but are due to differences in reflectivity (albedo) along the lunar surface FIGURE 8.2. The most obvious examples are maria — large dark regions on the moon. These are large enough to be seen by the unaided eye. They are what form the familiar "man in the moon" feature. Since they are not due to differences in elevation, maria are actually easiest to see when the moon is full. Of course, this is the only time when all the maria on the Earth-facing side of the moon can be seen.

The term "maria" [or "mare" singular] comes from the Latin meaning "seas." In fact, maria are large flat basins that have filled in with magma — now solidified basalt. There are not nearly as many craters in the regions of maria. Presumably, the maria are more recent than the rest of the lunar surface, and have obliterated any craters that were previously there. Curiously, almost all lunar maria are on the Earth-facing side of the moon. It is commonly believed that this is because the lunar crust is thinner on the Earth-facing side. It is enjoyable to learn to identify the various maria. Maria are often surrounded by high ridges. However, these can only be seen when the sunlight shines at an angle (i.e., not during the full phase).

Another feature which is not due to lunar relief is ejecta. Ejecta are very light-colored (they appear almost "white" by contrast) streaks which radiate away from some craters. They are formed, presumably, by the debris ejected from a crater at the time of impact. When the moon is full, the ejecta are just about the only way to see any craters since the shadows are gone at that time. The best example of ejecta is found surrounding

the crater Tycho, which occurs on the south side of the moon. Tycho is an easy binocular (or telescope) target, and is best seen when the moon is full or nearly so. The ejecta pattern from Tycho extends very far away from the crater. The next most obvious examples of craters that are bright due to ejecta are Copernicus and Aristarchus. Copernicus is about halfway between the center and the left limb of the moon. Aristarchus is even closer to the left limb.

◇Lunar Libration

As discussed in chapter 2, the moon appears to "wobble" a bit from our perspective as it orbits the Earth. The left-right wobble is caused by the fact that the moon's rotation rate is constant but its orbital revolution is not — the moon speeds up when closer to the Earth, and slows down when farther away. Over the course of an entire orbit, the rotation and revolution rates have the same average. But at any given moment, the rotation can be slightly faster or slightly slower than the revolution rate. When the moon is near perigee, its revolution rate speeds up (faster than the rotation), and the moon appears to turn slightly to the

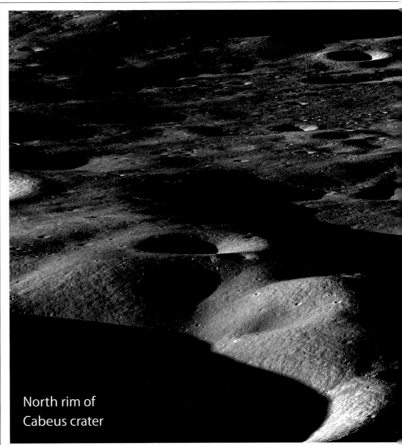

North rim of
Cabeus crater

NASA/GSFC/Arizona State University

left, allowing us to see a bit more of its right side. Conversely, at apogee, the moon appears to turn slightly to the right, exposing more of its left side.

The amount of libration is small, but it is noticeable. I have found that one of the most useful lunar features when looking for libration is Mare Crisium. This mare is on the upper right-hand side of the moon, rather close to the limb **FIGURE 8.3**. When libration shifts the moon to the left, Mare Crisium is well-separated from the limb, and appears fairly circular — only slightly compressed. However, when libration shifts the moon to the right, Mare Crisium appears very close to the limb, and is noticeably flattened by foreshortening.

The moon also experiences a north-south wobble due to the fact that its rotation axis does not exactly match its orbital axis. So from our perspective on Earth, we sometimes are looking a bit up toward the moon from slightly underneath its equator, whereas other times we are slightly above the moon's equator looking down. The north-south libration is slightly less severe than the east-west libration, and a bit harder to detect. Perhaps Tycho is the best surface feature to use to detect north-south libration. Tycho can be fairly close to the south limb of the moon at times, whereas it can also appear to drift a bit closer to center due to libration. Although we only see 50 percent of the moon's surface at any one time, with the help of libration it is possible to see a total of up to 59 percent of the moon's surface from Earth. Some amateur astronomers keep careful track of lunar libration, and use the effect to spot challenging lunar features which are normally (just barely) on the far side of the moon.

◇The Projection Method

The projection method of viewing a celestial object works very well for the sun and the moon. For the moon, a bigger telescope (larger aperture) works

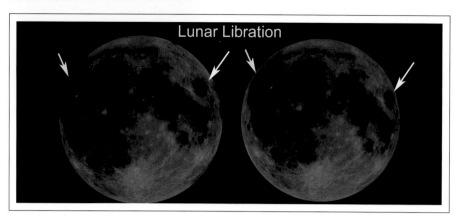

Lunar Libration

8.3 Libration of the moon is evident in these two images of the full moon, taken at different times of the year. Mare Crisium appears closer to the limb on the right image. Oceanus Procellarum appears to touch the limb on the left image, but is slightly separated on the right image.

better, because projection requires a lot more light than direct viewing. To project the moon, point the telescope at the moon just as if you were going to look at it as usual. Use a low magnification eyepiece. Then place white paper a few feet away from the eyepiece. While holding the paper at a constant distance, focus the telescope until a sharp image of the moon forms on the paper. This method will allow several people to look at the moon at the same time using the same telescope. It will also allow you to point to and identify specific surface features.

Note that the projection method creates a reversed (left becomes right) image from what you would see in the eyepiece. You can adjust the size of the image by moving the paper closer to or farther from the eyepiece. You will have to refocus the telescope when you move the paper. The tradeoff is brightness. A larger image of the moon will be fainter. The projection method works best when the moon is in its brighter phases, such as gibbous or full.

◇The Moon Illusion

Another interesting effect is the unusual appearance of the moon when it is very near the horizon. Sometimes it can appear red or orange due to Rayleigh scattering — the same reason sunsets are red. That is a real effect. But there is also a psychological effect that makes the moon seem much bigger when it is near the horizon. It's sometimes called the "moon illusion," and that's exactly what it is: an illusion. In fact, if you measure the angular size of the moon near the horizon, you will find that it is no larger than when the moon is higher in the sky. Either way, the moon is about one-half degree across.

But somehow the moon seems larger when it is near the horizon. The reason for this has to do with the way the mind interprets the shape of the sky. Instead of assuming the sky is a hemisphere, the brain tends to picture it as a flattened dome, not very high but very, very wide. So when the moon is high in the sky, the mind tends to perceive that it is close, and therefore relatively small. But when the moon is near the horizon, there are often other objects for comparison — trees, houses, etc. The moon is behind all these, and so the mind perceives that the moon must be at great distance and therefore very large.

You can break the illusion by removing the reference objects. For example, do this by looking at the moon through the central roll of paper towels. When no comparison objects are visible, the mind tends to assume that the moon is relatively close, and therefore relatively small. The moon illusion is very powerful, but it is purely psychological. The moon can be more than blocked by your finger at arm's length no matter where the moon is found in the sky.

◇Other Nighttime Objects

In the remaining chapters in this book, we will discuss other objects visible in the night sky. Usually, I don't look just at the moon. I start with the moon and then move on to fainter objects. Since the moon requires no dark adaptation, it is a great object with which to begin an observing session. But keep in mind that the brightness of the moon itself can delay your eye from dark adapting, or can ruin the dark adaptation you have already achieved. I therefore suggest using your nondominant eye for moon viewing if you plan on looking at fainter objects later on.

◇The Sun

The most important thing to remember about solar observing is *safety*. The sun emits dangerous ultraviolet radiation, and it emits lots of it. *Never look directly at the sun*, because the ultraviolet radiation is very damaging to the retina. It can cause permanent eye damage. Therefore, you will need to consider safe ways to view the sun. Basically, there are two: projection and filters.

In the projection method, you use a small telescope or one side of binoculars to project an image of the sun on a piece of paper. Paper will absorb much of the ultraviolet rays, and so you can safely look at the image of the sun as it is projected on the paper. Details on how to set up solar projection are included in the eclipse section in chapter 5.

Example of a "moon illusion" showing Rayleigh scattering (reddish coloring)

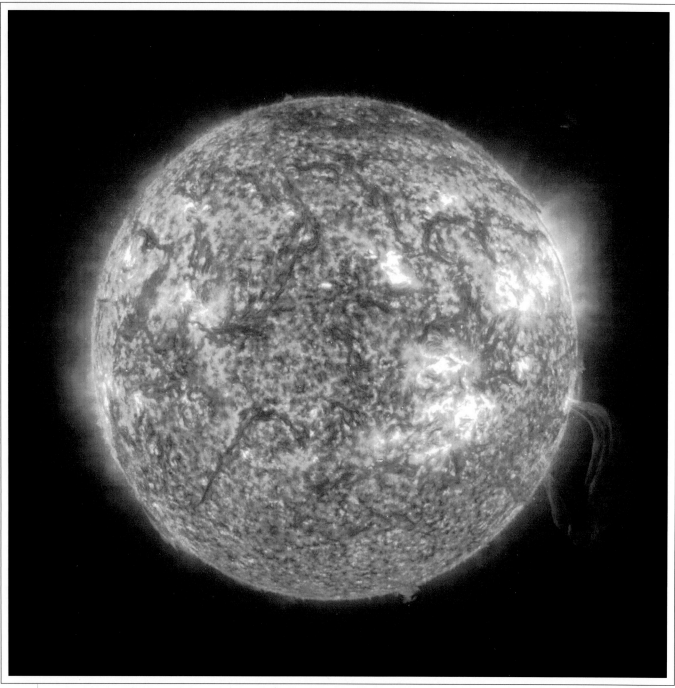

8.4 | A narrowband image of the sun. The wavelength selected here is 3040 nanometers, which corresponds to ultra-violet light. Several regions of plage are visible. A large solar prominence extends from the lower right side of the sun. Image credit: SOHO (ESA & NASA).

In this chapter I would like to address the solar filter method. This is generally better for observing details on the solar disk. There are several different kinds of solar filters you can get. They are not expensive, and so I recommend thinking about getting a solar filter for your telescope or binoculars. Often they have a

silvery appearance, and look just like a perfect mirror — but in fact, they allow a small fraction of the photons through. You can even hold the filter up directly between you and the sun, and look at the sun safely that way.

It is important that the filter has no cracks or defects in it that might allow dangerous ultraviolet radiation through. Always examine it carefully before each use. It is also important that the filter is designed to fit over the complete aperture of the telescope — not just the eyepiece. All other filters go on the eyepiece end, but that would be dangerous for solar viewing, due to the high energy levels involved. The light must be filtered *before* it goes through the telescope. Do not use a "solar" filter that is designed for the eyepiece — it's not safe.

There are solar filters that can enhance certain solar features by selecting a particular wavelength of light. These are narrowband filters FIGURE 8.4. A great example is an H-alpha filter, which selects the wavelength corresponding to the first (alpha) line in the Balmer series, the result of electrons transitioning from the third energy level to the second in a hydrogen atom. An H-alpha filter will allow you to see the upper regions of

the sun's visible surface. And there are certain features that are associated with that. A filter that is not tuned to a specific solar wavelength is a continuum filter FIGURE 8.5). It allows you to see the sun safely, approximately as it would look to the unaided eye, though sometimes the color is shifted. The silvered glass/mylar filters are continuum filters; they are more common.

◇ Limb Darkening

One feature that can be seen even without a telescope (but not without a solar filter!) is limb darkening. The center of the sun is noticeably brighter than the limb (this is clearly seen in FIGURE 8.5). This is because the sun is gaseous, and is hotter in the interior than the exterior. So when you look at the sun's center, you are seeing deeper into the sun (where the temperatures are hotter) than when you look at the limb. (If the sun got cooler as you went deeper in, then the limb would

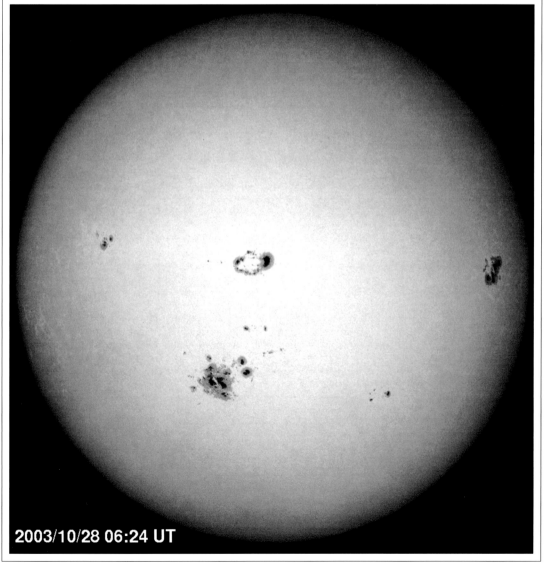

2003/10/28 06:24 UT

8.5 A continuum image of the sun. Several groups of sunspots are visible. Limb darkening is also apparent. Image credit: SOHO (ESA & NASA).

be *brightened*.) Limb darkening is most noticeable in the outer 10 percent or so of the solar disk. It can be seen with either a continuum filter or an H-alpha filter.

◇Sunspots and the Solar Magnetic Field

Sunspots are easily visible with a continuum filter under binoculars or a small telescope. Sunspots are darker regions on the sun caused by intense magnetic fields. Energy in the outer layers of the sun is transmitted by convection; plasma moves up from the hotter interior, carrying energy with it. Magnetic fields suppress plasma motion; they trap the plasma where it is, which prevents the flow of energy. Magnetic regions therefore cool off, since they radiate energy to space and have no source of new energy. The temperature of the sun's surface is around 6,000 degrees Celsius, but in a sunspot the temperature drops to about 4,000 degrees. Sunspots have an inner darker region called the umbra, and an outer lighter region called the penumbra — the same terms used for eclipse shadows.

Sunspots often occur in pairs, usually oriented in an east-west fashion. This is due to the orientation of the magnetic toroidal field, which we will discuss below. There are spectroscopic methods to measure the magnetic field associated with sunspots. These methods confirm that sunspot pairs have opposite polarity.

Sunspots have an 11-year cycle. Every 11 years or so the sun has very few sunspots — sometimes none are visible. Then sunspots begin to occur at middle solar latitudes (around 30 degrees north of the solar equator, and 30 degrees south). It is as if the sun has two "belts" of sunspot rows. Over the next few years, the number of sunspots increase and the latitudes at which they preferentially occur move toward the equator. Toward the end of the 11-year cycle, the sunspots lie fairly close to the equator, and their numbers drastically reduce. Then, at the end of 11 years, we have another solar minimum, and the cycle begins again.

These properties of sunspots can be understood in light of the nature of the solar magnetic field. The sun's

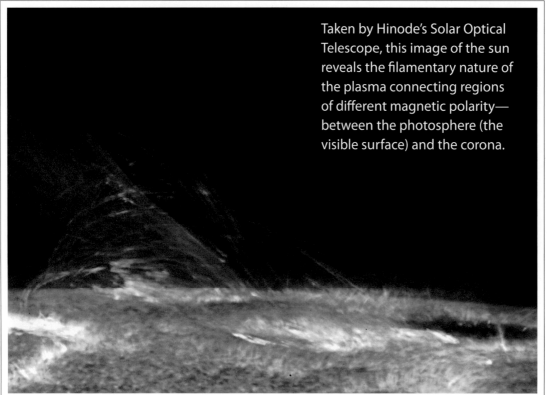

Taken by Hinode's Solar Optical Telescope, this image of the sun reveals the filamentary nature of the plasma connecting regions of different magnetic polarity—between the photosphere (the visible surface) and the corona.

Image credit: JAXA/NASA

magnetic field is far more complex than Earth's. The Earth has a dipole magnetic field — a north magnetic pole and a south magnetic pole that are roughly aligned with the Earth's rotation axis. The sun also has a dipole magnetic field. However, the sun's dipole field reverses polarity every 11 years. This is linked to the sunspot cycle. In other words, if the North Pole of the sun has a north magnetic polarity one year, then 11 years later it will have a *south* magnetic polarity. So the complete magnetic cycle is actually 22 years.

In addition to the dipole field, the sun also has a toroidal magnetic field for which there is no equivalent on Earth. The toroidal field lies below the

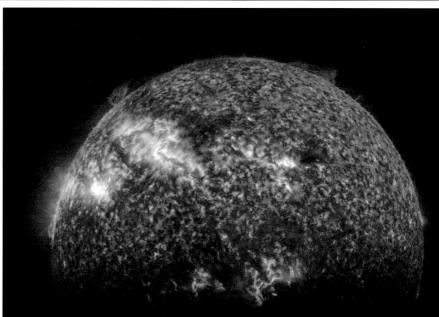

The mottling pattern covering the entire surface is supergranulation. The bright regions are plage. A few small prominences are visible along the limb.

surface of the sun. This field is oriented in an east-west direction, and wraps completely around the sun like a belt, so there are no "poles" — the toroidal field makes a complete loop. There is at least one such belt in the sun's northern hemisphere, and at least one in the southern hemisphere. These belts correspond to the preferred latitudes at which sunspots occur. A sunspot occurs when a fragment of the toroidal field is lifted up above the surface, forming a small arc. Sunspots occur at the two places where the arc intersects the sun's surface.

The magnetic pairs of sunspots that occur in a given hemisphere generally all have the same orientation. That is, if the north-charged sunspot is west of the south-charged sunspot, then all other sunspot pairs in that hemisphere will be the same way. In the other hemisphere, the situation is reversed (e.g., the south-charged sunspots are west of the north-charged spots). This indicates that the two primary toroidal belts in each hemisphere have opposite polarity.

The toroidal belts are slowly pulled toward the equator by a slow-scale solar flow called "meridional circulation." This circulation is away from the equator and toward the poles at the surface of the sun. But beneath the surface (where the toroidal fields are located) that is reversed; it's essentially the return trip of the convey-

er belt. When the two toroidal belts reach the equator, they are neutralized since they have opposite polarity. Newer toroidal belts then form at higher latitudes and have the opposite polarity of the originals. This model explains why sunspots occur when and where they do.

If you look at the sun one day after another and keep track of where the sunspots are, you will notice that the sun rotates. The sunspots are carried along from the eastern limb to the western limb. So the sun rotates counterclockwise as viewed from its North Pole — just like Earth. The sun takes about 25 days to rotate once at its equator. The rotation rate is a bit slower at the poles — taking a little over 30 days to rotate once. This is called "differential rotation" — the rotation rate being different at different latitudes. The sun can do that since it isn't solid. Differential rotation may be partly responsible for the generation of the toroidal magnetic fields, and the 22-year cycle of the dipole field.

◇Other Solar Features

At medium to high magnification, using a continuum filter, you may see a very small-scale mottling pattern completely covering the surface of the sun (except for where the sunspots are). This is called "granulation." It is caused by large convection cells which form an irregular "honeycomb" pattern on the sun. If you are using

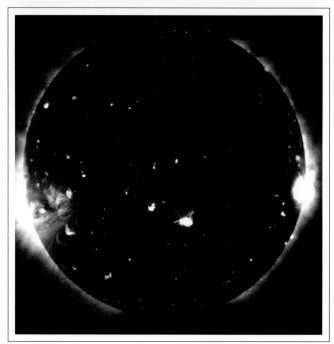

An image of the sun taken by an X-Ray Telescope showing the outer atmosphere or corona

A close-up of the solar photosphere shows a cellular pattern called granulation

an H-alpha filter, you may see a similar but larger-scale mottling called "supergranulation." It is exactly the same phenomenon as granulation, but on a larger, slower scale. Supergranulation cannot be easily seen with a continuum filter.

An H-alpha filter will also allow you to see bright regions of the sun near sunspots. These regions are called "plage" [pläzh]. The word is French and means "beach" or can refer to any luminous surface. Plage can also sometimes be seen with a continuum filter, though it doesn't stand out as much.

One of the most spectacular solar features (and one which can only be seen with a narrowband filter) is called a solar prominence. These are large faint streams of plasma that extend beyond the limb of the sun **FIGURE 8.4**. They are regions where a portion of the sun's magnetic field has lifted up plasma and constrains it from dispersing into space. People sometimes mistakenly called these "flares" but that is a different phenomenon. A flare is a temporary extremely bright spot on the sun, caused by the reconnection of magnetic fields. Flares might trigger a prominence, but they are two different things.

Sometimes prominences display a helical structure due to the twisting of the magnetic field lines. They can extend a substantial fraction of the sun's diameter out beyond the solar limb. They will change from one day to the next, and will be carried around by solar rotation. The way to search for a prominence is to pan very methodically around the solar limb. Prominences are often faint, but there are almost always a few present, and sometimes you'll find a really spectacular one — really bright, really large, or both.

An H-alpha filter will also allow you to see solar filaments. These are slightly darker thin lines or arcs that occur on the surface of the sun (several are visible in **FIGURE 8.4**). They are caused by plasma being lifted above the solar surface by magnetic fields — just like a prominence. In fact, physically, there is absolutely no difference between a prominence and a filament; they are the same phenomenon. But when the structure is viewed against the brighter solar surface, it appears dark by contrast, and is called a filament. When the structure is viewed against the black of space, it appears bright and is called a prominence. In some situations you can actually see the prominence connect to a filament at the solar limb. It becomes clear that the two are simply different perspectives on the same physical structure.

◇Other Daytime Objects

When you have the telescope out during the day for sun viewing, it is a lot of fun to attempt to locate and view other celestial objects as well. Some of the brighter stars and planets can be viewed in a telescope in broad daylight. And that is an enjoyable challenge for people who have some experience with telescopes. The planets and stars won't look as impressive as they do at night to be sure. The fun is in the challenge of locating them, and seeing them in the unfamiliar bright blue surroundings. One word of caution: once you take off the solar filter, be careful not to accidentally point the telescope at the sun. Think through where your celestial target is located, and make sure that it is a safe angle away from the sun.

The moon is lovely during the day. In a telescope, the terminator will not be as distinct and it will gradually fade to blue rather than black. The light parts of the moon look the same, but all the dark features become sky blue. Since the contrast is decreased the features won't be as distinct. But from an aesthetic perspective, it is beautiful.

Venus might be the one telescopic gem that actually looks better during the day than it does at night. The reason is that during the day you can find Venus very high in the sky (if you pick the right time of day), whereas at night it never gets too far from the horizon. And in astronomy, higher is better because you're looking through less atmosphere. Venus is plenty bright enough to be seen in broad daylight. So there is very little drawback to day observations of Venus, except perhaps that it can be harder to find.

It surprises some people to learn that Venus can actually be seen by the unaided eye in broad daylight — if you know exactly where to look. You'll need the sharpest resolution of your cones to see it, which means the image must fall nearly on the fovea. So it's just the opposite of viewing very faint objects. With Venus, you can't see it unless you are looking directly at it.

If the moon is out, remember that Venus will be roughly in line with the sun and the moon. You can check with computer software to find exactly where Venus falls along the sun-moon arc. Polarized sunglasses may help in finding Venus. Rotate them so that the sky appears darkest, and this will increase the contrast. Binoculars will make finding Venus in the day much easier. The only difficulty here is that getting them focused can be a bit of an issue since there is no reference point other than Venus itself.

Jupiter and Mercury are also good daytime planets to view through a telescope. They are fainter and more of a challenge to find than Venus. I can't quite make them out with my unaided eye, but I can in binoculars. Daytime views of Jupiter will not look nearly as good as nighttime views, but you can definitely tell what it is. Saturn is also faintly visible in a telescope during the day, however it is faint and not as impressive as one might hope.

Some of the brighter stars can also be seen during the day: Sirius, Arcturus, Betelgeuse. This is one case where I almost always do use the computer controls. These objects are challenging to find manually — likewise with Jupiter and Saturn. When you see a red star like Betelgeuse against the blue sky, the contrast is striking.

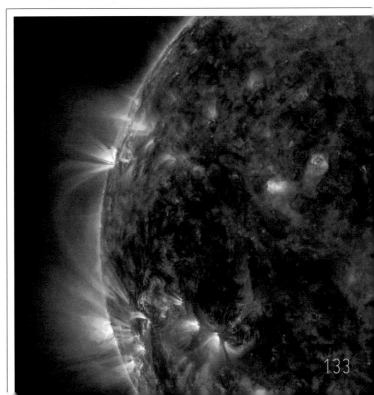

Studying the sun's magnetic fields; this image shows a series of arcs connecting two active regions of the sun's surface. Active areas are magnetically intense and can appear as sunspots.

133

Chapter 9

The Planets

In this chapter, we investigate tips on observing planets. Most of this will address telescopic views of planets, but we will also consider what can be seen with the unaided eye, and what can be seen with binoculars. We will begin with an overview of how to locate planets, and then we detail some specifics beginning with the planets that are easiest to find and most enjoyable to observe, and then move on to more challenging targets.

◇Locating the Planets

Since planets move, you cannot simply memorize their position relative to the background stars. That will

work for a few weeks or months perhaps, but next year the planet will be in a different location entirely, so you need to learn how to find them. Unfortunately, planet positions are not something you can easily estimate in your head. Their apparent motions are complex (since Earth also orbits the sun), and each planet has a different period. It can be hard to keep track of them all.

A computer program like "Stellarium" is a fast easy way to find out exactly where the planets will be tonight, or a popular astronomy magazine like *Sky & Telescope*. Also, consider that planets don't move all that fast, so the planets tomorrow night will be in roughly the same position as they were tonight with respect to the

Ultraviolet images from NASA's Galaxy Evolution Explorer showing a star named Mira, shedding material.

background stars. This works particularly well for the outer planets. Jupiter takes about one year on average to move from one constellation to the next. And Saturn takes more than twice as long. For this reason, I find that I normally know where Jupiter and Saturn are in the sky without having to think about it. I have a harder time keeping track of Venus and Mercury.

But even if you don't consult a computer program, you at least know the possible location where planets will be. Remember that planets lie (roughly) in the ecliptic. The ecliptic marks the path that the sun appears to travel with respect to the background stars (see chapters 1 and 2). It is also the orbit of the Earth around the sun, and the approximate plane of all the planets and even the moon. For this reason, planets will always be in a straight line with the sun and moon (unless they are so close in angle that their slight deviation from the ecliptic becomes very noticeable). If you use a planisphere or a star chart, it will usually show the ecliptic as a dashed arc. All the star charts in this book show the ecliptic as a yellow arc. If you go outside at night and see a "star" on (or very near) the ecliptic that is not indicated on your star chart, it's probably a planet.

◇Overview

Some planets are more obvious than others. You will have no trouble finding Venus when it's out. It will appear as an extremely bright star in the west just after sunset or in the east just before sunrise. The difficulty with Venus is this: you can only observe it for a relatively short time because it is always close to the sun. Venus is an early evening object, or a just-before-sunrise object. You can't see it late at night.

Jupiter is also an obvious and easy-to-locate planet. It is extremely bright — much brighter than any star. In reality, Venus is much brighter than Jupiter. But, psychologically, I find that Jupiter looks about as bright as Venus. This is because Jupiter can be out much later in the evening, when the sky is very dark, whereas Venus is visible only at twilight. So the relative contrast is similar. However, if Jupiter and Venus were side by side, Venus would outshine Jupiter by far.

Mars and Saturn are less obvious, but are still easily visible to the naked eye. These planets don't stand out like Venus and Jupiter, with the exception that Mars is bright for only a month or two every 2.1 years when it

9.1
Jupiter and the Galilean satellites. These four moons always appear in a nearly straight line next to Jupiter, since they orbit around Jupiter's equator. Sometimes, one of the moons will cast its shadow on Jupiter, as Ganymede is doing here.

comes close to the Earth. Otherwise, it is an unremarkable star, but it is always noticeably red. Saturn, on the other hand, shows no distinct color. Saturn is not nearly as bright as Jupiter, and can be confused with the background stars if you don't know the constellations. So if you see an unremarkable "extra" star in a constellation that is on the ecliptic: if it is red it's Mars and if it is white it's Saturn.

Mercury is also visible to the unaided eye, but you have to know just where to look, and you have to find it close to its greatest elongation (farthest position away from the sun). Otherwise it is lost in the sun's glare. Mercury is only visible just after sunset, or just before sunrise. It's a nice naked-eye or binocular object, but tends to look pretty lousy in a telescope. It's small, unremarkable, and always blurry because it is so low in the sky.

Uranus and Neptune are a bit more challenging because they are not visible to the unaided eye. Well, perhaps Uranus is visible under ideal conditions, but just barely. Uranus is an easy binocular object. Neptune is a slightly more challenging binocular object, but will be easily visible in a small telescope. Finding it can be tricky because it doesn't stand out from among the background stars. We will also discuss finding Pluto in this chapter. Even though it is no longer designated as a planet, it is a fun and very challenging telescope target.

In general, you will want to use medium to high magnification on planets. They are plenty bright enough, but they are small and will benefit from some magnification. Remember that there is a trade-off here: greater magnification makes the object appear fuzzier. I try to use the highest magnification in which the planet still appears relatively sharp. Experiment with different magnifications to find the one that gives the best view. Remember to have patience and wait for a moment of good seeing. Such moments (though infrequent) will allow you to see features that you couldn't otherwise see.

◇ Jupiter

Jupiter is always a delight. It is an easy planet to find because it shines brighter than any star. Only Venus, the moon, and the sun shine brighter than Jupiter. It really stands out, and so it is a great object for beginners. But it continues to delight expert astronomers as well. It never looks exactly the same way twice. Its cloud formations are constantly changing, and its moons constantly orbit about Jupiter, occasionally casting their shadow on the surface of the planet FIGURE 9.1.

The best time to see Jupiter is when the planet is in opposition; this occurs when the Earth is in between Jupiter and the sun. At this time, Jupiter reaches its highest point in the sky around midnight, and this is the ideal time to observe the planet. But since Jupiter is a large planet and since its distance to the Earth does not change dramatically, Jupiter also looks good for several months before or after opposition. From a practical perspective, a little bit after opposition is desirable because Jupiter then reaches its highest point in the sky before midnight; therefore you don't have to stay up as late to get a great view. Jupiter reaches opposition every 13 months. So if Jupiter is in opposition in the middle of July one year, it will be in opposition in the middle of August the next year.

With a backyard telescope, here is what you can expect to see with Jupiter. The most obvious thing is that Jupiter has some size to it. It's not a little shimmering dot like a star; it is noticeably large. The planet is ten times larger than the Earth in diameter. So even at a distance of about 500 million miles, it shows as quite large in a small telescope at modest magnification.

Next you may notice that Jupiter (usually) has two dark, orange horizontal stripes on it. One is just above the equator, and the other is just below. These are the northern and southern equatorial belts. They are essentially giant cloud features which encircle the planet. There are thinner, smaller belts above and below these belts, but you may not notice them right away (or at all if the seeing is poor). The light regions in between the belts are called "zones." The zones consist of higher altitude clouds made primarily of ammonia. The belts are methane-based and occur at lower elevations, and so you are actually looking deeper into Jupiter when

you look at its belts. The belts and zones are labeled in FIGURE 9.2.

Jupiter's belts and zones are dynamic; they change with time. Most of these changes are somewhat subtle. But occasionally one of Jupiter's equatorial belts will disappear for a year or so. It completely changes the look of the planet when this happens. But most of the time, you will see two very prominent horizontal stripes on Jupiter.

Another thing that nearly jumps out at the observer are Jupiter's four largest moons. These will appear as small stars next to Jupiter FIGURE 9.1. They always appear in a nearly straight line parallel to Jupiter's equator. Sometimes you won't see all four. Often one of them (usually Callisto) is so far to the left or right of Jupiter that it can be out of the field of view, and you will have to pan to find it. But also a moon can be directly in front of or behind Jupiter, in which case you will not see it. A third possibility is a moon that is in Jupiter's shadow; even though the moon is not blocked by Jupiter from Earth's vantage point, there is no sunlight falling on the moon to illuminate it. So if you only see three moons, or two, you'll know why. Very rarely will all four moons be invisible, but you will have to consult an astronomy magazine or computer software to find out when this unusual event will happen. Jupiter actually has over 60 known moons. However, all but

9.2
Belts and zones on Jupiter

North Polar Region

North-North Temperate Zone
North-North Temperate Belt
North Temperate Zone
North Temperate Belt
North Tropical Zone

North Equatorial Belt

Equatorial Zone

South Equatorial Belt

South Tropical Zone
South Temperate Belt
South Temperate Zone
South-South Temperate Belt
South-South Temperate Zone

South Polar Region

four are tiny and therefore faint. You will only be able to see the big four through a backyard telescope.

These four large moons are called the Galilean satellites since they were discovered by Galileo in the year 1610. In order of increasing distance from Jupiter, they are Io, Europa, Ganymede, and Callisto. Remember that their angular distance from Jupiter as we observe these moons from Earth may not be indicative of their true distance. In other words, all four moons may appear very close to Jupiter when they are in certain parts of their orbit. This means it is not always obvious which moon is which. However, if one of the moons is far from Jupiter, you can conclude that it is not Io or Europa, because these moons never depart very far in angle from Jupiter.

Io is about the same size as the Earth's moon. Europa is slightly smaller. Callisto is a bit larger than the moon, and Ganymede is a bit larger than Callisto. Ganymede is the largest moon in the solar system; it is even larger than the planet Mercury. And so if it orbited the sun directly instead of Jupiter, it would no doubt be classified as a planet. Since they have different sizes, and different surface reflectivity, the Galilean satellites do not all have exactly the same brightness. The difference is subtle, but I find that Ganymede does appear a bit brighter than the others. Jupiter's moons are easily visible in binoculars. They would be visible to the unaided eye if they weren't so close to Jupiter; they are certainly bright enough. In fact, if you have exceptional vision, you might just be able to see one or two of Jupiter's moons with the unaided eye.

The Galilean satellites orbit Jupiter relatively quickly. Io takes only 1.77 days to make an orbit. Europa takes only 3.55 days, Ganymede takes 7.16 days, and Callisto takes 16.7 days. Notice that Europa's period is almost exactly twice Io's period. And Ganymede's period is about twice Europa's. This is called an orbital resonance, and is apparently a very stable configuration. Callisto is not in resonance with the other three. Since Jupiter's moons orbit so quickly, they will appear in different places night after night. In fact, you can actually watch the inner moons move over the course of an evening. It is particularly obvious when two moons are very close to each other in angle. Look at Jupiter again an hour later and you will see that these two moons have noticeably moved!

One thing that people expect to see on Jupiter — that in fact you will only occasionally see — is the great red spot. Jupiter has a permanent storm in its southern hemisphere, just below the southern equatorial belt. This red spot is about twice the diameter of the Earth, but it's not always as easy to spot as people think. First of all, Jupiter rotates. So if you observe at a random time, there is a 50 percent chance that the great red spot will be on the back side of Jupiter, hidden from view. You might think then that you have a 50 percent chance of seeing the spot. But in fact, even when the

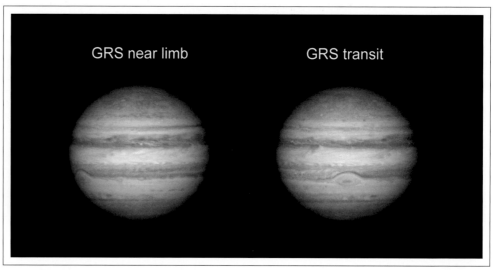

GRS near limb   GRS transit

9.3

When the Great Red Spot is near the limb as in the left image, it can be very difficult to see in a small telescope. The best time to see the Great Red Spot is when it transits, as in the right image.

9.4 Jupiter is slightly elliptical due to its rapid rotation, and does not appear as a perfect circle (shown in yellow).

day. Granted, you may not want to stay up late enough to see it. But on a given week, you will be able to find a day where the red spot transits at a convenient time, and that is when you should try to look for it.

Another thing to note about the red spot is that it changes in appearance from year to year. This strongly affects how easy it is to detect the feature. In the 1970s, the red spot was a very deep red, and quite large. It was extremely easy to see. In the late 1980s, Jupiter's red spot had faded to a light pink color, and was extremely difficult to see. Also, since the spot is sandwiched up against the southern equatorial belt, the lack of contrast can add to the difficulty. Sometimes you can see the distortion in the southern belt caused by the red spot easier than you can see the red spot. In 2010, Jupiter's southern equatorial belt disappeared for some time, and that made it much easier to see the red spot.

red spot is on the visible hemisphere of Jupiter, it is still not always easy to see. When it is close to the limb, foreshortening makes the red spot nearly impossible to view **FIGURE 9.3**. The bottom line is this: only when the red spot is near center is it easily visible.

This means that if you go out at a random time, you have only a 10 to 20 percent chance of seeing the great red spot. But there is some good news here. First of all, it's possible to estimate when the red spot will be centered. This is called the red spot transit time. You can look this up in *Sky & Telescope* magazine, or check the Internet to find the next transit time. This is one of those strange cases where a computer program will not be able to help you, unless it has Internet access and is designed to check transit times. The reason is that Jupiter's red spot (being a giant storm) moves around on Jupiter. It doesn't change latitude very much because it is sandwiched between the southern equatorial belt and the southern tropical zone, but it does move a bit in longitude. And just like weather on Earth, this is chaotic and not predictable very far in the future. So astronomers must actively keep track of the red spot's longitude and update the transit tables from time to time.

Jupiter has a very rapid rotation. It rotates in less than ten hours — faster than any other planet. This means the red spot transits several times per (Earth)

Using color filters may improve your view of Jupiter's features. Most eyepieces allow you to attach a color filter to the bottom, which allows only certain wavelengths of light through and changes the appearance of the target. I'm not big on using color filters. I usually prefer to see the object in its true color. However, there are a few cases where putting a colored filter on the eyepiece will help you to detect certain subtle features. In this case, a blue or green filter will increase the contrast of Jupiter's red spot, and will also increase the contrast between the belts and zones. If you are having trouble seeing the red spot, give it a try. Remember also to have patience and wait for a moment of good seeing.

Another thing to notice about Jupiter is that it is not exactly round. Jupiter rotates so quickly that it bulges at the equator. This effect is slight, but it is noticeable by eye when looking through a telescope **FIGURE 9.4**.

There are some other very interesting things to look for when observing Jupiter. Note that the red storm is not

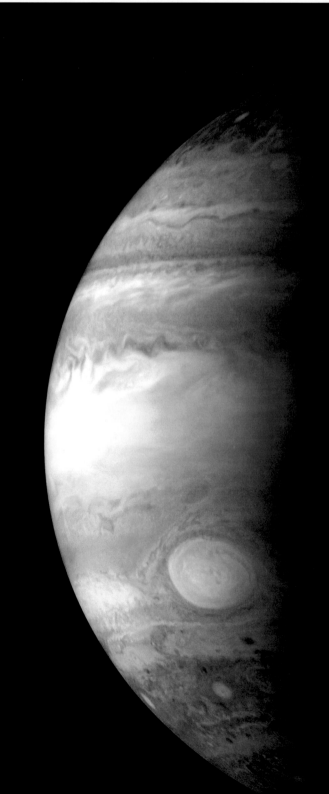

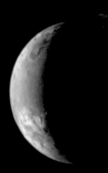

A montage of the planet Jupiter and one of its moons, Io. The great red spot appears as a white oval in this infra-red image. The blue area on Io is an active volcanic eruption which took place in 2007 when the photo was taken.

the only storm on Jupiter; it's just the only permanent storm. Other storms come and go and can have different colors. Look for these, especially right around the equatorial belts. Sometimes these storms will distort the otherwise smooth appearance of the belt. They are fun to watch. In 1994, comet Shoemaker-Levy 9 broke into 21 fragments which then plunged into Jupiter. As they descended into Jupiter's atmosphere, the explosive release of energy generated large black "welts" at the impact sites. These were easily visible in a backyard telescope. Over the course of weeks, the black spots smeared into lines and then eventually faded. It was incredibly fun to observe Jupiter at this time. And stay tuned, because that sort of thing could certainly happen again.

Another very enjoyable thing to look for on Jupiter is the shadow of one or more of Jupiter's moons. Since Jupiter is tilted only slightly relative to its orbit around the sun, and since its moons orbit around its equator, it is very common for the moons to eclipse Jupiter, or for Jupiter to eclipse the moons. When a moon casts its shadow on Jupiter, even a small telescope can reveal this little black spot **FIGURE 9.1**. They are not quite as distinct as you might hope, but with some practice and patience, you can definitely learn to see them. The positions of Jupiter's moons and the timing of their eclipses are all perfectly predictable by computer software. (Be sure to include the light-travel time delay between Jupiter and the Earth, or the estimated time will be off by about 30 minutes.) Alternatively, you can look them up on the Internet or in *Sky & Telescope* magazine.

Another interesting way to observe the motion of Jupiter's moons is to watch them disappear or (subsequently) reappear as they go behind or in front of Jupiter. This is all perfectly predictable from computer software, or you can look it up online or in an astronomy magazine. So you can predict the very minute that a moon will disappear into the limb of Jupiter or reappear on the other side. (You will not be able to see a moon directly in front of Jupiter, because there is not sufficient contrast.) Likewise, you can also predict when the moon's shadow will begin to fall on Jupiter. Since the Earth is not exactly where the sun is, Jupiter's moons will not block their own shadow.

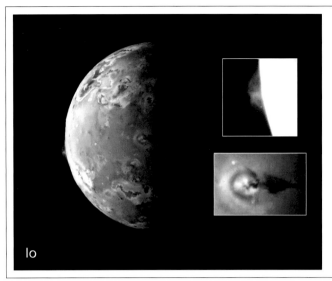

Io

Also, you can compute when and where Jupiter's shadow will fall on one of its moons. Again, since Earth is not exactly where the sun is, it is possible for Jupiter to block sunlight for one of its moons even though it is not blocking the Earth from view. In this case, from our perspective, Jupiter's moon is not blocked by Jupiter, but we still cannot see it because no sunlight is falling on it. This can lead to some interesting situations. I recall one time I was watching one of Jupiter's moons come out from behind the planet. But then a few minutes later it disappeared! I was perplexed at first because I knew the moon was coming out from behind Jupiter, so I was expecting it to get farther from the planet and become even easier to see. Why had it disappeared again? Upon checking the table though, I found that this moon had indeed come out from behind Jupiter, only to enter Jupiter's shadow four minutes later. There was only a four-minute window where this moon was visible from Earth and not in eclipse. It is interesting to watch celestial motions in real time like this.

Another example of watching celestial motions in real time is when Jupiter's moons eclipse each other. Jupiter is tilted only slightly with respect to its orbit around the sun. And thus, the orbits of the Galilean satellites (these moons orbit around Jupiter's equator) are only slightly tilted. This is why they always appear in a nearly — but not exactly — straight line. This slight offset means that the shadow of one moon will normally pass just a bit above or below the shadow of another moon. However, since Jupiter has a (nearly) 12-year orbital period, every 6 years its orbital plane intersects the sun (Jupiter's vernal or autumnal equinox). When this happens, the Galilean satellites begin to mutually eclipse each other. You can literally watch the shadow of one moon fall upon another. This makes the shadowed moon slowly fade to dim, and then re-brighten over the course of about 15 minutes or so. This period of potential mutual eclipses happens every 6 years (when Jupiter is "edge-on" relative to the sun) and lasts for several months. Jupiter is "edge-on" in May 2021, and so mutual eclipses take place several months before and after this. You can compute other years by adding any multiple of six (5.93 to be more precise) to May 2021.

◇Venus

Like Jupiter, Venus is exceptionally bright, which makes it easy to locate in our night sky. Only the sun and the moon are brighter than Venus. Unlike Jupiter, Venus is only visible in the west shortly after sunset or in the east shortly before sunrise. Venus is at its best when the sky is still twilight. The best time of year to view Venus is when the planet is near its greatest elongation (see chapter 2). The date is different from year to year. However, Venus will also look pretty good within

a month or perhaps two before or after this date. Use a computer program, the Internet, or *Sky & Telescope* magazine to find when Venus will be at greatest elongation. When Venus is at greatest eastern elongation (it is east of the sun), it will appear in the west just after sunset. Conversely, when Venus is at greatest western elongation, it will appear in the east just before sunrise.

Venus is often called "the evening star" or "the morning star" since it dominates the sky when near greatest elongation. It is a stunning naked-eye object, and looks even brighter and more magnificent in binoculars. Through a telescope you will be able to see that Venus goes through phases, just like the moon. In fact, people seeing Venus for the first time through a telescope often remark that it looks like the moon — not that it has visible craters or maria; by this they mean that it has a phase, such as the crescent phase. Only the inferior planets (Mercury and Venus) go through all phases as seen from Earth; the superior planets can never be seen in the crescent or quarter phases (see chapter 2).

Phase will be the main thing to notice when you look at Venus. It will appear only half illuminated: perhaps a bit more, perhaps a bit less. Moreover, when Venus

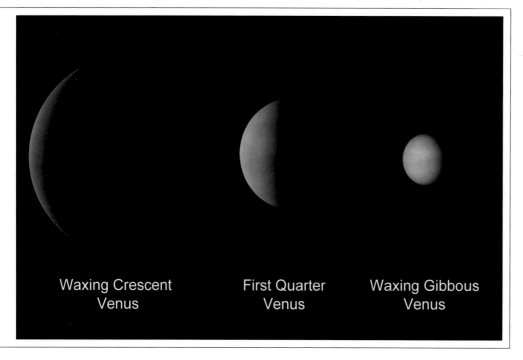

Waxing Crescent Venus   **First Quarter Venus**   **Waxing Gibbous Venus**

9.5
The size of Venus as seen from Earth is related to its phase

is in its crescent phase, it is always quite large since it is close to Earth. And when it is in its gibbous phase, it appears quite small since it is farther from Earth. This was one of the earliest indications that Venus orbits the sun rather than the Earth. It is very enjoyable to observe Venus over the course of a month or two. You can actually watch it change size and go through its phases at it orbits the sun. It really gives you a feel for where the planet is in relation to the sun. When in its crescent phase, Venus will appear about the same size as Jupiter. When in its gibbous phase, it will be only about one-third as large. See **FIGURE 9.5**.

The phases of Venus are "backward" from the moon in a couple of ways. First of all, when the moon is in its waxing phases, it is illuminated on the right side (from the perspective of Northern Hemisphere observers). However, Venus is illuminated on its *left* side during the waxing phases. Although both the moon and Venus orbit in the same direction, Venus orbits the sun, whereas the moon orbits the Earth. So when Venus is in between the sun and Earth (at new phase), it is moving westward, whereas the moon would be moving eastward at that time. This accounts for the reversed phases of Venus (and Mercury as well). Also, we normally think of waxing as "getting bigger" in the sense the phase is increasing. While this is true of Venus as well, the planet itself seems to shrink in size during the waxing phases (even though a larger percentage of its surface is illuminated), and grows during the waning phases.

Venus isn't quite as exciting to watch as Jupiter. Venus has no moons. Venus will not show any surface features in a backyard telescope. This is because Venus is permanently enshrouded in thick clouds. Its surface features are never visible in ordinary light. The clouds are not divided into belts and zones like on Jupiter. Instead they form a perfectly uniform blanket. So Venus always appears as a perfectly smooth yellowish-white sphere. This in itself is interesting. We are used to seeing the cratered surface of the moon going through phases. But a perfectly smooth polished sphere going through phases looks quite strange. Venus is almost the same size as Earth. So this is fun to think about when observing that world; if you could somehow observe Earth from Venus, it would be the same size in your telescope!

Artifacts of Earth's atmosphere are often seen in views of Venus. Since Venus is never far from the sun in angle, it will always be low in the sky when you observe it at twilight. This means you are looking through a lot of Earth's atmosphere, and this causes distortion. For this reason, generally speaking, your view of Venus will not be as sharp as your views of Jupiter, or other objects that are high in the sky. Sometimes you can actually see the motion of air currents as the image of Venus dances around. Poor seeing can also split light into its constituent wavelengths, which produces a "rainbow" of sorts. This effect is very noticeable on Venus due to its inherent brightness and the fact that it is usually low in the sky. Note that all these effects can be reduced by observing Venus as early in the evening as possible, and when it is closest to greatest elongation.

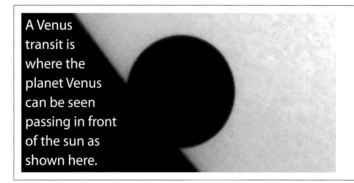

A Venus transit is where the planet Venus can be seen passing in front of the sun as shown here.

One really interesting and very rare observation you can make of Venus involves a solar transit. A transit (in this context) is when a small object passes in front of a larger one. In this case, Venus occasionally passes directly in front of the sun as seen from the Earth. This is only possible with an inferior planet (Venus and Mercury) since the outer planets are never between the Earth and the sun. This event does not happen often since the orbit of Venus is tilted relative to Earth's orbit. So Venus normally passes just a bit above or below the sun. However, very occasionally, the orientation is just right and Venus crosses directly in front of the sun. By safely viewing the sun, you can watch a tiny dot move across its surface. The event lasts a few hours. Transits of Venus happen only twice per century, and the two events are always separated by eight years. This last happened in June 8, 2004, and again on June 5–6, 2012[1]. If you missed these, you're probably out of luck — the next Venus transits will happen in December 2117, and again in December 2125.

The moon with Venus shown smaller at right

Another interesting thing to note about Venus is that it can be seen during the middle of the day if you know where to look. Being the third-brightest object in the sky, Venus looks quite lovely as observed through a telescope against a bright blue sky. It is also visible in binoculars in daylight. And if you have good eyesight (and with some practice), you can see Venus with the unaided eye in the middle of the day. This is easiest when Venus is near greatest elongation — far from the sun. Polarized sunglasses can help you find it. Turn the sunglasses so that the sky appears darkest, and this will increase the contrast, making it easier to spot Venus. Quite the opposite of night vision, you must look almost directly at Venus to see it during the day. This can make finding it quite a challenge. It helps when the moon is out as well, because the moon and sun indicate the orientation of the ecliptic: you know Venus will be lined up with the sun and moon.

◇Saturn

There is nothing quite like Saturn. The usual reaction people have when seeing Saturn in a telescope for the first time is: "Wow!" The rings are easily visible in a backyard telescope, even at low magnification. This gives Saturn a unique 3-dimensional appearance unlike any other object in the heavens. It just doesn't look quite "real." It also is smaller than beginners sometimes expect (but no less beautiful). It is physically about nine times the diameter of Earth, and nearly as large as Jupiter. But it lies twice as far away as Jupiter, so the body of the planet will appear less than half the size of Jupiter though the rings will extend farther out. We are used to seeing large Hubble/ Voyager images of Saturn. And though views from a backyard telescope will not have quite that quality, there is something majestic about

While it may not appear as clearly as on this image, amateur astronomers are often amazed at being able to see the rings of Saturn for themselves through almost any backyard telescope.

seeing the planet for real with your own eyes, something that cannot be captured in a photograph.

Like any outer planet, Saturn appears at its theoretical best at opposition observed at midnight. And from a practical standpoint, it's nice to view this planet about a month after opposition, when it reaches its highest point in the sky well before midnight. However, since Saturn is about a billion miles away, its distance from Earth really doesn't change very much throughout the year. What that means is this: as long as Saturn is high in the sky, it's going to look good! You really don't have to wait for it to reach opposition. Saturn orbits very slowly. It takes over two years on average for it to drift from one constellation to the next. So if you know where Saturn is tonight with respect to the stars, its position really isn't going to change all that much over

the next year. This also means that Saturn reaches opposition only a few weeks later every year. If you know when and where Saturn looked good this year, you know where and when it will look good next year.

Like Jupiter, Saturn is a gas giant with cloud features that are stretched into belts (dark) and zones (light). However, the belts and zones on Saturn are much more subtle than those on Jupiter, and are harder to see. Like Jupiter, Saturn often develops storm systems in its atmosphere. It does not have a permanent storm like Jupiter's red spot. But some of the larger transient storms can be seen in a fairly good quality backyard telescope. A giant white storm formation often appears in Saturn's northern hemisphere every 30 years or so when that hemisphere is experiencing summer solstice. It was seen in 1933, 1960, and 1990. If the trend holds, it should reappear in 2020. A giant storm also appeared in 2011, so they can occur in "off years" as well.

The rings are the most visually stunning feature of Saturn **FIGURE 9.6**. They are comprised of trillions of tiny moonlets which orbit around Saturn's equator. They are divided into three

A ring

C ring

Northern Equatorial Belt

Encke Gap

B ring

Cassini Division

9.6   Saturn and its ring system

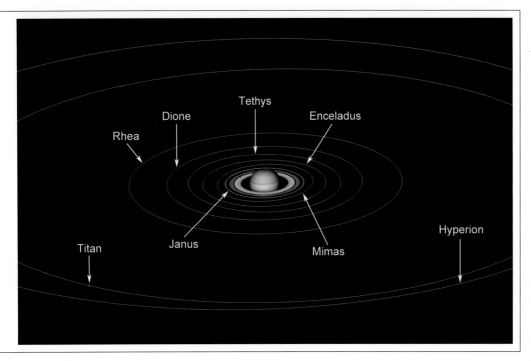

9.7
Saturn and its inner moons. These are the brighter moons which can be seen in a backyard telescope.

main systems, the A, B, and C rings. The C ring system is closest to the planet, then B, and A is the outermost. A small telescope will allow you to see the A and B rings with ease. The C ring system is much fainter, and a larger telescope with more light-gathering power will be helpful in detecting this system. Many additional ring systems have been discovered, but the A, B, and (perhaps) C rings are the only ones you are going to see with a backyard telescope.

There is a division between the A and B rings, a "gap" which appears dark from Earth because far less material is found in that region. This is called the "Cassini division," after Giovanni Cassini who discovered this division in the year 1675. On a night of good seeing, when Saturn is well-tilted, you should be able to see this division at medium to high magnification. It will be easiest to see on the left and right extremes of Saturn's rings where foreshortening is not a problem. This is the most noticeable feature within Saturn's rings, and marks the difference between the A and B rings. The Cassini division is caused by an orbital resonance with one of Saturn's moons: Mimas. Material orbiting within the Cassini division orbits twice for every one orbit of Mimas. This creates instability, and would cause any

material in that division to eventually be pulled out. In some situations, orbital resonances can increase stability (e.g., Jupiter's moons), but in other situations the resonance is unstable. Saturn has a number of smaller gaps and divisions, and additional rings. But none of these will be easily visible in a backyard telescope.

Like Jupiter, Saturn has over 60 moons. Most of these are quite small, and beyond the range of a typical telescope. But you will always be able to see at least one, and usually four or five. Unlike Jupiter, Saturn's moons are not normally in a straight line since Saturn is tilted with respect to its orbit around the sun. (The exception to this is when Saturn undergoes its edge-on transition, which we will cover shortly.)

Titan is the largest moon of Saturn and the second largest moon in the entire solar system. It appears as an orange star about five ring diameters away from Saturn. It orbits in the same plane as the rings. So if Titan is above or below Saturn, it will appear rather close; but if it is to the left or right, it will appear rather distant from Saturn. Titan is even visible in binoculars. In a telescope Titan is distinctly orange. It is the only moon in the solar system with a thick atmosphere. And it is this hazy atmosphere that produces the orange hue.

Most of the other moons that can be seen with a small telescope orbit much closer to Saturn than Titan orbits; they are within about two ring diameters of Saturn FIGURE 9.7. They are also quite a bit fainter than Titan. But their proximity to Saturn makes them relatively easy to spot. In order of decreasing brightness, they are Rhea, Tethys, Dione, Enceladus, and Mimas. All of these can be seen in a 12-inch telescope, and most of them are visible in an even smaller telescope. Rhea is the outermost of these inner moons, and the easiest to spot. Since these all orbit in the plane of Saturn's rings, they will appear closest to Saturn when above or below Saturn (i.e., in front or behind the planet), then when they are to the left or right — at greatest elongation. With a large backyard telescope, a skilled observer might also be able to glimpse the fainter moons Hyperion and Janus.

There is one other moon of interest in the Saturn system. Iapetus is a little moon which seems to break all the rules. It is about the same brightness as Dione or Enceladus — faint, but well within the range of a moderate backyard telescope. But it does not orbit in the plane of Saturn's rings and its orbit is larger than Titan's, so Iapetus is not always in the same field of view as Saturn. This makes it harder to locate than the other moons. The easiest time to spot Iapetus is when its orbit brings it close (in angle) to Saturn. You will have to use a computer program or consult an astronomy magazine or website to find the location of Iapetus. Otherwise, it will be nearly impossible to distinguish it from a background star.

Another interesting aspect of Iapetus is that it is much brighter and thus easier to see when it is to the west of Saturn than when it is to the east of Saturn. The reason for this is that Iapetus is very dark on one side, and white as snow on the other. And since it rotates at the same rate it revolves around Saturn (it's tidally locked just like the Earth's moon) its white side faces Earth when it is west of Saturn, and its dark side faces Earth when it is east of Saturn.

Another thing to look for when observing Saturn is the interplay of shadows between the planet and the rings. If the Earth were exactly where the sun is, the rings of Saturn would always block their own shadow. In fact, this is nearly what happens around the time of opposition. At opposition, Earth is between Saturn and the sun, and so the rings essentially block their own shadow. However, at other times, the Earth is not exactly between the sun and Saturn. This puts us at a slight angle between Saturn's rings and their shadow on Saturn. I always look for this shadow when I am viewing Saturn.

First, try to see if the rings cut in front of Saturn on the top half or the bottom half. As long as the seeing is decent, you can usually tell. If for example, Saturn

is tilted such that its rings cross in front on the lower half of the planet `FIGURE 9.8`, then we look for the ring shadow on this lower portion. If Earth is just a bit above the Saturn-sun plane, then we will see the shadow of the rings on the planet just above where the rings cross in front `FIGURE 9.8 B`. If on the other hand the Earth is just below the Saturn-sun plane, then we will see the shadow of the rings just below the rings as they cut across the planet `FIGURE 9.8 A`. If the Earth is in the Saturn-sun plane, then the rings will block their own shadow, and you won't be able to see it.

Another thing I always look for is the shadow of Saturn on its rings. This is most visible when the Earth is to the east or west of the Saturn-sun line. In other words, it's most obvious when Saturn is far from opposition. Saturn casts its shadow on the back portion of its rings of course. So if Saturn is tilted such that its rings cut in front of Saturn on the bottom half, then you will look for the planet's shadow on the top portion of the rings, just to the left or right of where

the planet intersects the rings `FIGURE 9.8 A` and `B`. It will look like a piece of the rings is missing there. It's almost always possible to see this, except when Saturn is very near opposition, or when seeing is very poor.

From our perspective on Earth, Saturn seems to change its tilt from year to year `FIGURE 9.9`. Though the true tilt of Saturn's axis of rotation remains constant at 26.7 degrees, our perspective on Saturn changes as it orbits the sun. As Saturn approaches its vernal equinox, we see the planet from a less-tilted perspective. The rings seem to collapse into a thin line as Saturn goes through its equinox `FIGURE 9.9 C`. After this time, the tilt increases again, though in the opposite direction. So if we were "above" Saturn's rings looking down on the planet before it crossed through equinox, we would be "below" Saturn's rings looking up at the planet after its equinox.

9.8

The shadow of Saturn's rings on the planet and the shadow of the planet on the rings are often visible from Earth. Where the shadows appear depends on the orientation of the sun and the Earth relative to Saturn.

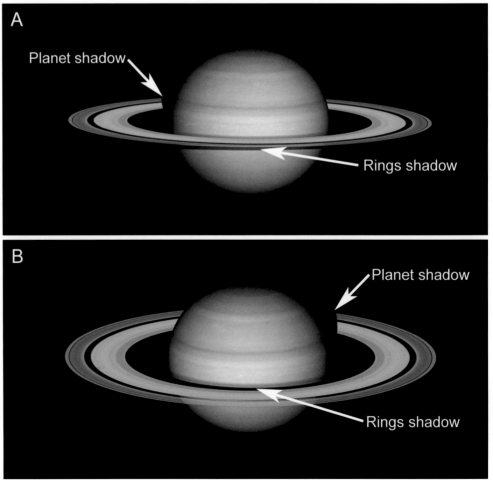

9.9
(A) Saturn at its maximum possible tilt as seen from Earth
(B) Saturn at an intermediate tilt
(C) Saturn as seen edge-on

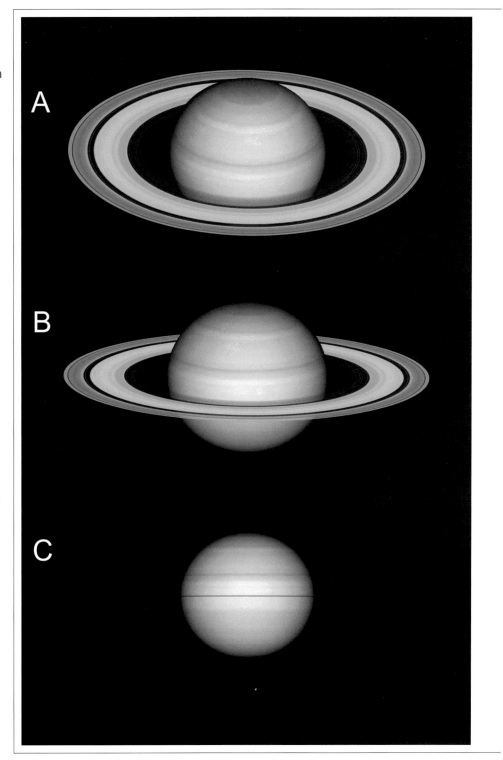

From our perspective on Earth, Saturn's tilt appears to go from a maximum of 26.7 degrees FIGURE 9.9 A down to zero FIGURE 9.9 C, then to -26.7 degrees, then to zero again, and finally back to 26.7 degrees, completing the cycle. Since Saturn takes 29.5 years to orbit the sun, this is how long its ring-tilt cycle lasts. It takes a little more than 7 years for Saturn to go from maximum tilt to edge-on from our vantage point. Seven years after that, Saturn is viewed at its maximum tilt again. So as you observe Saturn year after year you get to enjoy the planet from different angles. No doubt, the prettiest view is when Saturn is at its highest tilt. The strangest view is when Saturn is edge-on. In fact, when Saturn is precisely edge-on from our perspective, the rings cannot be seen at all for a period of a few weeks. It is really odd to view Saturn and not see rings. But this situation only happens every 15 years (twice per orbit). It last happened in 2009.

There is one additional complexity to consider. The main change in Saturn's apparent tilt is because the planet is orbiting the sun and is seen at different angles. But we must also consider that the Earth is orbiting the sun, too, and the plane of Earth's orbit is not exactly the same as Saturn's orbital plane, though it is very close. What this means is that Earth is some-times above the Saturn-sun plane, and other times it is

below. While Saturn makes a complete circuit around the sun every 29.5 years, which causes the apparent change in tilt from our perspective, there is a smaller change in apparent tilt on a one-year cycle due to Earth's orbit around the sun.

In practice, what this means is the following. Suppose Saturn appeared edge-on two years ago. In that case it is becoming more tilted every year. But this increase

This false color image of Saturn indicates varying heights and compositions of cloud layers. The image also captures two of Saturn's moons: Tethys, upper right, and Dione, at lower left.

is not constant due to Earth's orbit around the sun. Saturn's tilt may slightly decrease for a few months, and then increase by a much larger amount after that. The net result is after one year the tilt has increased, but there is a smaller wobble that may cause a temporary change in the opposite direction. This smaller wobble isn't obvious except when Saturn goes edge-on. During this time, a very small change in perspective can have a large effect on the appearance of the planet.

Sometimes when Saturn goes through its edge-on transition, it happens in the middle of the wobble caused by Earth's orbit. When this happens, Saturn goes edge-on from our perspective three times in a row. A spectacular example of this happened in the 1990s. Saturn appeared edge-on in May 1995, then again in August, and once more in February 1996. Earth must be in the proper part of its orbit when Saturn goes through its equinox for this situation to occur. In 2009, this was not the case, so Saturn went through its edge-on state only once. The next time Saturn will appear edge-on is in March 2025. It will transition only once, though it will come very close to

edge-on again in late November of the same year due to the "wobble" caused by Earth's orbit.

When Saturn is edge-on, take advantage of the rare opportunity to see a "ring-less" Saturn. It is an interesting sight. A few weeks before or after the edge-on perspective, the rings look like a "pin" going right through the planet. When the rings are exactly edge-on from our perspective, they cannot be seen at all. However, the Earth's perspective is not exactly the same as the sun. Therefore, you might still be able to see the shadow Saturn's rings cast on the planet, even when the rings themselves are invisible from our vantage point.

One advantage to viewing Saturn in its edge-on configuration is that it suddenly becomes very easy to spot the moons. Since the moons orbit in the same plane as the rings (except Iapetus, and some of the small outer moons), they all form a straight line, just like the Galilean satellites. It is much easier for the eye to pick out the moons under these circumstances. Also, any glare that is normally produced by the rings is gone, so it becomes easier to spot faint moons.

◇Mars

All of the large outer planets (Jupiter, Saturn, Uranus, and Neptune) look pretty good throughout most of the year, and experience opposition about once per year. Mars breaks the mold. Mars only looks good when it is very near opposition. And to add insult to injury, it only experiences opposition every 2.1 years. So the point is this: when Mars reaches opposition, don't miss it! You can enjoy the other planets almost year-round. But you only get a really good view of Mars for a month or so, and then you have to wait two years for the next good view.

If Mars is not near opposition, it's going to look fairly lousy in the telescope. The reason is simply the change in distance. Mars is *much* closer to the Earth at opposition than it is at any other time of the year. It can appear over five times larger at opposition than it does at more distant parts of its orbit FIGURE 9.10. And since Mars is only half the diameter of the Earth, it needs to be very close in order for us to see any detail at all. With Mars, image size makes all the difference in the world. It will either look spectacular, or it will be a tiny red circle.

With the other outer planets, you can wait for a month or so after opposition, and get your best view of the planet when it crosses the meridian at a comfortable time well before midnight. With Mars, you don't dare wait. Observe it on the weeks of and surrounding its opposition. Even if you don't want to wait for it to reach its highest point in the sky at midnight — that's okay. It's fine to observe Mars in the east before it crosses the meridian if you don't want to stay up late. But make sure you don't miss the date of opposition.

There is another weird rule about Mars oppositions. Some oppositions of Mars are far better than others. That's not the case with any other planet. The reason is that the orbit of Mars is elliptical; it is farther from the sun at some points than others. When the Earth passes Mars (which it does every 2.1 years), sometimes it makes a very close pass, and other times it doesn't come as close due to the elliptical nature of Mars' orbit. For example, in August 2003, the Earth came as close to Mars as it ever has in recorded history! Mars reached an angular size of 25 arc-seconds, and looked spectacular in a telescope. However, when Mars reached opposition in January 2010, the largest it ever reached

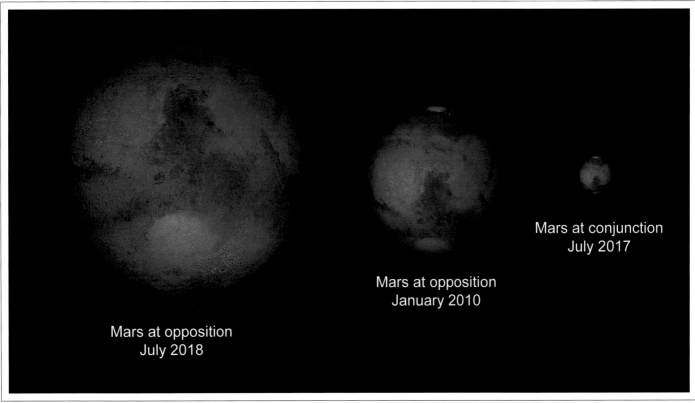

Mars at conjunction
July 2017

Mars at opposition
January 2010

Mars at opposition
July 2018

9.10   The apparent size of Mars changes greatly with time due to its distance from the Earth

was 14 arc-seconds — just a little more than half as big as it appeared in the 2003 opposition.

So there's bad news and there's worse news. The bad news is that Mars only looks good every 2.1 years. The worse news is that even then it doesn't always look its best. Mars only experiences a really great opposition every 15 years or so, though the oppositions that precede and follow it are also pretty good. The next really good opposition of Mars is in July 2018, when Mars will reach 24 arc-seconds in size; however, the October 2020 opposition will also be decent (22 arc-seconds). Notice the incredible change in size between the 2010 opposition and the 2018 opposition in **FIGURE 9.10**.

You may have read a popular hoax that has been widely circulated on the Internet. It claims that Mars will appear in August as large as the full moon. Of course, this could never happen because the orbits of Mars and Earth never bring either one close enough to the other. The myth is based on a misunderstanding of a real event. The original notice said that in August of 2003, Mars will appear as large _through a telescope at 75 times magnification_ as the moon appears _without any magnification_. That is, Mars will look as big with a telescope as the moon looks without a telescope. This did happen of course (in 2003!!!), but it's not quite what the myth conveys.

To the unaided eye, Mars appears a vivid red color. It is usually not one of the brighter stars, hovering around magnitude 2. But at opposition, it becomes very bright and can shine as bright as magnitude -2.9. This puts it on par with Jupiter, temporarily at least. At such time, it is a delightful naked-eye object. And you will have no difficulty at all locating it. But in a month or two, it will fade back down to its dreary non-opposition brightness. Again, you can use a computer program to compute when Mars will undergo opposition, and where it will be located. You can also look up opposition dates of Mars on the internet, or in an astronomy magazine such as _Sky & Telescope_. I suggest you view Mars at least once at its non-opposition date just for the experience of it. Then you can contrast this with how much better the view is during opposition.

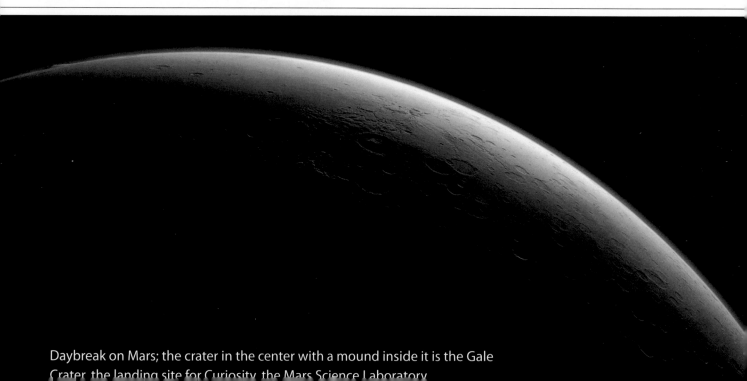

Daybreak on Mars; the crater in the center with a mound inside it is the Gale Crater, the landing site for Curiosity, the Mars Science Laboratory

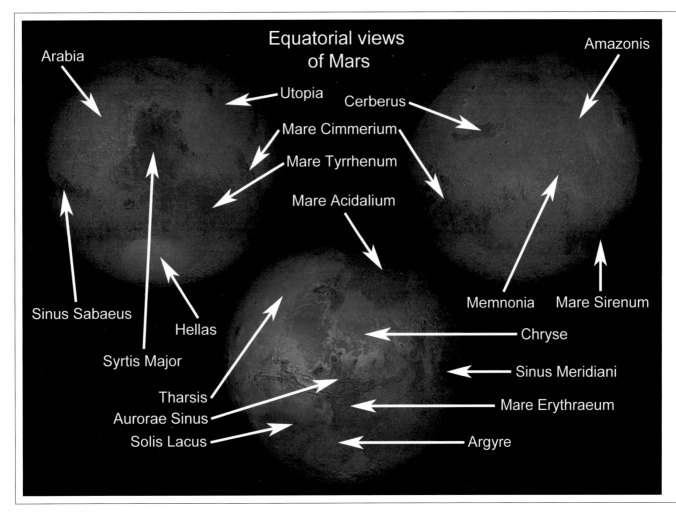

9.11 The surface features of Mars as viewed edge-on, at three different longitudes

Now that you know when and where to look for Mars, what can you expect to see? As with other planets, you will want to use medium or high magnification when viewing Mars. It will appear as a disk with noticeable size. Assuming you are observing during opposition, you will usually be able to see some surface features on Mars, as shown in **FIGURE 9.11**. In particular, Syrtis Major, Hellas, and one of the polar ice caps are often visible. It is very helpful to use computer software to compute which side of Mars will be visible at the time you are planning to observe it. Knowing what to expect will help you to see the features.

Syrtis Major is a large dark feature with a more or less vertical orientation which passes through Mars' equator. It is the darkest feature on Mars, and is therefore usually the easiest to see. Just below Syrtis Major is the large valley Hellas. This valley often fills with fog, giving

it a very bright appearance — almost white. In fact, many beginners mistake Hellas for the southern ice cap. The southern ice cap is even further below Hellas.

Mars has polar ice caps, much like Earth. These are nearly white, and so it is usually easy to see one of them. Which one you see will depend on how Mars is tilted relative to the Earth. But clearly, if one polar ice cap is visible, then the other one will be hidden on the opposite side of the planet. If you think you see two ice caps, you are probably seeing the northern ice cap and Hellas. The ice caps change size with the Martian seasons. Sometimes over the course of a month or so around opposition, you can observe a noticeable change in the extent of one of the polar caps.

Mars has a 24-hour, 37-minute rotation period — just a bit longer than a day on Earth. So you can actually watch Mars rotate over the course of an evening. And it is rotating at about the same rate you are. At opposition, Mars is visible all night. So you can watch nearly a half rotation of the planet on or around that date, if you are willing to stay up all night.

Since Mars' day is about the same as Earth's, if you observe Mars tomorrow night, you will see approximately the same side as is visible tonight at the same time. But since the Martian day is slightly longer than an Earth day, Mars will appear at a slightly earlier point in its rotation tomorrow night than it does tonight at the

same time on Earth. If you took a picture of Mars every night at the same time, and then played those images in sequence, you would see Mars rotating backward. If, on the other hand, you took pictures of Mars every few minutes in a single evening and played the sequence, you would see Mars rotating normally.

By selecting the date and time of night, you can determine which side of Mars to view. I recommend finding the time when Syrtis Major will be centered. It is one of the easiest features to see, and Hellas lies just below

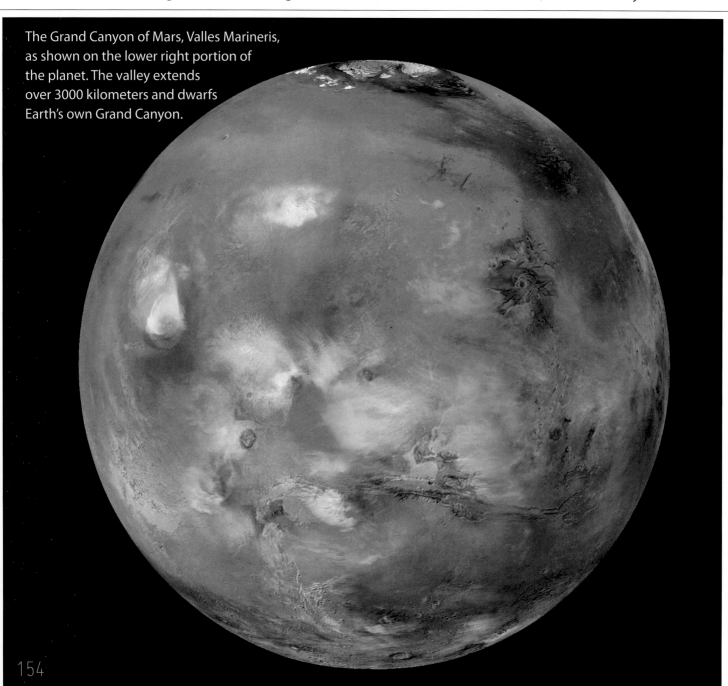

The Grand Canyon of Mars, Valles Marineris, as shown on the lower right portion of the planet. The valley extends over 3000 kilometers and dwarfs Earth's own Grand Canyon.

it. Even a six-inch telescope will be able to pick out those features. Mars may be the most important object to wait for a moment of good seeing. Be patient, and watch for those few precious seconds of crystal clarity that happen only every few minutes.

Mars' moon Deimos

Color filters may help you see various features on Mars. A blue filter will increase the contrast between red and white. This will make it easier to see the polar ice caps, as well as the Hellas basin. Try experimenting with other colors as well, and see which features can be seen with each filter.

Like Earth, Mars has weather. This is sometimes visible from Earth. Clouds can form in the Martian atmosphere; however, they tend to be much thinner and fainter than Earth clouds. I'm not certain that I have ever clearly seen a cloud on Mars (not counting the fog in the Hellas Basin). But skilled Mars watchers love to watch for these subtle features. Various color filters may help bring out these hard-to-detect transient markings.

One very obvious form of weather on Mars is the dreaded dust storm. Mars experiences both regional and *global* dust storms. When the global dust storms happen, they obscure the entire surface of the planet in a blanket of orange muck. It is very obvious. All of the surface markings disappear and you find yourself looking at a completely featureless orange sphere. These global dust storms often begin as a regional storm in a specific location on Mars, and then gradually envelop the entire planet over the course of a few weeks. Most regional dust storms never become global. However, the global dust storms can last for months. They will obscure almost all of the surface features, and there's really nothing you can do about it. Fortunately, these global storms are not terribly common.

Mars has two tiny moons: Phobos and Deimos. Each

is only a few miles in diameter. They are very faint, but they are within the detectable range of a moderately large backyard telescope (such as a 12-inch) — when Mars is at opposition. If Mars is not at opposition, you can forget observing these moons. Even at opposition, these moons can be a challenge. So Phobos and Deimos are not good targets for beginners. But they are a fun challenge for experienced observers. The problem is not so much that the moons are too faint for the telescope. They aren't, and would be fairly easy to spot if they weren't so close to Mars. Mars is 200,000 times brighter than Phobos! It's hard to see something faint next to something so bright.

If you want to try your luck at Mars' moons, the first thing to do is to calculate (or look up) when these moons will be at greatest elongation, which puts them at the largest angle away from Mars. Mars' moons orbit very fast, so you will likely have several opportunities in a given evening. Deimos takes only about 30 hours to make one orbit and Phobos takes less than 8 hours to orbit once! It has the shortest period of any known moon. I recall looking at Phobos one evening when it was at elongation on the right side of Mars. A few hours later, I saw it again at elongation on the left side of Mars. The key is to catch it at its farthest distance (in angle) from the planet.

Another tip in observing Phobos and Deimos is to get Mars out of the picture. You can create an occulting bar within the telescope to block Mars. Alternatively, the easiest thing to do is to move the telescope so that Mars is just barely outside the field of view, just touching the right or left side of your field, but with its moon just inside the field of view. Use high magnification. Remember that moving the telescope very slowly may enable you to see these faint moons better. The eye is sometimes able to detect moving faint objects better than stationary ones. Deimos is a bit fainter than Phobos. But it is also farther from Mars, and this makes it easier to detect.

◇Mercury

As the closest planet to the sun, Mercury takes only 88 days to complete one orbit. It's hard to keep track of something that moves so fast. It is pointless to memorize where Mercury is relative to the background constellations for two reasons. First, it's not going to stay there very long, and second, Mercury is always very close to the sun, and can only be seen in relatively bright twilight. Fortunately, Mercury is fairly bright and cuts through twilight pretty well. You won't need any other stars to find it. We need to spend some time discussing how and when to look for Mercury, because with Mercury, timing is everything.

The key to spotting Mercury is to look for it within about one week of greatest elongation (see chapter 2). With Venus, it's not so crucial to be close to the date of greatest elongation, because Venus orbits the sun at a greater distance. But Mercury never gets farther than 28 degrees away from the sun. Mercury is visible to the unaided eye, but the window of time is rather narrow. Mercury is only visible very shortly after sunset (for eastern elongation) or very shortly before sunrise (for western elongation). If (like me) you are not a morning person, you will want to look for the date of greatest eastern elongation, and look for Mercury in the western sky shortly after sunset. Fifteen minutes after sunset is probably a reasonable guideline. Before that time the sky is still too bright. But if you wait too much later, Mercury will be very low and possibly will have set. It is crucial to pick a viewing location with a low horizon. Avoid locations which have trees or hills to your west.

Use the sun and the ecliptic as your guide. Having just watched the sun set, you know where the sun is. Indeed it should still be illuminating the horizon. If there is another planet out that evening, like Jupiter or Venus, they will fall along the ecliptic. The moon does, too. Mercury will be (roughly) in line with the sun, moon, and any other planets. If other planets are not visible, you will need to think through how the ecliptic is oriented. For example, in spring the ecliptic is at a

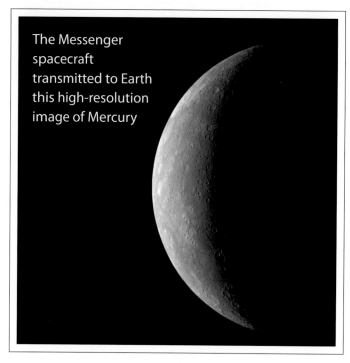

The Messenger spacecraft transmitted to Earth this high-resolution image of Mercury

high angle above the setting sun. But in the fall, the ecliptic swings far south of the setting sun.

Some greatest elongations are better than others. There are two factors that can influence how good an elongation of Mercury will be. These are (1) the angle of the ecliptic relative to the horizon, and (2) how close Mercury is to its aphelion (the point in the orbit farthest from the sun). Let's consider these in order.

The angle of the ecliptic can either help or hamper your view of Mercury (and Venus for that matter). When the ecliptic is at a high, steep angle, Mercury and Venus will tend to be higher in the sky at greatest elongation, which is better for viewing. This is called a "favorable elongation." If the greatest eastern elongation of Mercury or Venus occurs in the *spring* it will be a *favorable* elongation. Conversely, when the ecliptic is at a low angle, Mercury and Venus will tend to be farther south and lower in the sky at greatest elongation, which is worse for viewing. This is an unfavorable elongation.

If the greatest eastern elongation of Mercury or Venus occurs in the *fall*, it will be *unfavorable*. It's just the opposite for western elongations. So if you are an early riser, and want to look for Mercury or Venus in the east just before sunrise, try to find a western greatest elongation that takes place in the fall. This will be favorable, and will give you the nicest views of these planets, whereas a spring western elongation will be unfavorable. This doesn't matter as much with Venus. It is well separated from the sun, and so it is not as important to seek a favorable elongation. But with Mercury it can make a big difference.

One other important aspect of Mercury is that its orbit is very elliptical. Its distance to the sun changes by 14 million miles throughout its orbit. So Mercury is actually physically closer to the sun at some times than at other times. This is a very noticeable effect, and will drastically change Mercury's angular separation from the sun from one elongation to the next. Sometimes at greatest elongation, Mercury will be as much as 27.5 degrees away from the sun (if elongation happens when Mercury is near aphelion). Other times, it will be merely 18 degrees away from the sun (when elongation happens when Mercury is near perihelion). That's a huge difference, and will certainly affect your view of the planet. This effect is at least as important as the ecliptic angle, and perhaps more so.

Mercury's orbit is such that if greatest eastern elongation occurs in late March, Mercury will be near perihelion, and will be separated from the sun by only 18 degrees. Although such an elongation is called "favorable" (in the Northern Hemisphere) since the ecliptic is at a high angle, unfortunately Mercury will still not be very high in the sky after sunset since its sun angle is only 18 degrees. So with Mercury you need to consider not only whether the elongation will be favorable, but how large is the angle between the sun and

The extensive rays of Debussy stretch across this image of Mercury's limb

Mercury when it reaches greatest elongation. It will differ from one elongation to the next. These two effects tend to partially cancel for observers living in the Northern Hemisphere. That is, favorable elongations tend to occur around Mercury's perihelion. The two effects add for observers in the Southern Hemisphere.

Since Mercury is only visible just after sunset or just before sunrise, it is always low in the sky. For this reason, telescopic views of Mercury tend to be pretty lousy. Atmospheric turbulence will strongly distort your view of Mercury. To make matters worse, Mercury is a small planet only a third the diameter of Earth. So you will have a distorted view of a tiny object. Nonetheless, a backyard telescope at high magnification should allow you to resolve Mercury as a disk. It will not have the point-like structure of a star; it has some size, albeit not very much. Mercury has no moons, and it lacks any noticeable color. If you see color when viewing Mercury, it is because of the distorting effects of Earth's atmosphere.

Like Venus, Mercury goes through phases. This is about the only detail of the planet you will likely notice when viewing it through a backyard telescope. Unlike Venus, Mercury has no atmosphere, so its surface features are always theoretically visible. However the small size of Mercury and its great distance make it very unlikely that you will be able to distinctly see any surface features. The main thing to appreciate about Mercury is that it's there. It is fun to be able to say you've seen this little world, even though it really doesn't look that impressive with a telescope. Mercury is best thought of as a good naked-eye or binocular target. It is a fairly bright planet, but can be a bit challenging to find since the window of viewing time is so narrow.

◇Uranus

We now transition to those planets which cannot be seen easily (or at all) with the unaided eye. These will be more of a challenge to locate. But that's part of what makes it fun. Uranus has a visual magnitude just a bit less than 6. This is very close to the limit of human vision. We normally think of magnitude 6 stars as the faintest stars that can be seen without aid. So, if you have really good vision, are well dark-adapted, and have very dark skies, it is entirely possible to see Uranus with the unaided eye — but just barely.

A standard pair of binoculars will allow you to easily see Uranus, if you know where to look. In binoculars, Uranus appears as a faint blue star, and is not easily distinguished from the background stars, so you will have to know where it is in relation to the background stars. The best way to find this planet is to look it up on a current star chart or use computer software to plot its current location relative to the

Two images of Uranus, the one at left is true color; the one at right, false color created by using special filters

9.12   The planet Uranus is relatively featureless, but does show significant limb darkening

constellations. The star-hopping method described in a previous chapter is ideal for locating Uranus. Of course, computer-controlled telescopes will be able to automatically locate Uranus. But there is no challenge there. The fun thing is to find it manually.

Uranus does not move quickly, so if you memorize its location relative to the stars for a particular date, this information will be useful for months. You can often pan around that area with binoculars and locate Uranus long after it is past the date you selected. If you are uncertain whether you are looking at Uranus or a background star, zooming in with a telescope will make it obvious.

With a six-inch or larger telescope, at high magnification you will notice that Uranus has some size to it. It's small, but you will be able to resolve the disk. It will appear as a little blue sphere, not a shimmering point as a star would. That little blue sphere is four times the diameter of Earth and lies at a distance of around 1.8 billion miles. One additional thing to look for is limb darkening. I am usually able to see that the limb of Uranus is darker than its center FIGURE 9.12. This is primarily because sunlight is striking the limb at a glancing angle, and fewer photons are reflected back in our direction there than those that are reflected from the center of the disk. Limb darkening on Uranus looks similar to limb darkening on the sun, but the cause is totally different.

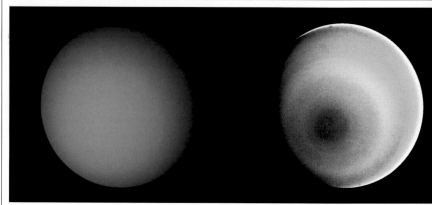

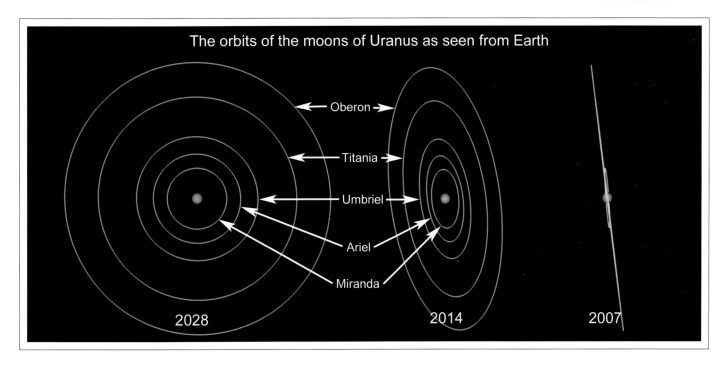

The orbits of the moons of Uranus as seen from Earth

Oberon
Titania
Umbriel
Ariel
Miranda

2028   2014   2007

9.13   Orbits of the five brightest moons of Uranus, as seen in different years

Aside from seeing the disk and some limb darkening, I am rarely able to see any other details on Uranus. It is a relatively featureless blue sphere; and since it appears so small, any features would be difficult to detect anyway. One possible exception is transient clouds that form (infrequently) in the atmosphere of Uranus. Such clouds are occasionally visible from a (high-quality) backyard telescope on nights of good seeing, at high magnification. But more often than not, you will see a perfectly featureless tiny pale blue sphere, with slight limb darkening.

Uranus has a system of moons. Most are tiny and are far too faint to be detected in a small telescope. Five are within the theoretical limit of a moderately large backyard telescope: Miranda, Ariel, Umbriel, Titania, and Oberon FIGURE 9.13. Of these, I have only ever distinctly seen two: Titania and Oberon. These are brighter than the others and easier to detect. Nonetheless, they are still a challenge, and are not good targets for beginners. They require a good size telescope under very dark skies, and some experience at detecting faint objects. Titania and Oberon have a visual magnitude of about 13. Ariel also has a magnitude around 13, but lies closer to Uranus, making it hard to detect. Umbriel is magnitude 14, and Miranda is by far the most dif-

ficult at magnitude 15. Although they are challenging objects to see, Uranus's moons are relatively easy to image with a CCD.

Another interesting aspect of Uranus is its axial tilt. Uranus is "tipped on its side" with a rotation axis tilt of 97.8 degrees. It is possible to look almost directly down the planet's north or south pole from Earth. As Uranus orbits the sun, our perspective of it changes — just as Saturn's apparent tilt changes from our perspective. Since Uranus orbits the sun with a period of 84 years, it can be seen "edge-on" every 42 years. This last occurred in 2007.

Since the five largest moons of Uranus orbit around its equator, they appear in a straight line only when Uranus is edge-on from our perspective. When this happens, they will be lined up vertically (in a roughly north-to-south orientation), rather than horizontally like Jupiter's moons. Conversely, when Uranus is perceived at its maximum tilt (as will occur in 2028), the moons will appear to orbit in nearly perfect circles from our perspective. This is because we are looking directly "down" on the system. At in-between tilts, the moons are found in an ellipse around Uranus. This is illustrated in FIGURE 9.13.

◇Neptune

At magnitude 8.2, Neptune definitely cannot be seen with the unaided eye. Good binoculars can pick it up, but even then it will be very faint and indistinguishable from the background stars. The method for locating it is the same as for locating Uranus. Use a good star chart or computer software to plot the position, and then use the star-hopping technique. Unless you use a computer-controlled telescope, this planet will be a challenge to find for beginners. But that's part of the fun.

Neptune is essentially a twin of Uranus. Its physical size is nearly the same, and it has a similar color. However, its distance is greater (2.8 billion miles), and so it will appear even smaller than Uranus FIGURE 9.14. And since less sunlight is available at that distance, Neptune will appear darker/fainter than Uranus as well. Its angular size is about 2 arc-seconds, which is pretty close to the limit of what a typical backyard telescope can detect. Nonetheless, I have found that under high magnification, using a 12-inch telescope, I can resolve the disk.

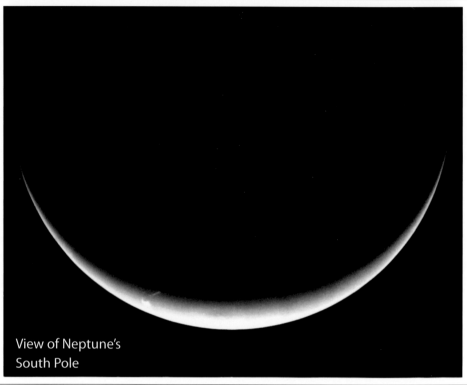

View of Neptune's
South Pole

Neptune will look like a tiny little sphere. However, using a 6-inch or smaller telescope, I find it very difficult to resolve the disk of Neptune.

The fun of looking at Neptune is (1) the challenge of finding it (manually) and (2) the challenge of resolving the disk. It will appear dark blue, or sometimes greenish-blue in color. Neptune does have occasional surface features. These include white clouds and great

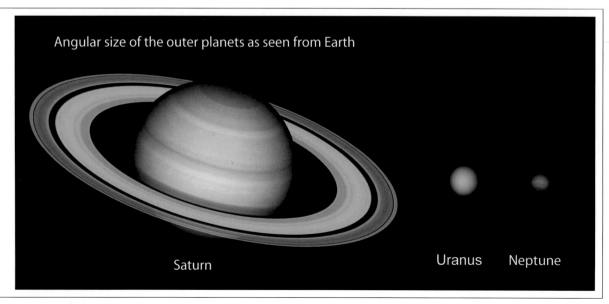

Angular size of the outer planets as seen from Earth

Saturn

Uranus   Neptune

9.14
Uranus and Neptune appear as very tiny disks in a backyard telescope

dark spots which have been seen in both hemispheres. However, a typical backyard telescope simply is not going to be able to resolve these features. Just be happy you are able to see the planet at a distance of nearly 3 billion miles!

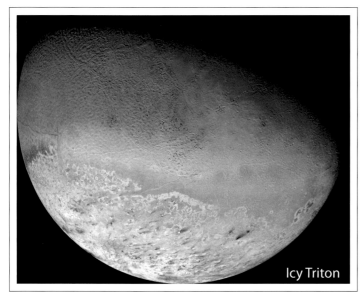

Icy Triton

Neptune has a number of moons, but only one of these will be visible with a moderately-sized backyard telescope: Triton. It has a visual magnitude of 13.5, which is pretty faint and on par with the brighter of Uranus's moons. It will be a challenge to detect this moon, so it's not a good target for beginners. Besides Earth's moon, Triton is the only large moon that does not orbit around its planet's equator. It has a highly inclined retrograde orbit. In fact, Triton is the only large moon to orbit its planet backward. Consult computer software or Internet applets to find where in its orbit Triton will be at a given time.

◇Pluto (Yes, It Still Exists)

When I first saw Pluto in the 1990s, it was classified as a planet. However, as astronomers began discovering many objects of similar size in the outer regions of the solar system, it became clear that Pluto is actually one of the largest mem-

bers of a new class of objects: the Trans-Neptunian Objects or TNOs. In 2006, the International Astronomical Union (IAU) declared that Pluto is no longer classified as a planet, but is considered a "dwarf planet." The newly discovered Eris was what prompted this decision. Eris is an icy world, slightly larger than Pluto and orbiting at a greater distance from the sun. For consistency, either Eris would have to be added as the tenth planet, perhaps along with several other TNOs, or Pluto would have to be dropped. The IAU chose the latter. For what it's worth, I agree with their decision. (In case you are wondering, at visual magnitude 18.7, Eris will definitely *not* be visible with a backyard telescope under any circumstances. However, it can be imaged with a CCD under ideal conditions.)

It's not the first time a planet has been demoted. When the first asteroids were discovered in the 1800s, they were classified as planets. However, when it became apparent that asteroids are much smaller than the (other) planets, and that there are many of them, it made more sense to classify them as a new type of object. This is just what happened with Pluto. The only difference is this: Pluto was classified as a planet for over 70 years! Clyde Tombaugh discovered Pluto in 1930, and it was considered the ninth planet until 2006.

Though it is not classified as a planet, Pluto is still a fun object to find. The joy of observing Pluto lies entirely in the challenge of it. It is a hard object to locate and it's definitely not a target for beginners. Pluto will appear as a tiny star-like speck, even in larger telescopes, but it's fun to say you've seen it. I would not hesitate to use a computer-controlled telescope to locate Pluto, because even then it will be tricky to locate.

With an angular diameter of only 0.1 arc-seconds, Pluto shows absolutely no disk. Even through a large

Showing the dwarf planet, Pluto, at left; its moon, Charon, at right. Pluto was discovered in 1930, but Charon was only found in 1978. They are so close (only 12,200 miles apart) they often appear as one image when viewed from Earth-bound telescopes.

telescope, it is indistinguishable from the background stars. So which one of those faint specks in your field of view is Pluto? You will have to use a detailed star-chart or computer software to answer that. The only alternative is to jot down (or take a CCD image of) the star field. Then you can come out a few nights later and look again. Pluto will be the one that moved. A 12-inch or larger telescope is desirable to use in spotting Pluto. It is theoretically possible to see it in smaller telescope; however, you will need very sharp vision and ideal dark skies.

Pluto's apparent magnitude changes from year to year. This is because it has a highly elliptical orbit. Near peri-helion, Pluto is actually slightly closer to the sun than Neptune. This was the case between 1979 and 1999. At perihelion Pluto reaches its highest brightness at visual magnitude 13.7. But at aphelion, Pluto is 4.58 billion miles away and its brightness drops to magnitude 16.3. Its average magnitude is around 15. Pluto takes 248

years to orbit the sun once. It reached perihelion in 1989. I was very fortunate to be able to first see Pluto in the 1990s shortly after perihelion when Pluto was closest to the sun and at its brightest. Pluto is now getting slightly fainter every year and will continue to do so until it reaches aphelion in 2113.

Pluto has one large moon, Charon — about half the size of Pluto itself. Four tiny moons, named Styx, Nix, Kerberos, and Hydra, orbit farther out. Charon orbits close to Pluto and contributes substantially to the brightness of Pluto. If you've seen Pluto, you've seen Charon, too. But it is very unlikely that you will be able to separate the two. Their angular separation never exceeds one arc-second.

The two tiny dots to the right of Pluto and Charon are two newly discovered moons around the dwarf planet. They are named Nix and Hydra.

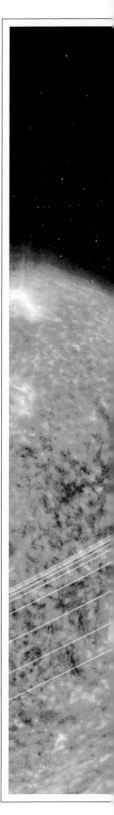

A graphical presentation of our sun and solar system. Distances are not to scale.

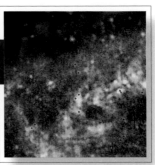

Chapter 10

Star Classification and Telescope Viewing

After planets and the moon, bright stars are the next easiest target for telescope beginners. They are naked-eye objects, and so it is always possible to locate them on a clear night. Most stars do not look terribly impressive through a telescope. They show no true angular size, and so they appear as a shimmering point. Nonetheless, telescopes make bright stars appear much brighter, which brings out their intrinsic color. Additionally, binary stars are delightful telescope objects. In this chapter we will cover how stars are classified. And then we will discuss some of the more impressive binary stars and how to locate them.

◇ The Magnitude System

Since ancient times, the brightness of a star as we see it from Earth has been classified according to its "apparent magnitude." The apparent magnitude is reversed from what many beginners expect, with lower numbers representing brighter stars, and higher numbers representing fainter stars. A very bright star in our night sky like Vega has an apparent magnitude of about zero. The faintest stars visible to the unaided eye are around magnitude 6. Binoculars will allow you to see stars down to magnitude 9, and a backyard telescope will go down to 12 or more, depending on its size. The Hubble Space Telescope could reach visible magnitudes of 31.

The magnitude system is logarithmic in nature, not additive. This means that a magnitude 5 star is *not* twice as bright as a magnitude 10 star. Rather, the magnitude 5 star is *one hundred times* the brightness of the magnitude 10 star. By using this logarithmic system, we are able to describe an extremely large range of brightness values without using a large range of numbers. By definition, a difference in 5 magnitudes represents a brightness factor of exactly one hundred times. So a difference in one magnitude is a brightness factor of the fifth root of one hundred, which is about 2.51 times. So a magnitude 4 star is 2.51 times brighter than a magnitude 5 star, which is itself 2.51 times brighter than a magnitude 6 star.

For each magnitude difference, you multiply the brightness by 2.51 times. For example, a magnitude 0 star is how much brighter than a magnitude 3 star? The answer is 2.51 x 2.51 x 2.51 = 15.8 times brighter. And a difference of 5 in magnitude means a difference of one hundred in brightness. So you can figure out the brightness ratio for any two stars given their magnitudes. A bright star like Vega (magnitude 0) is 251 times brighter than the faintest star we can see (magnitude 6). We know this because a difference of 5 magnitudes is a ratio of one hundred, and a difference of one magnitude is 2.51. So 100 x 2.51 = 251 times.

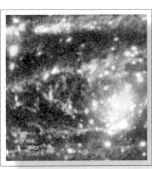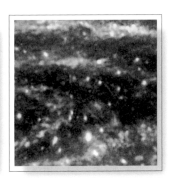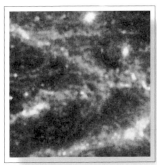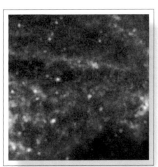

Stars brighter than Vega have a negative magnitude. Sirius, the brightest star in our night sky, is magnitude -1.46. The planet Venus can reach a brightness corresponding to magnitude -4.89. The full moon is around magnitude -12.7, and the sun has a magnitude of -26.7. Always remember that the scale is logarithmic in nature, so what may seem like a small difference can actually be quite large. For example, the 14 magnitude difference between the sun and the moon represents a brightness ratio of 400,000 times! This makes it all the more impressive that the Hubble Space Telescope could reach magnitudes of 31, which is ten billion times fainter than the faintest star visible to the un-aided eye!

Of course, the apparent magnitude does not really tell you much about the true properties of the star. Does a star have a negative apparent magnitude because it is truly luminous, or merely because it is very close to Earth? There is no way to know. Therefore astrono-mers sometimes use another system, the *absolute magnitude,* which is an indication of the true intrinsic brightness of the star. The absolute magnitude of a star is the apparent magnitude that the star *would have if it were placed 10 parsecs* (32.6 light-years) away from the observer. If the sun were placed 10 parsecs away, its apparent magnitude would be 4.83; therefore, we say the sun has an absolute magnitude of 4.83. For comparison, the blue supergiant Deneb has an absolute magnitude of -7.2.

Usually, if the term "magnitude" is used without the apparent/absolute prefix, the *apparent* magnitude is intended. In this book, all references to magnitude will be apparent magnitude unless the absolute prefix is specified. There are other complications as well, since the magnitude can be different as measured in different wavelengths of light. However, these details go beyond the scope of this book. Our main purpose here in using the magnitude system is so that the reader will have a feel for how much of a challenge the target object will be.

◇ Stellar Classification

Stars are classified based on their spectral features — the presence or absence of certain wavelengths of light as seen in a spectroscope. These spectral features reveal the temperature of the star, and can also provide information on its size. But even without spectral features, it is possible to estimate at least roughly the temperature and class of a star by eye, simply by looking at its overall color. Blue

The bright star Vega and the other stars of the constellation Lyra. Credit & Copyright: Eckhard Slawik

Spectral class and color are determined by temperature.

| O | B | A | F | G | K | M |

HOTTEST   < — >   COLDEST

stars are the hottest. Red stars are the coolest. White and yellow stars are intermediate. Stars are organized into one of seven classes based on their temperature, which is indicated by their color. These seven classes, in order from hottest to coolest are: O, B, A, F, G, K, and M.

The O and B stars are noticeably blue. The A-type stars show a hint of blue, but are paler than O and B stars. F stars are white. G stars are white, or yellowish white. K stars are noticeably reddish or orange. And M stars are quite red. Colors in stars tend to be rather muted compared to what most people are used to in everyday life. So don't expect a blue star to be as blue as the sky, or a red star to be as red as blood. The colors are subtle, but they are definitely there.

The seven classes are subdivided into a range of ten categories within each class, which is represented by a number after the letter. So, an A0 star is hotter than an A1 star, and so on. The coolest A-type star would be classified as A9, and then the next slightly cooler star would be classified as F0. The sun is classified as G2. Since hotter stars give off more energy than cooler stars, it is generally the case that blue stars are much brighter than red stars. The only way a red star could outshine a blue one is if it were physically larger (which does sometimes happen).

In addition, stars are classified based on their size within a given temperature class. The smallest type of star is called a main sequence star. It is given the Roman numeral V. The sun is a main sequence star, so it is listed as G2V. The sun is therefore the smallest type of star in its temperature class (e.g., there are no G2 stars that are significantly smaller than the sun). However, other temperature classes have a different range of sizes. An M-type main sequence star will be much smaller than the sun, and much, much fainter. Proxima Centauri, the nearest star to the sun, is such a star. Conversely, blue main sequence stars are larger

than the sun. About 90 percent of stars in the solar neighborhood are main sequence stars. The remaining 10 percent are larger.

Stars significantly larger than the sun are classified as "giant" and given the Roman numeral III. A class intermediate between main sequence and giant star is called the "sub-giant" class and is assigned the Roman numeral IV. Arcturus is a red giant star, class K2III. Stars even larger than giants are called "bright giants" and are assigned the Roman numeral II. The largest type of star within a temperature class is called a "supergiant" and is assigned the Roman numeral I. Supergiants are sometimes further divided into a larger class designated Ia, and a smaller class designated Ib. An intermediate class Iab is sometimes used as well. The star Betelgeuse is a red supergiant, class M2Ib.

Again, supergiants are the largest type of star within a temperature class, but supergiants in different temperature classes will have different sizes. A red supergiant will be much larger than a blue supergiant, although the blue supergiant will be much brighter. So red stars have a much greater range of sizes than blue stars. The largest stars in the universe are red (red supergiants), and the smallest stars in the universe are also red (red main sequence).

Since main sequence stars are the smallest within their temperature class, they are sometimes referred to as "dwarf" stars, particularly with red dwarfs which are the smallest type of true star. So the sun could be called a "yellow dwarf." There is an exception to this: white main sequence stars must *not* be referred to as "white dwarfs," because that term is already used to describe another object entirely. White dwarfs are thought to be the central core of a collapsed star. They are only the size of the Earth, and do not generate new energy by fusion, so they are not a true "star."

Red stars far outnumber white or blue stars. However,

most of the stars you see in the night sky are blue. This paradox is resolved by recognizing that blue stars are much brighter than red stars (of similar size) since they are hotter, and thus are much easier to see. A blue dwarf star ten light-years away is easily visible to the unaided eye, but a red dwarf star at the same distance would not be. Most stars are red dwarfs, and are just not easily seen in our night sky.

If you do see a red star with your unaided eye, you can be certain that it is not a main sequence star. Virtually every red star visible to the naked eye is at least a giant, or possibly a supergiant. If it weren't, you'd never see it. The same cannot be said for white and blue stars. They may be main sequence stars that are relatively nearby, such as Sirius. Or they may be supergiants at great distance, such as Deneb.

◇Telescopic Views of Stars

A backyard telescope will not allow you to resolve the disk of any nighttime star. They are all simply too far away. Even the best world-class telescopes must use some fairly advanced technology to resolve the disk of stars; and only the largest ones like Betelgeuse can be resolved at this time — and just barely. So you will not see any size to stars in a backyard telescope. Any apparent size will be due to the inherent diffraction of light in the telescope. But telescopes will enhance a star's brightness, making it easier to see the color. You may want to look at some of the more colorful stars in a telescope, just for the experience of it.

Some of the bluest bright stars in our night sky are found in Orion's belt. They are all O and B class, so they are about as blue as stars get. They are just about the easiest stars to locate in the winter sky. In the summer (Northern Hemisphere), about the best you can do for a bright blue star is Vega, which is class A0V. It is cooler, and therefore less blue than the stars of Orion's belt. But it does appear to have a bluish tint to me. (Sirius in our winter sky is very similar: class A1V.) Deneb is class A2Ia, a blue-white supergiant. In the spring, Spica is one of the bluest bright stars, class B1V. Fomalhaut is

a modestly blue-white star far south in the autumn sky, class A3V.

Red stars are the ones that show their color best. Betelgeuse is a great example of a red supergiant in our winter sky. It is class M2Ib. Its summer-sky counterpart is Antares, which is class M1Ib. Since Betelgeuse has higher apparent brightness, it will usually appear a bit redder than Antares. Both are spectacular. Also in the winter sky, not far from Betelgeuse, is Aldebaran. It is a K5III, red giant. Since it is K-class, it is not as red as Betelgeuse, but it is still noticeably reddish. Its spring-time counterpart is Arcturus, also a red giant: class K2III. Arcturus is noticeably less red than M-type stars like Betelgeuse. It often appears orange, or sometimes even a yellow-orange in a telescope. For a delightful challenge, try finding T Lyrae. It's not far from Vega, but at magnitude 8.5 it is not visible to the unaided eye, so you'll have to use a star chart or computer. It is faintly visible in binoculars. Through a telescope, T Lyrae is about as red as stars can possibly be. If you find it, you'll know it.

To round out the experience, try finding a few white-yellow stars. There's not much color to them. But it is interesting to see what the sun would look like from several light-years away. Capella is a fine example of a yellow giant star (actually two — too close to be resolved). They are G0III and G5III respectively. For Southern Hemisphere observers, Alpha Centauri is a yellow main sequence binary star. The two components are resolved in a backyard telescope; the brighter one is a G2V star, just like the sun. The fainter component is K0V, a bit redder than the sun. Canopus is a fine example of a white star. It is a supergiant, class F0Ib. Procyon is a great example of a white main sequence star, class F5V.

Alnilam, the center star in Orion's belt, is a blue supergiant

◇Binary Stars

It is good to know about some of the brighter and more impressive double stars, as these make wonderful telescope objects. The ones we will discuss here are all quite bright. They can be seen early in the evening, even during twilight. When doing observing sessions, I usually go to some good binary stars early in the evening. Since they are bright, it's not so important to have a dark sky or to be fully dark-adapted.

There are many types of double stars. These include optical doubles (where the two stars only appear to be close together in the sky, but are in fact at different distances), visual binaries (true binaries, where the two

stars can be separated in a telescope), spectroscopic binaries (which cannot be separated in a telescope, but are known to be binary based on their spectra), eclipsing binaries (which cannot be separated, but show a change in brightness as one star eclipses the other), or astrometric binaries (where the companion star cannot be seen, but is deduced by the motion of the visible star). Only the first two are interesting telescope objects, so these will be the only ones covered here: binary stars for which you can actually see two (or more) stars with a telescope.

Albireo may be my favorite double star. It is the "head" star for Cygnus, the swan (or the base of the Northern Cross if you prefer) and is shown in FIGURE 10.1. The star

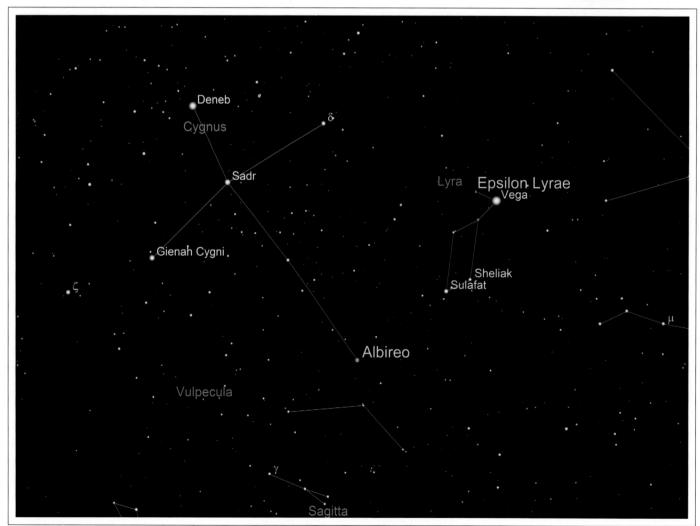

10.1   The bright blue-and-yellow binary star Albireo is found high in the sky in late summer evenings. Another often-viewed binary is Epsilon Lyrae – the "double double."

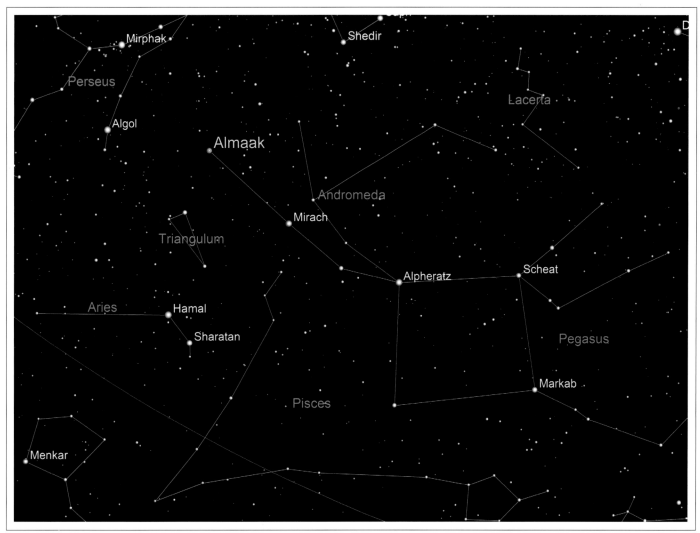

Mirphak
Perseus
Algol
Almaak
Shedir
Lacerta
Andromeda
Mirach
Triangulum
Alpheratz
Scheat
Aries
Hamal
Pegasus
Sharatan
Markab
Pisces
Menkar

10.2   A late-autumn blue-and-yellow binary star is Almaak (Gamma Andromedae)

is easily visible to the unaided eye, though it appears single. Good binoculars will reveal two stars. And a telescope will show Albireo in all its glory. The two stars are both bright, and are easily separated in a small telescope since they are 35 arc-seconds apart. But the lovely thing about Albireo is the striking color contrast. One star is blue (B8V), whereas the other is yellow (K3II). It's not currently known whether they are a true binary, or merely an optical double. Either way, it's a fantastic summertime double star.

In the late autumn sky is the star Almaak (Gamma An- domedae). It is the final star in the lower arc of the con- stellation Andromeda FIGURE 10.2. It is bright, and easily visible to the unaided eye as a single star. A telescope will split this (true) binary star into two components — blue and yellow, just like Albireo. However, the two components are not as widely separated (10 arc-sec-

onds), and the difference in brightness is greater than with Albireo, so it isn't quite as impressive but it is still a great example of a colorful binary. The blue star itself is actually a three-star system, though only the blue star is easily seen. Almaak is therefore a quadruple star system.

A good optical double is found in the middle of the handle of the Big Dipper. Mizar (the bright star) and Alcor (the faint one just next to it) can be easily split by the unaided eye **FIGURE 10.3**. Mizar itself is a true binary, and can be split with a backyard telescope. The two components are nearly equal in brightness. Recently, it has been suggested that Alcor is gravitationally bound to Mizar, and not just an optical double.

For Southern Hemisphere observers, Alpha Centauri is a good visual binary **FIGURE 10.4**. The naked eye cannot resolve the two components, but good binoculars

sometimes can, and it is an easy telescope binary. The two stars take 80 years to orbit each other. From our perspective on Earth, their angular separation changes during that orbit from 2 to 22 arc-seconds. Acrux — the southernmost star in the Southern Cross — is also a visual binary **FIGURE 10.4**. The two components are separated by 4 arc-seconds, which is within the resolving power of a good backyard telescope.

Epsilon Lyrae, the famous "double-double" mentioned in chapter 4, is an excellent visual binary. The star is faint, but easily visible to the unaided eye just north-

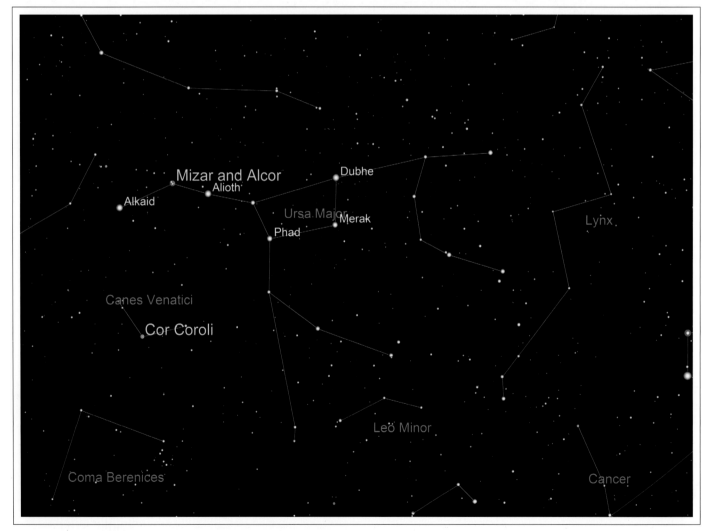

10.3 Mizar and Alcor are an optical double found as the middle star in the handle of the Big Dipper. Mizar is itself a true binary, and both components can be seen in a small telescope. Cor Coroli is also an impressive binary.

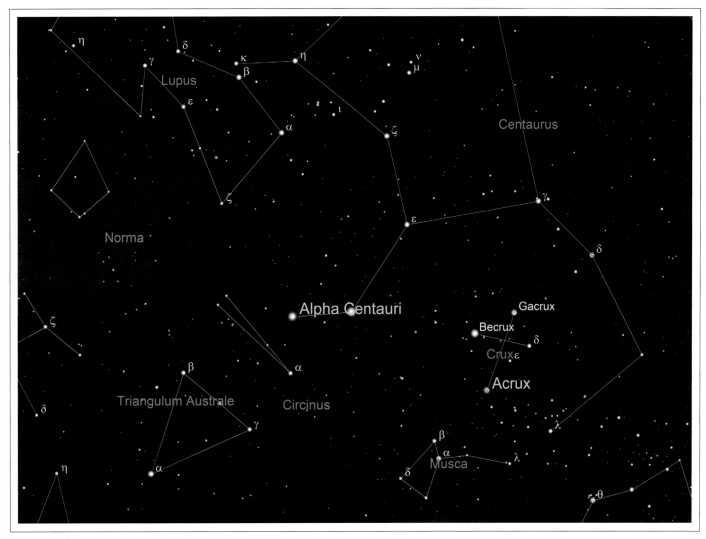

10.4 For Southern Hemisphere observers, Alpha Centarauri is an impressive binary star, as is Acrux

east of Vega FIGURE 10.1. The two components can be seen by the unaided eye if you have good vision, and easily in binoculars. But each of these two components is also a binary. So a decent backyard telescope will resolve four stars. The two main pairs will appear widely separated. However, the stars within each pair are split by just over 2 arc-seconds, so they require good seeing to resolve. Note that the two pairs are oriented orthogonally (at a perpendicular angle), so one pair is "horizontal" and the other is "vertical." Sometimes, if the seeing is not good enough to resolve the stars within each pair, you can still notice that one pair looks elongated horizontally, and the other pair looks elongated vertically. The two pairs are thought to be

Two galaxies, M82 and M81, as they appear in infrared wavelengths.

gravitationally bound to each other, so the system is a true double-double.

Regulus is a good example of a binary where the two components have very different luminosities FIGURE 10.5. Both components are main sequence stars, but their temperature is very different, resulting in different brightnesses. Regulus A is class B7V. Regulus B is a substantially fainter K2V, lying 177 arc-seconds away. So it is a widely separated binary. Within a few arc-seconds of Regulus B is found a much fainter companion: Regulus C, a red dwarf (M5V). At magnitude 13.5, Regulus C is a challenging target, but is within the range of a decent backyard telescope.

Cor Coroli (the brightest star in the constellation Canes Venatici) is a binary star with a separation of 19.6 arc-seconds, making it easily resolvable in a small telescope FIGURE 10.3. The brighter star is a type A0, whereas the fainter component is a type F0V. It is a nice target for late spring/early summer for Northern Hemisphere observers.

For an example of a good optical double, consider Alpha Capricorni FIGURE 10.6. This double star is separated by 6.6 arc-minutes, which is resolvable to the unaided eye. For comparison, that's about half the angular separation between Mizar and Alcor. With Alpha Capricorni, the two stars are definitely *not* a true

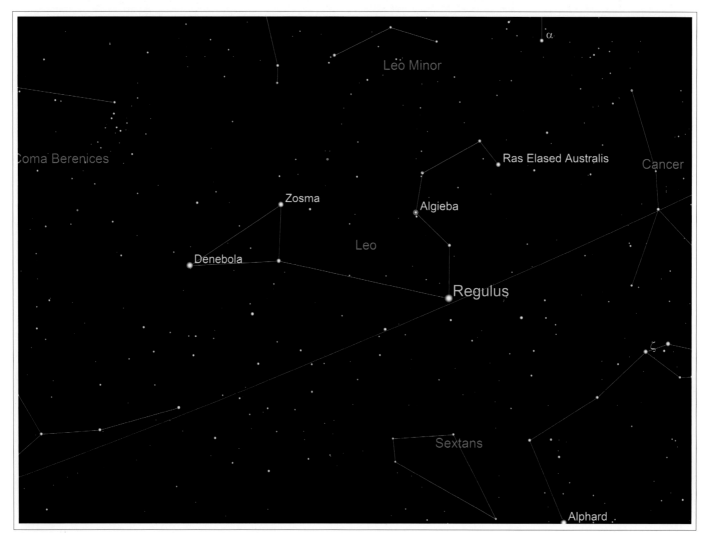

10.5 Regulus is a widely-separated binary star in the constellation Leo, high in the spring sky. Regulus is very close to the ecliptic (shown in yellow).

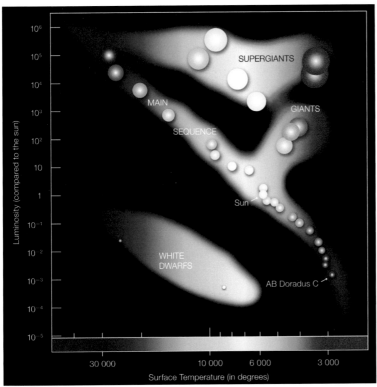

Stellar classification using a Hertzsprung-Russell diagram, a graph that plots the absolute magnitude (luminosity relative to the sun) of a star against its surface temperature. This shows most stars on the main sequence curve (decreasing from upper left to lower right). A star's position on the sequence depends upon its mass: low mass stars are cool and red, medium mass stars are yellow and high mass stars are hot and blue. Giants and supergiants (upper right) are less dense than main sequence stars. They are brighter and larger for a given mass. White dwarfs (lower left) are stars that have contracted to become hotter but dimmer.

Credit & Copyright: EUROPEAN SOUTHERN OBSERVATORY

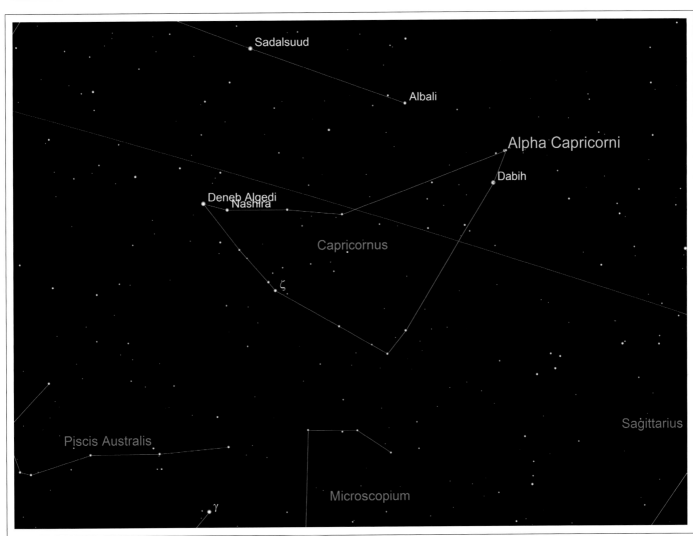

10.6　Alpha Capricorni is a good optical double for viewers in either hemisphere

binary; they only appear to be close together in the sky. The fainter star (Alpha[1] Capricorni) is actually six times farther away from the Earth than the brighter star (Alpha[2] Capricorni).

Sirius, the brightest star in our nighttime sky, is a visual binary FIGURE 10.7. However, it can be a very challenging telescope target to resolve, and is best attempted with a 12-inch or larger telescope. The separation of the two compo-

nents varies from 3 to 11 arc-seconds depending on where the two stars are in their orbit. That's close, but would still be widely separated enough for any backyard telescope if both stars were bright. The problem is the contrast between the two objects. Sirius A is a bright main sequence star, whereas Sirius B is a white dwarf, and is much, much fainter. It's a fun challenge.

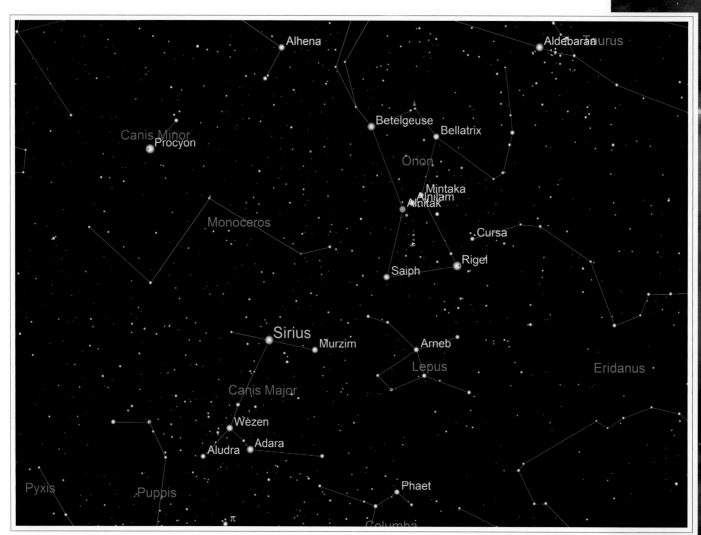

10.7 | Sirius – the brightest star in our nighttime sky – is a visual binary. However, the companion star (Sirius B) is a white dwarf and is often lost in the glare of Sirius A in all but high-quality telescopes.

A cosmic cloud called the Orion Nebula; this chaos includes four massive stars near the center called the "Trapezium".

Chapter 11

Deep-Sky Objects

The moon, the bright planets, and bright stars are a great start for beginners because they are so easy to find. However, most objects of interest will be too faint to be visible to the unaided eye under normal circumstances and require a little more skill to locate. Faint objects beyond the solar system other than individual stars are referred to as "deep-sky objects." These include open star clusters, globular star clusters, nebulae, and galaxies.

One of the nice things about deep-sky objects (in contrast to the planets) is that they do not move. Once you learn how to locate a deep-sky object relative to the constellations, it will always be right there. Again, I realize that many backyard telescopes are computer controlled and can locate deep-sky objects automatically. But it is very enjoyable and very useful to learn how to find these objects manually. This isn't to say that you should never use the computer controlled system to automatically find the target. But I highly recommend that you learn to find at least some deep-sky objects manually by star hopping. It is very rewarding to know where in the sky they are located.

Before we deal with any specific deep-sky objects, it is important to note that they are usually quite faint. So everything we covered about observing faint objects applies. A quick review: Avoid the weeks surrounding the full moon. Try to get away from city lights; it will make all the difference in the world. Allow yourself a half hour to get dark-adapted. Use only a red flashlight, and even then only when really necessary. Use low magnification (usually). Most important: use averted vision when looking at these faint objects. For some of the brighter deep-sky objects, these guidelines are not so crucial. But for the fainter ones (like galaxies) it may make the difference between getting a lovely view, and seeing nothing at all.

◇The Messier List

Some of the best galaxies, star clusters, and nebulae that can be viewed in a small telescope or binoculars are included in the Messier [**mes**-ee-ey] list. Published by Charles Messier in 1781, this list contains 110 of some of the brightest and prettiest deep-sky objects within the range of a small telescope. Since Messier himself used a 4-inch refractor to observe the cosmos, it follows that all Messier objects can be seen with a small telescope. That's why it is a great list with which to begin. Furthermore, if you live in the Northern Hemisphere, you have an additional advantage. Messier observed from France; therefore all Messier objects are visible from mid-northern latitudes. So if you have a small telescope under moderately dark skies in the Northern Hemisphere, all Messier objects are within

your grasp. That's not necessarily the case with other celestial catalogs, such as the NGC list.

The motivation behind the Messier list is an interesting story. Charles Messier was a "comet hunter." He discovered 13 comets in his career. Comets look like little indistinct "fuzzy" objects in a small telescope. But so do some deep-sky objects. The only difference is: comets move. Messier created a list to keep track of all the non-moving fuzzy objects so that he wouldn't mistake them for comets. These turn out to be some of the most spectacular celestial gems in the night sky, but to Messier, they were simply distractions from finding comets. The Messier list may be the ultimate example of the old adage "one man's trash is another man's treasure."

A Messier object is designated by a number (1 through 110) after the letter "M" for "Messier." So, M57 is the 57th Messier object. There is no scientific or positional significance to the number assigned to a given Messier object. Apparently, the number simply reflects the order in which Messier discovered these objects, so you can't tell from the number whether the object is a galaxy, a star cluster, or a nebula. And Messier didn't really care. To him, they were just non-comets. Some Messier objects are brighter and prettier than others. Certain ones you will want to memorize: like M13 — a beautiful globular star cluster in Hercules. Some Messier objects actually look better in binoculars than a telescope because they are so large that a telescope cannot necessarily fit the entire object in the field of view. This is often the case with the larger open star clusters such as M45.

◇Messier Marathon

One fun challenge for moderately experienced backyard astronomers is the Messier marathon. The goal here is to view as many Messier objects as possible in one evening. To do this right, you need to stay up all night since some Messier objects do not rise until early morning. The best time of year to attempt a Messier marathon is in mid-March to early April on the date of the new moon. During that period of time, from mid-northern latitudes, it is possible to view all 110 Messier objects in a single night. This is because the sun during those weeks is in a part of the sky devoid of any Messier objects.

It is crucial to observe in a west-to-east fashion to take advantage of the Earth's rotation. That is, you need to get the Messier objects in the western sky early on before they set. Then you move eastward all night until you are trying to observe the easternmost Messier objects before the sun rises. Observing west-to-east is a good habit to get into for this same general principle. You can't take longer than about 5 minutes (on average) to find each Messier object, or you will run out of nighttime before you run out of objects. If you really want to test your skill with a telescope, try doing a Messier marathon, finding all the objects by star hopping without using any computer aid. I have. It's fun!

◇Star Clusters

Stars are not distributed evenly within our galaxy. Some stars, like the sun, are relatively far from any neighbors. But sometimes stars are found in denser regions called a star cluster. There are two types of star clusters: open clusters and globular clusters. Open clusters consist of a few hundred or perhaps a few thousand stars in a relatively small region of space **FIGURE 11.1**. They are irregularly shaped. Globular clusters typically consist of about 100,000 stars, and are always spherical in shape with greater density near the core.

11.1 NGC 6791 – an open star cluster as imaged by the Hubble Space telescope. Image credit: NASA, ESA, and L. Bedin (STScI)

The Pleiades – a nearby open star cluster.
Image credit: NASA, ESA, AURA, and Caltech

◇Open Clusters

Open star clusters are found primarily in the disk of the galaxy, whereas globular clusters orbit around the center of our galaxy, and are not typically within the disk. This explains their relative distribution in our night sky. Since we are within the disk of our galaxy, we can see open clusters in virtually any direction; however, they are particularly abundant along the densest regions of the Milky Way. This is why many open clusters are visible in the late summer (Northern Hemisphere) evening when our night sky is centered on the heart of our galaxy. But late winter also has its share of open clusters because we are looking directly away from the galactic center, and many open clusters are found in the disk that lies beyond the position of our solar system. You can find open clusters any time of the year, but some of the best ones are visible in late summer or late winter. On star charts, open clusters are usually designated by a circle, sometimes with a single horizontal line through the middle. In this book they are designated by a yellow circle. The size of the circle is indicative of the angular size of the star cluster.

Some open star clusters are visible to the naked eye. One good example is the Pleiades — M45 FIGURE 11.2. It's part of the constellation Taurus, and is visible in the winter evening sky FIGURE 11.3. To the unaided eye, the Pleiades look like a tiny little dipper, consisting of about six or

seven stars. For this reason, the Pleiades are often called "the seven sisters." The Pleiades are a wonderful binocular object. Binoculars reveal many more stars than can be seen by eye. Not far from the Pleiades is another, large star cluster called the Hyades FIGURE 11.3. This cluster forms the head of Taurus — the bull. The brighter stars make this cluster look rather "V" shaped. The Hyades cluster is considerably larger than the Pleiades, which makes it a great naked-eye object.

This infrared image of the Pleiades makes it easy to see the surrounding cloud of dust

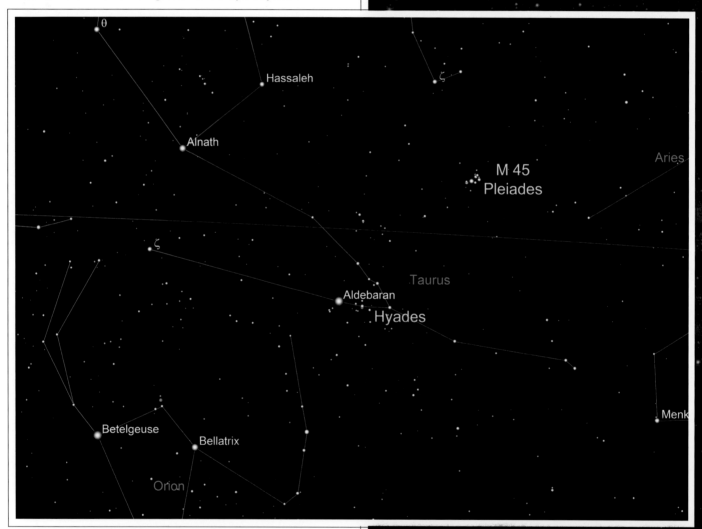

11.3 Location of the Pleiades (M45) and Hyades open star clusters. Both are found in the constellation Taurus, and are easily seen by the unaided eye.

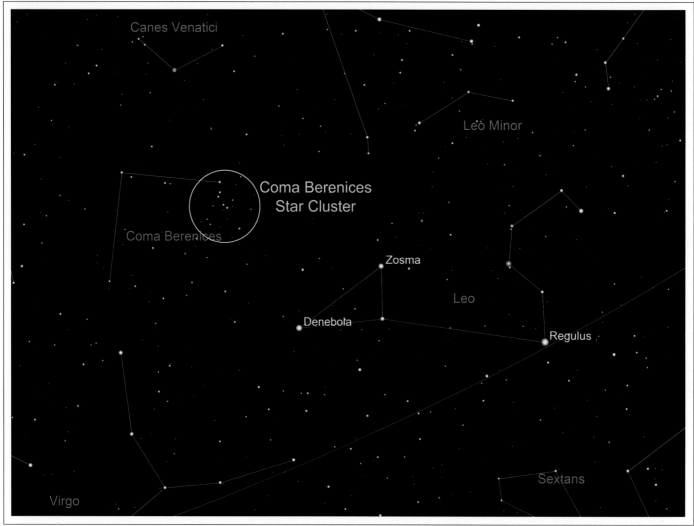

11.4 The Coma Berenices cluster is an open star cluster visible to the unaided eye under dark skies

In the spring evening sky, a nice naked-eye open cluster is the Coma Berenices star cluster **FIGURE 11.4**. This cluster is faint, but is distinctly visible to the unaided eye under dark skies. Binoculars reveal hundreds of stars. This cluster is found just to the east of the constellation Leo. The Coma Berenices cluster is about five degrees across, which makes it suitable for binoculars, but a bit large for most telescopes.

Some nice binocular/telescope open clusters are M6 and M7 in the summer evening sky **FIGURE 11.5**. Both are found in the constellation Scorpius and are small enough to look nice in a telescope at low magnification. M7 is the brighter of the two, and is sometimes

called the Ptolemy cluster. It can be seen with the unaided eye under dark skies. M6 is named the Butterfly cluster, since its shape vaguely mimics such.

In the early spring evening sky, the Beehive cluster (M44) is a classic **FIGURE 11.6**. It is particularly easy to locate, being nearly centered in the constellation Cancer, which is between Leo and Gemini. It can be faintly seen with the unaided eye under dark skies as a faint "cloud." It is also small enough to look nice in a telescope at low magnification.

A number of interesting open clusters are visible along the Milky Way in the summer evening sky. Many of

The Heart and Soul Nebulae as captured by NASA's Wide-field Infrared Survey Explorer (WISE), a space-based infrared telescope seeing into the deeper regions of the universe

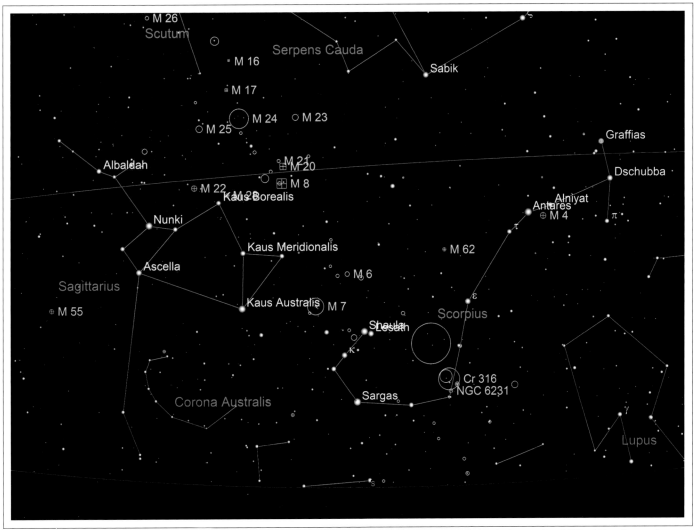

11.5 A number of Messier objects including nebulae and star clusters are found along the Milky Way in and around the constellations Sagittarius and Scorpius. Many of these are visible in binoculars, and make wonderful telescope targets.

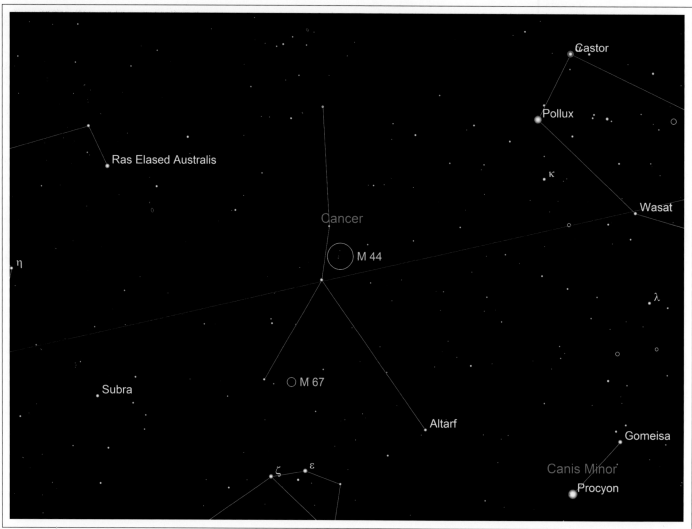

11.6 The Beehive Cluster (M44) is a large open star cluster in the constellation Cancer. The cluster is faintly
visible to the unaided eye under dark skies, and is an easy binocular object.

these are fine telescope objects. One of my favorites is M11 — the Wild Duck cluster FIGURE 11.7. It is so named because it appears to have distinct edges, giving it a "V" shape like a string of ducks in flight. This is a nice open cluster for telescopes because it is far more compact than many others. The cluster is faintly visible in binoculars near the south end of the constellation Aquila.

Two open clusters that look spectacular in a small telescope in our winter sky are H Persei and Chi Persei FIGURE 11.8. These are not Messier objects. In fact they follow the naming convention of stars because they are faintly visible to the unaided eye, and appear as small fuzzy blobs in binoculars. The really neat thing about these clusters is that they are so close together that you can often fit them in the same field of view of a telescope at low magnification. For this reason, H and Chi Persei are often referred to as "the double cluster." The double cluster is found in the northwest of the constellation Perseus, just southeast of Cassiopeia.

◇Globular Clusters

Globular clusters are usually considered far more spectacular than open clusters when they are viewed using a moderately sized backyard telescope. Instead of a few hundred stars, globular clusters have 100,000 or

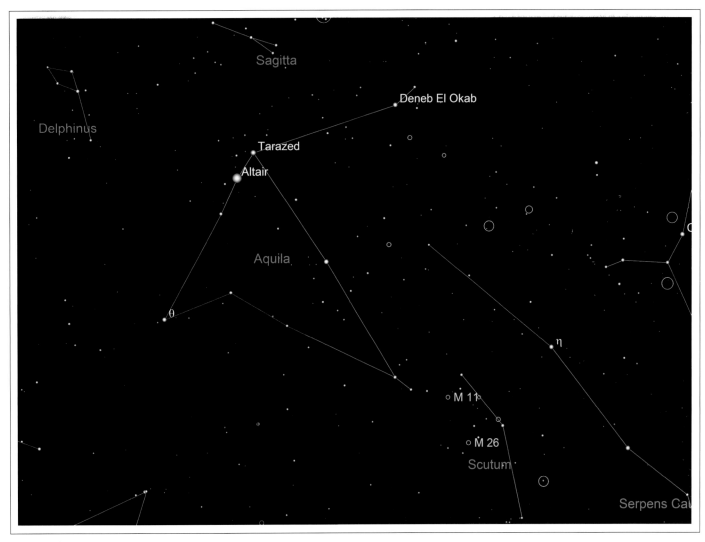

11.7 The Wild Duck Cluster (M11) is a fairly compact open star cluster just south of Aquila. The cluster appears as a faint smudge in binoculars, and is spectacular in a small telescope.

The M11, or Wild Duck Cluster, located 6000 light-years away

Image credit: NASA/JPL

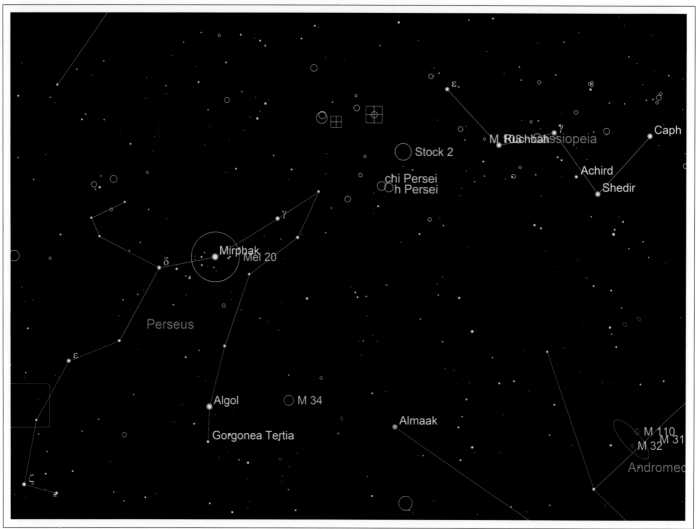

11.8   H and Chi Persei are two open star clusters which can be seen in the same field of view through a telescope at low magnification. They are often called "the double cluster."

more **FIGURE 11.9**. Most of the Messier globular clusters are visible in binoculars, but appear only as a faint blur. A telescope of at least 8 inches is needed to see the individual stars in most globular clusters. A smaller telescope may allow you to pick out individual stars on some of the brighter globular clusters if you have very good vision. On star charts, globular clusters are usually indicated by a circle with a vertical and horizontal line going through the middle. The charts in this book use this convention, and show globular clusters in green.

Globular clusters are always relatively faint, and so a bigger telescope will give you a better, brighter view

of them. It is always crucial to use averted vision to get the best view of globular clusters. Review chapter 3 for details in this. Globular clusters are perhaps the best targets to use to practice finding the best angle of averted vision. Too close to center and you will see nothing; too far from center and you won't see individual stars. But at the right angle, globular clusters are absolutely beautiful.

Globular clusters are excellent summer evening objects. They orbit around the central bulge of our galaxy, and most of them are closer to the center than our solar system is. And it is during summer (Northern Hemisphere) that our evening sky is directed toward the galactic center. Thus, virtually all globular clusters are found in the summer sky, or late spring/early fall. If you are observing during the winter evening, you are not going to see many globular star clusters. In fact, there is only one Messier globular cluster visible in our winter sky: M79. And M79 is not a particularly good one; it is rather faint and indistinct. But in the winter, it is your only option.

All globular clusters look pretty similar in terms of their basic structure. They are generally spherical in shape and consist of hundreds of thousands of stars with decreasing density as a function of the distance from center. Some have denser cores than others and some globular clusters are closer to our solar system and look more impressive as a result. The more distant ones are fainter and the stars tend to be less distinct.

11.9   M80 is a typical globular star cluster. This image is from the Hubble Space Telescope.

Image credit: The Hubble Heritage Team (AURA/STScI/NASA).

For example, M54 is a particularly distant and dense globular cluster in which it is nearly impossible to see any individual stars. Try observing several globular clusters and compare them.

One of the first impressive globular clusters to come into view in the spring is M3. This is found in the constellation Canes Venatici, next to the constellation Boötes, and not far from the star Arcturus FIGURE 11.10. At magnitude 6.2, M3 is easily seen in binoculars as an indistinct blur. The only difficulty in finding it is that there are no bright stars very close to it, which makes star hopping more difficult. I use Arcturus as a "jump-

ing off" star. M3 forms an almost equilateral triangle with Arcturus and Rho Boötis. M3 is a relatively small globular cluster with a dense core.

A month later an even better example is in prime position for viewing: M13. M13 is usually considered the best globular cluster for Northern Hemisphere viewers. Some would say that M22 competes, as it is also spectacular and is slightly brighter than M13. But M22 is far to the south FIGURE 11.5, which means it never gets terribly high in the sky for Northern Hemisphere viewers. M13 crosses nearly overhead for mid-northern latitudes.

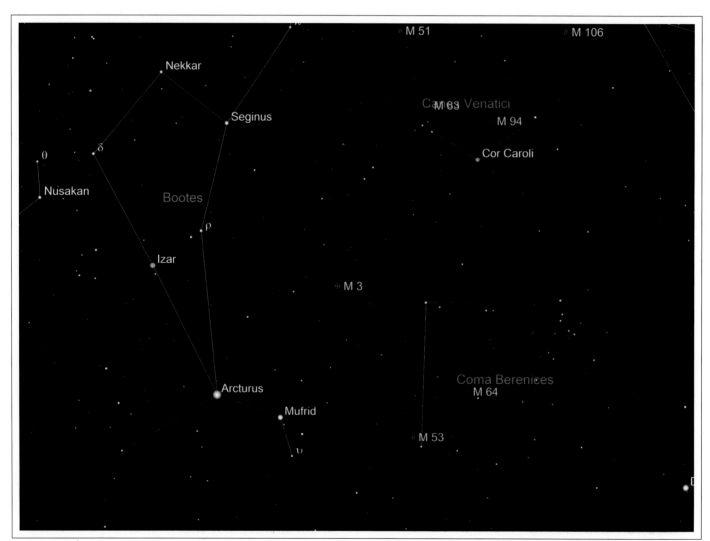

11.10 | M3 is a compact globular star cluster found to the northwest of Arcturus. It can be detected in binoculars, and is one of the earliest globular clusters visible in the spring for mid-northern latitudes.

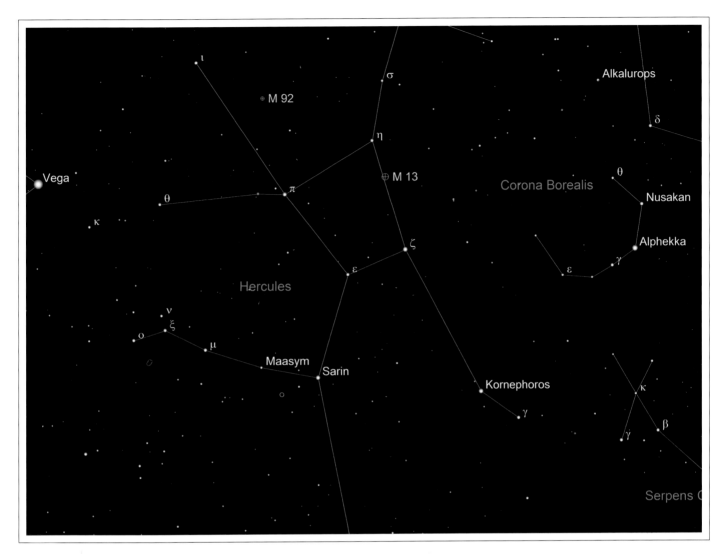

11.11   The constellation Hercules contains one of the best globular clusters visible in the Northern Hemisphere – M13

M13 is very easy to find FIGURE 11.11. It is in the constellation Hercules. To locate it, find the trapezoid corresponding to Hercules' torso. Hercules is broad-shouldered, so the stars marking his shoulders are farther separated than those forming his waist. Find the star corresponding to his westward shoulder and move precisely one-third of the way toward the star marking the west end of his waist. There you will find M13. It is easily seen in binoculars as a fuzzy blob. But a telescope will reveal one of the prettiest and most spectacular globular clusters in the northern sky. Notice that this cluster has a less dense core than M3, and the individual stars are easier to see. If you want to see individual stars in a globular cluster, but have only a six-inch or smaller telescope, M13 would be a good one to try.

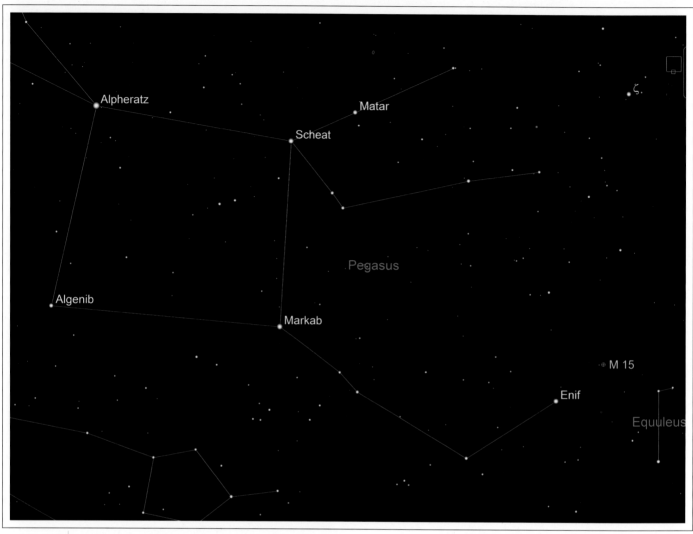

11.12   M15 is one of the easternmost decent globular star clusters visible in the autumn for Northern Hemisphere observers.

Another fairly bright globular of interest is M15 **FIGURE 11.12**. It is visible in the early fall in the constellation Pegasus and is easy to find because it is just slightly northwest of the star Enif (Epsilon Persei). The appearance is similar to M3 — a small but bright globular cluster with a very dense core. M15 is of interest because it also has a planetary nebula in it! It will require a fairly large telescope at high magnification and dark skies to see the nebula, which is named Pease 1. It is very rare to have a planetary nebula within a globular cluster; M15 is one of only few. (M22 also has one, but it is very difficult to detect.)

The most spectacular globular cluster visible from Earth is Omega Centauri **FIGURE 11.13**. This globular cluster is the largest and brightest associated with our galaxy; it is estimated to contain over a million stars. It is a wonderful object for those observing from the Southern Hemisphere of Earth, and can actually be seen by the unaided eye. This is why it is named after the star convention. Since Omega Centauri is far south on the celestial sphere, it is difficult to spot from northern latitudes because it never gets very far above the southern horizon. It cannot be seen at all from latitudes north of 42.5 degrees.

Omega Centauri – the largest globular cluster in our galaxy.

Credit & Copyright: LUKE DODD

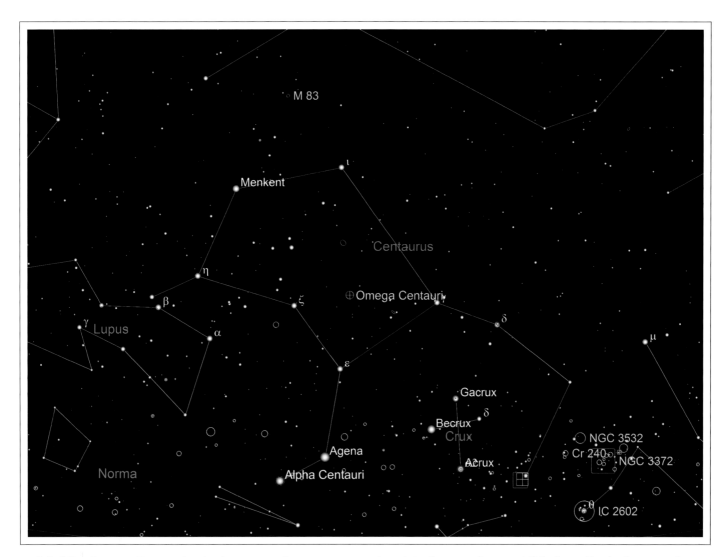

11.13 Omega Centauri – the largest and most spectacular globular star cluster visible from Earth. It can only be seen from latitudes south of +42.5°.

◇Nebulae

A nebula is a cloud of hydrogen and helium gas spread over a vast region of space. If stars are close to a nebula, they will heat it and cause it to glow. Otherwise, the nebula will be dark, and you will not be able to see it unless it is blocking something brighter in the background, such as a star field or a bright nebula. There are several different kinds of nebulae (plural of "nebula").

A diffuse nebula is one which is large and does not have a distinct boundary (as opposed to a planetary nebula which we cover below). Diffuse nebulae can be further divided into emission nebulae and reflection nebulae. Emission nebulae produce their own light because they are heated by nearby stars. The great Orion Nebula is an emission nebula. Reflection nebulae do not produce light, but they appear bright by reflecting light from nearby stars. The blue nebulosity seen in long-exposure photographs of the Pleiades is a beautiful example of a reflection nebula FIGURE 11.2. (However, it is not easily seen in a backyard telescope.) A diffuse nebula is usually indicated by a square on a star chart; the size of the square is indicative of the size of the nebula.

A planetary nebula is one which is produced by the ejected gas of a star. Planetary nebulae are therefore usually much smaller than diffuse nebulae. They tend to be either spherical in shape, or bipolar (having a two-lobed structure). The Ring Nebula (M57) is a classic and one of the best examples of a planetary nebula FIGURE 11.14. They are sometimes designated by a small square or diamond on a star chart; in this book we will use a small light blue circle with a horizontal line. Planetary nebulae are a lot of fun to observe, so we'll deal with them in more detail below.

Additionally, there are nebulae that are produced by an exploding star. These are called supernova remnants. The Crab Nebula (M1) is perhaps the best example of a supernova remnant FIGURE 11.15. It is in the constellation Taurus and can be readily viewed with a backyard telescope, but requires fairly dark skies. It is located just over one degree north of the star Zeta Tauri — the star marking the southern horn of Taurus FIGURE 11.16. The Crab Nebula was produced by a star

11.14 The Ring Nebula (M57) as imaged by the Hubble Space Telescope
Image credit: the Hubble Heritage Team (AURA/STScI/NASA).

11.15 The Crab Nebula (M1) as imaged by the Hubble Space Telescope.
Image credit: NASA, ESA, J. Hester and A. Loll (Arizona State University).

that exploded in the year A.D. 1054. This supernova was recorded by Chinese astronomers. It was so bright it was visible in daylight. If you look at two images of the Crab Nebula taken more than a decade apart, you can see that the Crab Nebula is still noticeably expanding. Through a backyard telescope, the Crab Nebula appears as a relatively featureless blur. I have never been able to see any of its internal structure with a small telescope.

Usually considered the most impressive nebula, as seen through a small telescope, is the great Orion Nebula (M42). It's the brightest nebula and one of only a handful where it is actually possible to clearly see some color in it. M42 is a winter object. It is found in the middle of Orion's sword, and is probably the easiest nebula to locate in a small telescope FIGURE 11.17. Orion itself is one of the most recognizable constellations. The three bright blue stars of Orion's belt are hard to miss on a clear winter night. The sword lies just below (to the south of) Orion's belt and is on the left side. To the unaided eye, the sword is easily visible as three stars, fainter and closer together than the three belt stars, and oriented in a roughly north-south fashion. The middle star is actually the combined light of M42 and the stars within it.

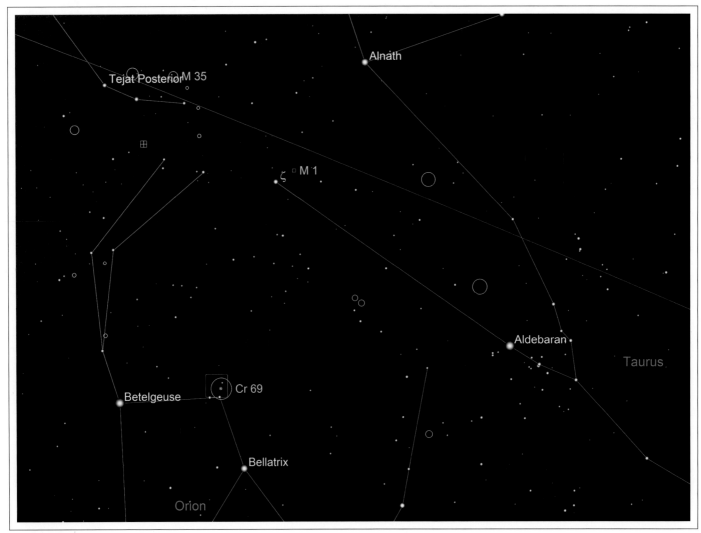

11.16   The Crab Nebula (M1) is located in the upper section of the constellation Taurus

So the nebula is easily seen to the unaided eye, though it is not easily distinguished from a star. Binoculars will show the nebulosity of the center sword star. A telescope centered on this position will reveal the Orion Nebula in all its glory. In the middle of the nebula are four very bright stars forming a sort of trapezoid. These four stars are called the Trapezium. They are responsible for heating the Orion Nebula and causing it to glow. Interestingly, two of these four stars are eclipsing binaries. (What are the odds?!)

M42 is enormous. Even at relatively low magnification, it will likely fill most of the field of view. However, it gets fainter as you go farther from the Trapezium; and you may not easily see the fainter, outer regions except with a really good telescope under very dark skies. The Orion Nebula is one of those very few objects that look more beautiful to the eye in a small–medium telescope than they do in photographs. The reason is the tremendous contrast. CCD images of M42 inevitably either (1) overexpose the Trapezium so that the outer regions of the nebula can be seen or (2) underexpose the nebula, making it hard to see, so that the Trapezium is in view. The human eye has the amazing ability to see both simultaneously, using a modest telescope. For this reason, I have never seen a photograph of the Orion Nebula that is as beautiful as the real thing.

◇Planetary Nebulae

Most of the other impressive nebulae are summertime objects. None are as bright as M42. Nonetheless, some are very beautiful. The Ring Nebula (M57) is one of my favorites FIGURE 11.14. It is a planetary nebula and looks

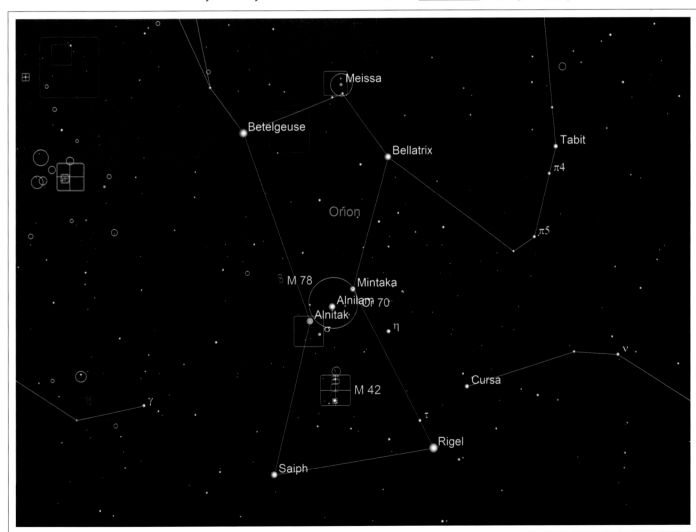

11.17 The Great Orion Nebula (M42) is located in the center of Orion's sword, just below Orion's belt. The nebula can be seen in binoculars and is the brightest nebula in our nighttime sky.

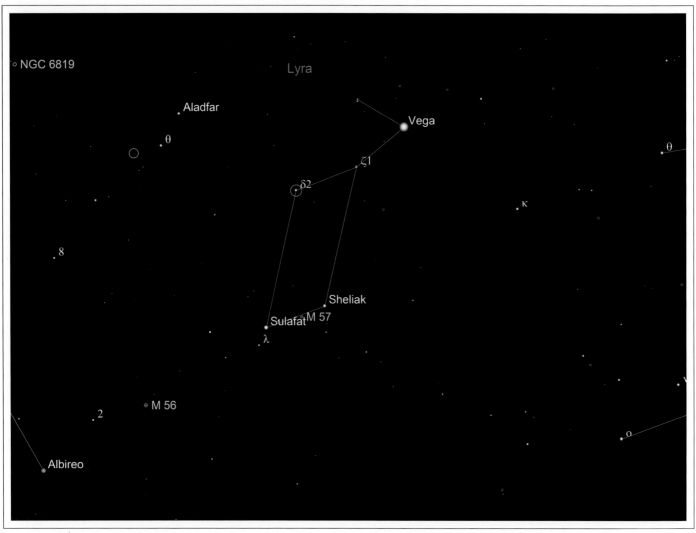

11.18   The Ring Nebula (M57) is located almost exactly in between Sulafat and Sheliak in the small constellation Lyra

just like a smoke ring that has been frozen in time. The nebula is small, but its shape is very distinct. M57 is located in the constellation Lyra FIGURE 11.18. This is a tiny constellation. It contains the star Vega — one of the brightest stars in the summer sky. This constellation is ideally suited for mid-northern latitude viewers, as it passes overhead each night. Next to Vega are four faint stars that form a nearly perfect parallelogram. Point a telescope directly in between the two stars on the end of the parallelogram farthest from Vega. These stars are Beta Lyrae and Gamma Lyrae (Sheliak and Sulafat). The Ring Nebula is almost precisely in between them. It won't quite be visible in the spotter scope. But if the

crosshairs are centered between Sheliak and Sulafat, you will see the Ring Nebula when you look through the telescope. It will look gray in all but the largest telescopes.

Not far from the Ring Nebula is another bright planetary nebula. M27 is called the Dumbbell Nebula because it has a quasi-circular, two-lobed structure. It is located in the constellation Vulpecula — a small, relatively faint constellation next to Cygnus. I actually use Cygnus to find M27 because Cygnus is bright and easy to locate FIGURE 11.19. I find Albireo, the bottom star in the cross or the "head" of Cygnus, and look 8 degrees to the east. Here is a tiny group of faint stars

Dumbbell Nebula
Credit & Copyright: MPIA-HD, BIRKLE, SLAWIK

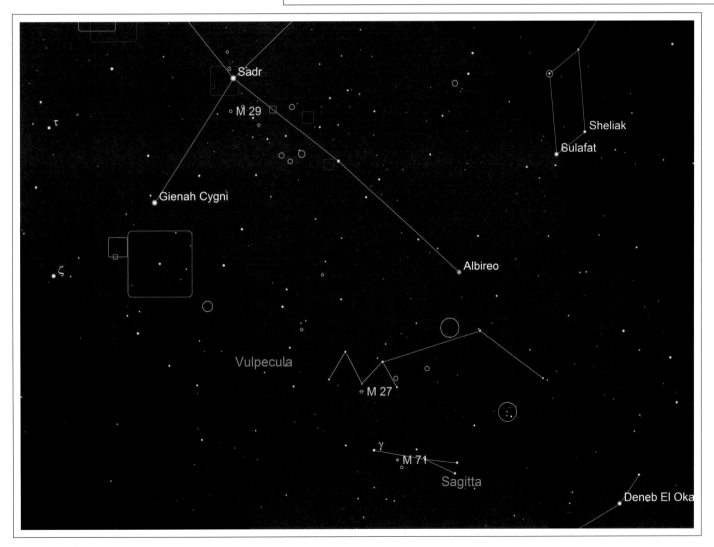

11.19 The Dumbbell Nebula (M27) is 8° east of Albireo, and lies at the bottom of an M-shaped asterism (shown in yellow)

(easily visible in the spotter scope, and faintly to the unaided eye) shaped like the letter "M." The top two vertices of the "M" are both optical double stars. M27 is just below the central star at the base of the "M." It may be faintly visible in the spotter scope on a dark evening. M27 is much less distinct than M57, but it is brighter and much larger. Under ideal conditions, this is another one of those rare nebulae where it is possible sometimes to see some color. If you have any light pollution whatsoever, I highly recommend that you get an Oxygen III filter for viewing planetary nebulae. Such filters can be a bit pricey, but they will dramati-

cally improve the appearance of planetary nebulae in a small telescope.

For a wintertime planetary nebula, the Eskimo Nebula (NGC 2392) is a good choice. It is in the constellation Gemini FIGURE 11.20. It is not a Messier object, and may be a harder challenge to locate. It is a small, blue circle, smaller than the Ring Nebula, and with a bright central star. The compactness of this nebula makes it relatively bright. As such, the blue color is often visible in larger backyard telescopes. It may look a bit like a blurry star, but right next to this nebula is another little blue star — without a nebula. This comparison star makes it

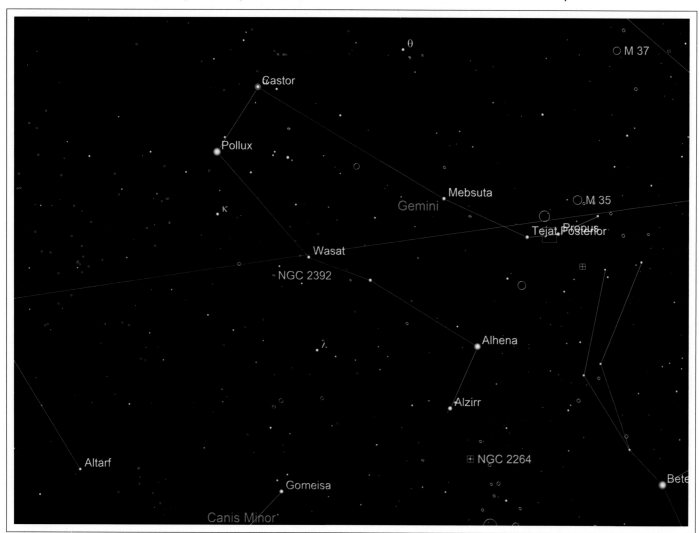

11.20 The Eskimo Nebula (NGC 2392) is a nice winter planetary nebula. It is small, compact, and blue.

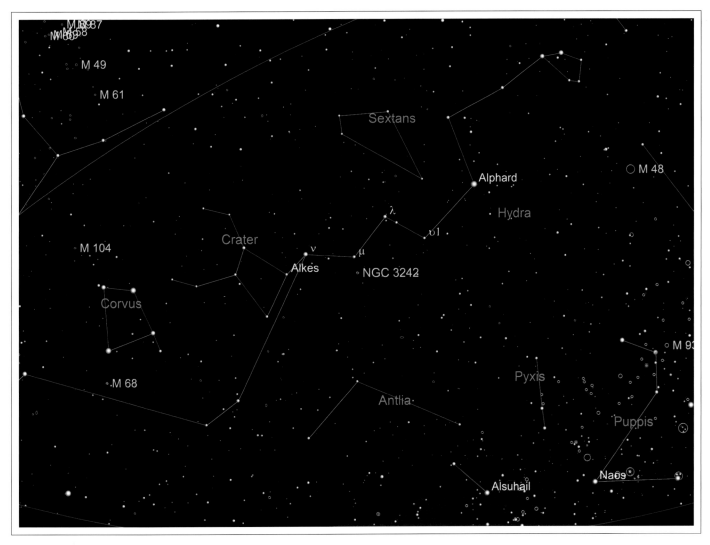

11.21 The Ghost of Jupiter (NGC 3242) is a fairly bright planetary nebula in the constellation Hydra, visible in spring (Northern Hemisphere)

very obvious that the Eskimo Nebula does have some size to it; it extends well beyond the central star.

A spring evening planetary nebula is called the Ghost of Jupiter (NGC 3242). It is not a Messier object, but it is bright enough to be detected in a backyard telescope. It is located in the constellation Hydra, just below the star Mu Hydrae **FIGURE 11.21**. It is a small, fairly bright bluish-green circle, similar to the Eskimo Nebula, but with some evidence of internal structure.

◇ Diffuse Nebulae

The Swan Nebula, M17, is another nice summertime object **FIGURE 11.5**. It is a diffuse nebula, and is sometimes called by other names, such as the Omega Nebula, or the Horseshoe Nebula. I prefer the "Swan

Nebula" because it really does look like a swan, as seen from the side as if swimming on a lake. It is in the constellation Sagittarius, right along the Milky Way. M17 can be detected as a faint glow in binoculars.

Perhaps the brightest summertime nebula is the Lagoon Nebula (M8). It is an emission nebula located very close to the (slightly fainter) Trifid Nebula (M20) along the Milky Way in the constellation Sagittarius **FIGURE 11.5**. The combined light from these two nebulae is bright enough to be seen as a faint glow to the unaided eye. Both nebulae can be seen in binoculars in the same field of view. The Lagoon Nebula is farther south, and is noticeably brighter than the Trifid Nebula. Both are lovely telescope targets. The Lagoon Nebula is particularly attractive because it also has a star cluster overlapping the nebula. In cases where nebulae and

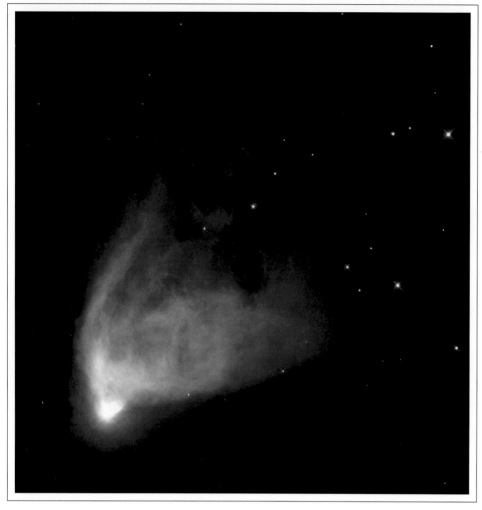

11.22 The Hubble Variable Nebula (NGC 2261) as imaged by the Hubble Space Telescope.

Image credit: Nasa and the Hubble Heritage Team (AURA/STScI).

star clusters overlap (which is fairly common), star charts often represent this as a square with crosshairs.

The Eagle Nebula (M16) is also found along the Milky Way, to the north of M8 and M20 in the constellation Serpens FIGURE 11.5. Like the Lagoon Nebula, the Eagle Nebula overlaps with an open star cluster. The Eagle Nebula is well known even among non-experts because there is a famous Hubble image of a section of it which shows large, beautiful pillars of hydrogen gas. The image is sometime called "the Pillars of Creation" because it is said that stars are forming in this region. However, this has never been observed, so the name is rather inappropriate. This famous image is false-color; the true color of the Eagle Nebula is red (though it is too faint to show color in most backyard telescopes). Although the nebula is comparable in brightness to

the Lagoon, it will appear much fainter, since the rods have low sensitivity to red (see chapter 3). As with most nebulae, it is helpful to view the Eagle Nebula at low magnification to enhance the surface brightness.

There are a few really interesting nebulae that are fainter and somewhat more difficult to detect than the ones we've covered so far. For example, in winter, Hubble's variable nebula (NGC 2261) is a lovely object which strongly resembles a comet — a brighter "nucleus" (the central star) with a very wide, wispy "tail" (see FIGURE 11.22 and FIGURE 11.23). In fact, it makes a better looking "comet" than most real comets; its "tail" is easily seen, whereas many comets have no visible tail. It is ninth magnitude, which puts it in the range of a good backyard telescope, though it is a more challenging target than most Messier objects. The really interesting thing about this nebula is that it changes appearance with time. It's a "variable nebula." In fact, it is the only variable nebula within range of a small telescope. The appearance can change in a matter of weeks. Since Hubble's variable nebula is a reflection nebula, it is thought that material orbiting the progenitor star is casting shadows on the nebula. Hence, as the material orbits, the shadows move, causing the appearance to change with time.

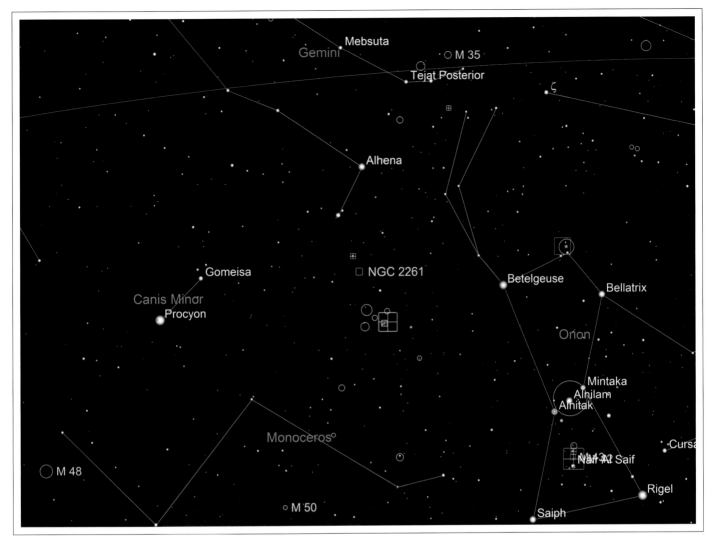

11.23 The Hubble Variable Nebula (NGC 2261) is found to the east of Betelgeuse.

◇Galaxies

A galaxy is a collection of around 100 billion stars. Some are smaller; some are larger. With the exception of our own galaxy (the Milky Way), galaxies are always very distant, and therefore very faint. They are usually represented by an ellipse or circle on a star chart; the shape sometimes indicates the orientation of the galaxy. In general, galaxies are the most difficult targets for backyard telescopes. With only a few exceptions, they require very dark skies if they are to be seen. It's when you are trying to observe galaxies that you'll wish you had bought a larger telescope with more light-gathering power. For beginners, galaxies are usually considered the most disappointing celestial object. Beginners are expecting to see glorious spiral shapes as are found in the textbooks. But these textbook images are all captured using long time-exposure techniques. Through a backyard telescope to the untrained eye, most galaxies will appear as a faint glowing smudge — if you're able to see them at all.

I don't say that to discourage anyone from looking at galaxies. They are a very enjoyable challenge. I simply do not want beginners to have unrealistic expectations about what they are going to see. With some practice at using averted vision you will be able to see some structure and details in many of the Messier galaxies. It is particularly helpful to know what to look for. Spend some time during the day studying textbook images of the galaxies you plan to observe at night. The eye can often pick out details when you know what to expect. You might be able to see a dark dust lane, or a trace of the spiral structure. However, you will *not* see any color.

The Pinwheel Galaxy (M33)

Credit & Copyright: Kurt Birkle / Eckhardt Slawik / Max-Planck-Institut f,r Astronomie, Heidelberg

Composite image (X-ray, visible, and infrared) of the Whirlpool Galaxy (M51)

◇ Spiral Galaxies

The way in which we classify galaxies was developed largely by Edwin Hubble. There are four basic kinds of galaxies: spirals, ellipticals, lenticulars, and irregulars. Astronomers once believed that one kind changed into another with time, but this is no longer thought to be true. Spiral galaxies are usually the most enjoyable to view. They are disk-shaped, with a brighter bulge at the center of the disk. The central bulge consists primarily of red stars, whereas the spiral arms contain a mixture of red and blue stars. We might infer that it would be easier to see the spiral arms than the core due to the increased sensitivity of the rods to blue light. However, the bulge is only slightly redder than the disk and is usually so much inherently brighter than the disk that it more than compensates for this effect. Therefore, the bulge will usually be far easier to see than the disk.

Spiral galaxies are further divided into subcategories based on several different criteria. Some spiral galaxies have a "bar" going across their central bulge, and are referred to as "barred spirals." It used to be the case that galaxies without bars were called "normal spirals."

However, with better imaging technology, we are now finding that many spiral galaxies once thought to be "normal" are in fact barred. It now appears that barred spirals actually outnumber the "normal" spirals two to one. So the terminology can be misleading. Perhaps "barred" and "unbarred" would be better terms. Our galaxy — the Milky Way — is now thought to be barred.

Additionally, spiral galaxies can be classified based on the ratio of bulge size to disk size. Type "a" spiral galaxies have a very large central bulge in comparison to their disk. Their spiral arms tend to be fairly tightly wrapped. The Sombrero Galaxy (M104) is a great example of a type "a" spiral, and is given the designation "Sa." At the other extreme are type "c" spirals. These have very small central bulges relative to their disk and their spiral arms tend to be fairly wide open. M101 — the Pinwheel galaxy — is a c-type spiral which is designated "Sc." (Note that M33 is also sometimes called the "Pinwheel galaxy.") Intermediate between these two is the Sb galaxy. M81 is a fine example of a type Sb galaxy — one of the best in range of a small telescope.

In addition, the presence or absence of a capital "B" in the galaxy classification is indicative of whether or not the galaxy is barred or unbarred. For example, since M81 has the classification Sb, it is an *unbarred* type b spiral galaxy. M91 is classified as SBb, so it is a barred type b. Sometimes astronomers will designate galaxies that fall in between two classes with two lowercase letters, so a galaxy intermediate between type a and type b is classified as Sab. In addition, some astronomers now add a "d" class for extreme examples of galaxies that previously would have been classified as type c. A very wide-open barred spiral galaxy with a tiny bulge might be classified as SBcd. Our Milky Way galaxy is thought to be an SBb galaxy, though it is difficult to know for certain since we are within it.

Additionally, spiral galaxies can also be divided into one of two types based on the structure of their spiral arms. Those galaxies which have well-defined spiral arms that can be traced continuously from the core to the periphery are called "grand design spirals." M51 (the Whirlpool galaxy) is one of the most spectacular grand design spirals. Only about 10 percent of spiral galaxies are grand design spirals. Conversely, those galaxies which have patchy traces of spiral arms, but where the spiral arms cannot be traced continually from core to periphery, are called "flocculent spirals." NGC 4414 in Coma Berenices is a good example of a flocculent spiral. They often have evidence of multiple spiral arms.

One of the delights of observing spiral galaxies is that we get to observe them from a variety of different angles. Some galaxies are oriented in a face-on fashion such as M51. This makes it easier to see the spiral structure. Other spiral galaxies are essentially edge-on, such as M108. They look like a faint smoky line when viewed through a telescope. I have found that the edge-on galaxies are usually a bit easier to see than the face-on galaxies of comparable brightness because the contrast is higher. Statistically, most galaxies are intermediate between face-on and edge-on. M81 is a nice example of a moderately tilted galaxy.

As an interesting historical note, spiral galaxies were once referred to as "spiral nebulae." Before the 1920s, astronomers did not understand what galaxies were. Many thought that galaxies were small and relatively nearby — that they were some sort of nebula. It wasn't until the 1920s that astronomers were able to see individual stars in other galaxies for the first time — confirming their status as "island universes." But terminology does not die overnight. You will often find the term "spiral nebulae" in early to middle 20th century astronomy literature. The term is now considered obsolete.

◇ Elliptical Galaxies

Most galaxies fall under the "elliptical" class because their basic shape as projected on the sky is an ellipse. The true shape of these galaxies is thought to be a prolate ellipsoid — a bit like an American football but with rounded edges. Some are more prolate than others; the degree of stretching varies from galaxy to galaxy. Some elliptical galaxies appear to be very close to a perfect sphere. Elliptical galaxies are designated by the capital letter "E" followed by a number from 0 to 7 which reflects the degree by which they deviate from a perfect circle (eccentricity). So a perfectly round elliptical galaxy is classified as E0, whereas a highly "stretched" one is designated as E7.

Note that this number reflects their two-dimensional appearance as seen from Earth, not necessarily the true 3-dimensional shape of the galaxy. For example, a galaxy that is very prolate would look circular from our vantage point if we happen to be lined up with the direction in which it is stretched. So an E0 galaxy may not actually be spherical; it simply looks circular from our point of view. M87 is a particularly large and bright example of an elliptical galaxy — class E0. Most elliptical galaxies are smaller and less massive than the average spiral galaxy. (M87 is an exception.)

When viewed using a backyard telescope, all elliptical galaxies look pretty similar: a faint indistinct glow, brightest in the center, with no discernible features. About the only differences you may note between them are differences in the overall size, brightness, and degree of eccentricity. They contain very little interstellar gas and dust. They are dominated primarily by red stars. Elliptical galaxies may not look like much, but consider that the faint smudge in that eyepiece is comprised of several billion stars at a distance of several million light-years!

◇Lenticular Galaxies

A lenticular galaxy is one that is a blend between an elliptical and a spiral. They often appear much like an E7 elliptical, but they have a definite disk. However, they contain no trace of spiral arms in their disk. Lenticular galaxies are given the designation S0. M84 and M85 are two examples of lenticular galaxies. When nearly face-on, lenticular galaxies can be difficult to distinguish from elliptical galaxies. When viewed nearly edge-on, lenticular galaxies can be difficult to distinguish from type Sa spirals.

◇Irregular Galaxies

Those galaxies that do not fit into any of the above shapes are classified as "irregular." They usually do not have a symmetric or well-defined shape. The physical characteristics of irregular galaxies are more similar to the disk of a spiral galaxy than elliptical galaxies. They have abundant gas and dust, and blue stars. They generally have no central bulge. Most irregular galaxies are small. They sometimes have traces of spiral arms.

Irregular galaxies are further divided into (at least) two subclasses. Irr-I galaxies are those which do have some trace of spiral structure, but not enough to be classified as a true spiral. Irr-II galaxies are those which do not have any trace of spiral structure. They are very rare. A third category called "dwarf irregulars" (dIrr) has been recently introduced as well.

For Southern Hemisphere observers, there are two spectacular examples of irregular galaxies: The Large Magellanic Cloud, and the Small Magellanic Cloud. These are both Irr-I galaxies, and are visible to the unaided eye as faint clouds near the south celestial pole. These are the two nearest bright galaxies to the Milky Way. They are never visible for mid-northern latitude observers.

Unfortunately, Northern Hemisphere viewers do not have such a splendid example of an irregular galaxy. In fact, only one Messier galaxy is classified as irregular: M82 FIGURE 11.24 — and there is some question as to whether it should really be classified as Irregular, or an

11.24 M82, the Cigar Galaxy, as imaged by the Hubble Space Telescope. Image credit: NASA, ESA, and the Hubble Heritage Team (STScI/AURA).

edge-on spiral. From my observations, it seems more like an edge-on spiral, albeit one with a very unusual appearance.

◇The Best Galaxies to Observe

For Northern Hemisphere observers, the best galaxies to observe are those in the Messier catalog. These are all within the range of a backyard telescope (under good dark skies), and some are very interesting. The biggest, brightest galaxy visible in the Northern Hemisphere is M31, sometimes called the "Andromeda Galaxy" due to its location in the constellation Andromeda. M31 is a type Sb spiral galaxy, similar to the Milky Way in overall shape. It is strongly tilted from our perspective, but not quite edge-on. M31 is larger than our galaxy, but has comparable or perhaps slightly less mass. It lies at a distance of around 2.9 million light-years, which makes it the nearest large galaxy. It is also one of only a handful of extragalactic objects that is blue-shifted, meaning it is approaching our galaxy. Virtually all other galaxies are red-shifted, meaning they are moving away from us (and from each other) due to the expansion of the universe. M31 is so close that its motion through space overcomes the small amount of expansion between there and here.

M31 is easily visible to the naked eye under moderately dark skies. It is a late autumn evening object. M31 is a wonderful object to find using the star-hopping technique FIGURE 4.16. Find the star Alpheratz (Alpha Andromedae), which is the northwest corner star of the great square of Pegasus. Then hop over two stars to Mirach (Beta Andromedae), then up to Mu and then Nu Andromedae. M31 is just slightly northeast of Nu Andromedae. It appears as a faint cloud to the unaided eye, and is a fantastic binocular object. Binoculars will clearly reveal the disk, which is about three degrees across.

Due to the large size of M31, it generally makes a pretty lousy telescope object because you cannot fit the entire galaxy in the field of view. The telescope's magnification reduces the overall surface brightness. I have found that M31 usually actually looks better in binoculars than in a typical telescope. Telescopes which have a very wide field of view, under lowest magnification will give the best views of M31. The central bulge will be the brightest part of the galaxy. The

The Great Andromeda Galaxy (M31). The small dwarf elliptical galaxies M110 and M32 are found above and just below M31 respectively.

Credit & Copyright: Celestial Image Co.

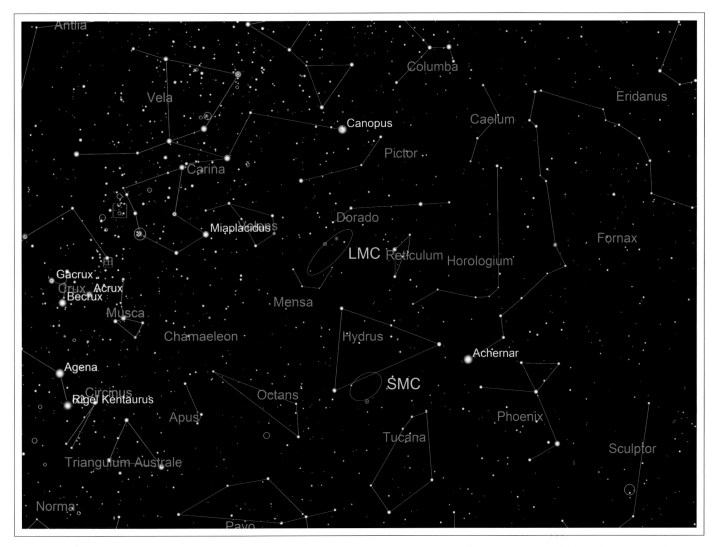

11.25 Location of the Large and Small Magellanic Clouds (LMC and SMC). These are visible to the unaided eye under dark skies for Southern Hemisphere observers.

disk is faint and I have never been able to see the spiral structure of the arms in a backyard telescope.

While you are in the area, look for M32 and M110. These are satellite galaxies of M31. They orbit M31 (or at least they *would*, given enough time). M32 and M110 are both dwarf elliptical galaxies. You will not have to look far away from M31 to find these satellite galaxies. M32 is found just south of the central bulge, grazing the outermost region of the disk of M31. Being class E2, it shows slight eccentricity. M110 is slightly fainter than M32, and is found on the opposite side of the bulge, at about twice the distance. At class E6, it shows considerable eccentricity.

If you have some experience with a telescope and are up for a challenge, you may want to try to locate

G1 — a globular cluster belonging to the M31 galaxy. At magnitude 13.7, G1 is within the range of a large backyard telescope under ideal conditions. G1 is actually intrinsically brighter than any globular cluster in the Milky Way, or for that matter any globular cluster in any of the nearby galaxies. You will need a detailed star chart to locate G1.

For Northern Hemisphere viewers, M31 is the only easy naked-eye galaxy. But for Southern Hemisphere observers, there are two: the Large and Small Magellanic Clouds (the LMC and SMC — **FIGURE 11.25**). These are satellite galaxies to the Milky Way, just as M32 and M110 are satellites of M31. Since they are located below Earth's South Pole, they are never visible at mid-northern latitudes. Both are irregular galaxies (Irr-I), much smaller than M31, but far closer. The LMC lies

at a distance of 160,000 light-years and crosses the border of the constellations Dorado and Mensa. The SMC (NGC 292) lies at a distance of 200,000 light-years and is located in the constellation of Tucana.

One of the most interesting and beautiful galaxies within range of a backyard telescope from the Northern Hemisphere would have to be M51 — the Whirlpool Galaxy FIGURE 11.26. It is one of very few galaxies where I can actually clearly see the spiral arms under dark moonless skies with a 10-inch or larger telescope. It is perhaps the best example of a face-on grand design spiral galaxy. It is a type Sc, so it has a very small central bulge, and widely spaced spiral arms. It is well-placed for viewing in the late spring or early summer, but can be seen at other times as well since it has a high declination.

M51 is actually two galaxies in the process of collision. The larger galaxy M51A is the grand design spiral, and is the brighter of the two. The smaller galaxy (M51B) seems to be lenticular, and is located at the end of one of the spiral arms of M51A. M51B and the core of M51A are each brighter than the spiral arms of M51A. Under moderate light pollution, you may not see the spiral arms, but only two faint glowing patches. The core of M51A is slightly brighter than M51B.

M51 is located in Canes Venatici, and is very close to the Big Dipper (part of Ursa Major). It's an easy galaxy to find by star-hopping FIGURE 11.27. First locate Alkaid (Eta Ursa Majoris) which is the last star on the end of the handle of the Big Dipper. Then

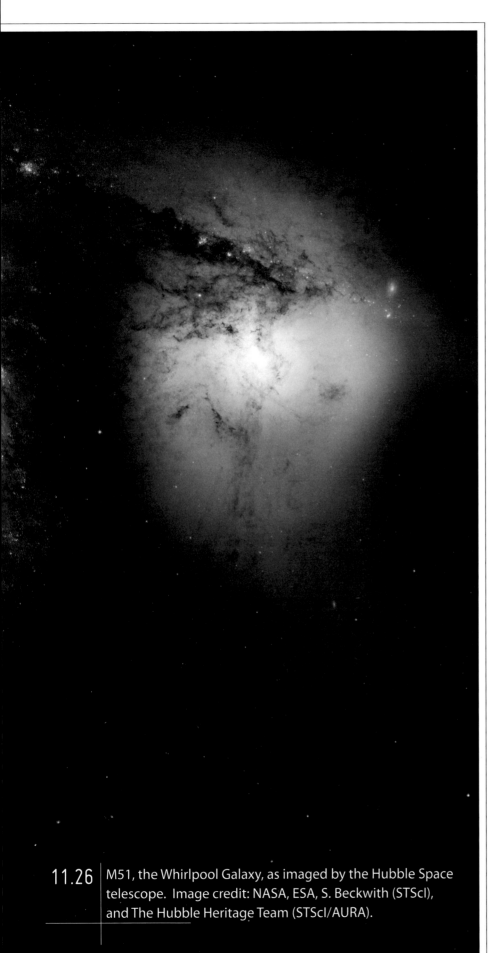

11.26 | M51, the Whirlpool Galaxy, as imaged by the Hubble Space telescope. Image credit: NASA, ESA, S. Beckwith (STScI), and The Hubble Heritage Team (STScI/AURA).

find Mizar, the middle star in the handle. M51 is just northwest of Alkaid at about half the distance between Mizar and Alkaid. In other words, the Alkaid-M51 line segment is about half the Alkaid-Mizar line segment, and is perpendicular to it. So Alkaid, M51, and Mizar form a right triangle, with Alkaid at the right angle.

M81 and M82 are well placed for viewing in late spring FIGURE 11.28. They are both in Ursa Major, rather close to the North Celestial Pole, so they are circumpolar for mid-northern latitudes and can be viewed throughout the year. These two galaxies are fairly bright and can be seen in binoculars under very dark skies. In a backyard telescope with low magnification, it is possible to view both galaxies in the same field of view. The two are an interesting pair, because M81 is one of the prettiest galaxies to observe, while M82 is one of the "ugliest." M81 (Bode's Galaxy) is a stunning Sab spiral, tilted well in between face-on and edge-on FIGURE 11.29. The orientation is usually quite noticeable. M82 (the Cigar Galaxy) is usually classified as Irr-I, though it appears as an edge-on spiral with dark obscuration near the center FIGURE 11.24. It looks almost like a ghostly line segment in a small telescope. Both are about 12 million light-years away.

There are several other places in the night sky where you can see two or more galaxies within the same field

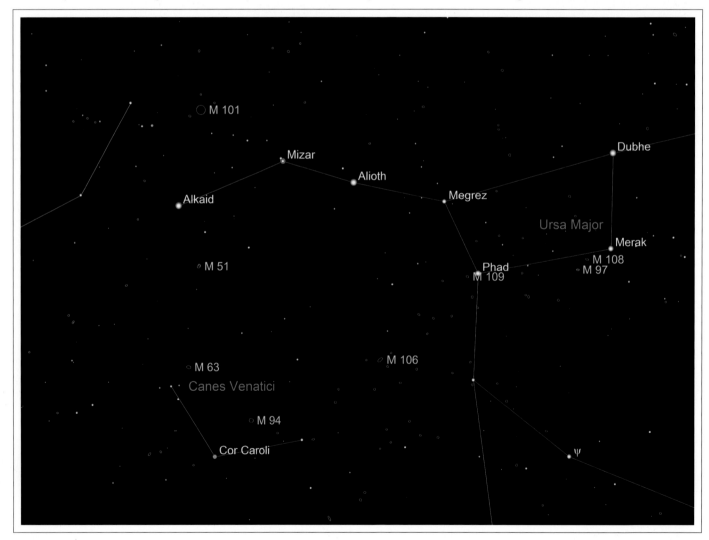

11.27   M51, the Whirlpool Galaxy, is found close to the star Alkaid – the final star in the handle of the Big Dipper

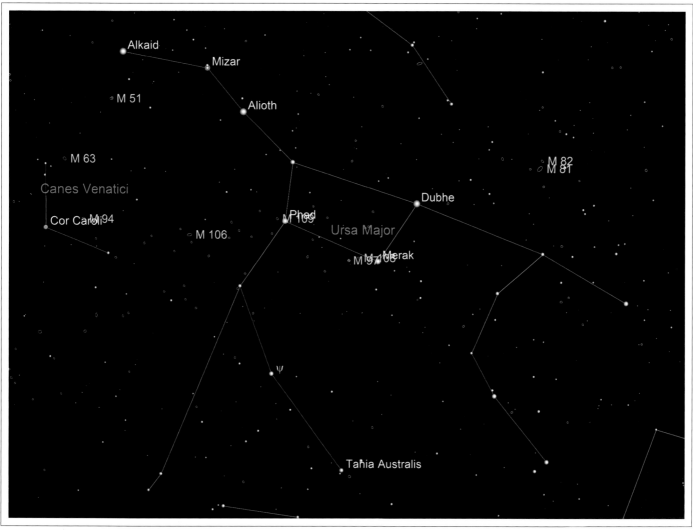

11.28 M81 and M82 are found just north of Ursa Major. They can appear in the same field of view for some telescopes at low magnification.

11.29 M81, Bode's Galaxy, as imaged by the Hubble Space Telescope. Image credit: NASA, ESA, and the Hubble Heritage Team (STScI/AURA).

of view at low magnification. The constellation Leo has some of these, and is well placed for viewing in spring. M65 and M66 are a fine example FIGURE 11.30. They are located halfway between Chort (Theta Leonis) and Iota Leonis. Slightly north of M65 and M66 at about twice their distance from each other is the galaxy NGC 3628. All three of these will fit within the field of view at low magnification and form a lovely triangle, sometimes called the "Leo Triplet." All three are spiral galaxies. M65 and M66 are strongly tilted from our perspective, and NGC 3628 is edge-on with a prominent dust lane. The triplet is 35 million light-years away.

Another often-viewed pair of galaxies in Leo is M95 and M96 FIGURE 11.30. These are farther separated (about twice as much) than M65 and M66. They are both spiral galaxies of intermediate tilt and appear nearly identical, except M96 is very slightly brighter. I was blessed to be able to observe a supernova in M96 which occurred in 1998. For several weeks, one star blazed as bright as the rest of that galaxy. North of M96 lies a third galaxy in this group: M105. It is an elliptical galaxy, type E1. To find this group, locate Chort and Rho (ρ) Leonis. M96 falls nearly on the line connecting these two stars, nearly halfway in between them, but slightly closer to Rho Leonis.

If you want to see as many galaxies as possible simultaneously, visit the Virgo cluster FIGURE 11.31. This is also a springtime object (autumn for Southern Hemisphere).

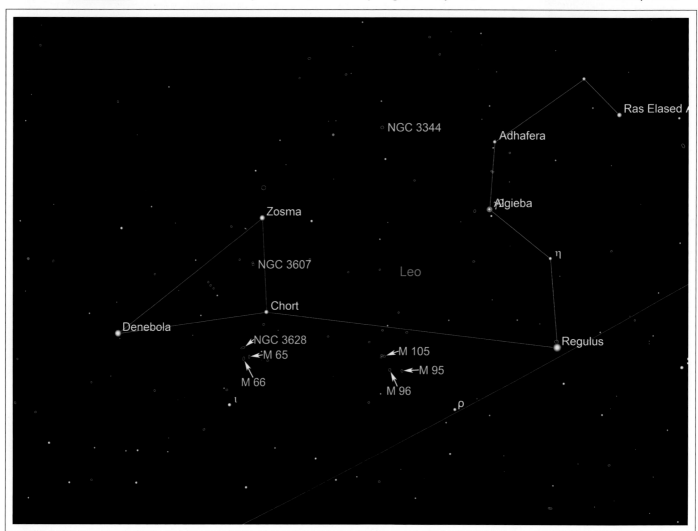

11.30   A number of bright galaxies are found in the constellation Leo, in the spring evening sky

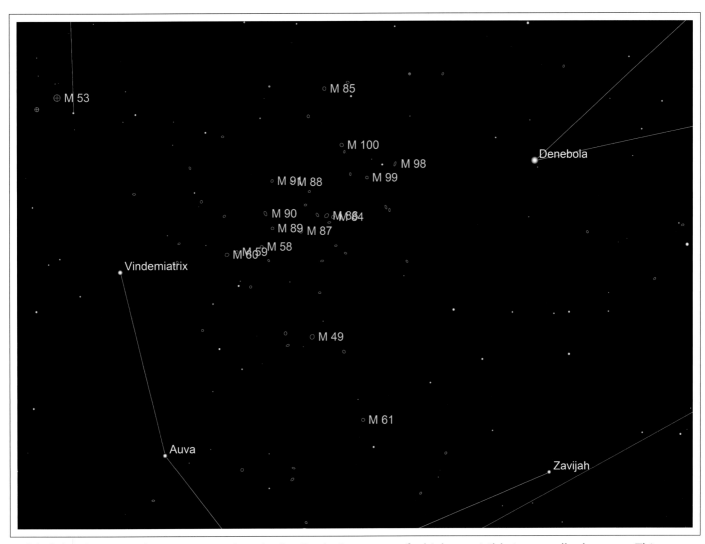

11.31 The Virgo cluster contains hundreds of galaxies, many of which are visible in a small telescope. This galaxy cluster is located east of Leo.

It is an enormous cluster of galaxies, more than ten degrees across. This is far larger than the field of view of a backyard telescope, but nonetheless you can often see several galaxies in the eyepiece at the same time. And by panning around the area, you can see several dozen. The center of the Virgo cluster lies about halfway between Vindemiatrix (Epislon Virginis), and Denebola (Beta Leonis). It is very enjoyable to just scan around this area with a telescope at low magnification, and see how many galaxies you can find. About 16 Messier galaxies belong to the Virgo cluster: M49, M58, M59, M60, M61, M84, M85, M86, M87, M88, M89, M90, M91, M98, M99, and M100. It also contains hundreds of non-Messier galaxies. The Virgo cluster alone makes the spring evening the best time of the year to observe galaxies.

At the center of the Virgo cluster you will find the giant elliptical galaxy M87. It is the largest and brightest member of the Virgo cluster. M87 is located on the line segment between Vindemiatrix and Denebola, just a little bit past halfway — closer to Vindemiatrix. At magnitude eight, it is an easy object to spot. The galaxy is a completely featureless sphere (E0 to E1), but it is probably the most massive thing you will ever see with your own eyes. It contains over one trillion stars. Research indicates that M87 has a massive black hole at its core, which is responsible for a large jet structure emanating from the nucleus of M87. The jet is not normally visible in a backyard telescope, though some amateur astronomers claim to have seen it under ideal conditions.

Another galaxy of interest can be found on the lower section of the constellation Virgo. This is the Sombrero

Galaxy: M104 **FIGURE 11.32**. It is found just to the left of the line segment connecting Algorab (Delta Corvi) to Porrima (Gamma Viriginis), about one-third of the way up **FIGURE 11.33**. A spotter scope is better than a telrad for this target, because the galaxy is not close to any bright stars. M104 is a stunning nearly edge-on type Sa spiral galaxy. It is a well-known and often-photographed galaxy because of the striking dust lane

11.32 The Sombrero Galaxy (M104) is a nearly edge-on spiral galaxy. The dark dust lane can be seen with a backyard telescope under dark skies. Image credit: NASA and the Hubble Heritage Team (SCScI/AURA).

around the galaxy's perimeter. This visually divides the galaxy into an upper and lower section. This dust lane is indeed visible in a backyard telescope under dark skies.

Other galaxies of interest include M64 **FIGURE 11.10**, M33 **FIGURE 4.16**, and M101 **FIGURE 11.27**. M64 (the Black Eye galaxy) is a spiral galaxy of intermediate tilt, located

just north of the Virgo cluster. It is famous because about half the spiral disk is obscured by dust, giving the galaxy a very unusual appearance and hence its name. M33 is a spiral galaxy in the constellation Triangulum. M101 is a spiral galaxy in Ursa Major. Interestingly, both M33 and M101 are sometimes referred to as "the Pinwheel Galaxy." M101 is nearly face-on, whereas M33 is moderately tilted. M33 is a fine late fall/early winter galaxy, not far from M31. M101 is well-placed in early summer.

About the worst time to look for galaxies is late summer (evening sky). The part of the sky that is well placed for viewing in late summer is conspicuously devoid of galaxies. It is called the "zone of avoidance." The reason is that gas and dust in our own galaxy obscure our view of other galaxies that are in line with the Milky Way. The zone of avoidance is basically anything within a few degrees of the Milky Way. Spring is the best time of year for galaxy detection.

◇Quasars

Before closing out this chapter, I need to mention one other deep-sky object of interest: the quasar. Quasars are small, blue objects which have enormous redshifts, suggesting that they are at great distance from our galaxy. Quasars are apparently the brightest type of active galactic nucleus (AGN). An AGN is a galaxy whose center is unusually bright and sometimes gives off powerful radio signals due to a highly energetic phenomenon taking place in the core. It is currently thought that a supermassive black hole at the center of some galaxies is able to generate copious amounts of energy from in-falling material in a process that is only partially understood. This causes the core of such galaxies to be brighter than the rest of the galaxy. For this reason, quasars look much like stars: point-like, without the fuzzy halo normally associated with a galaxy.

Since they look much like a star, these little blue objects with enormous redshifts are called QSOs (for "Quasi-Stellar Object"). A small fraction of QSOs also give off powerful radio waves, in which case we say that the object is "radio loud." These

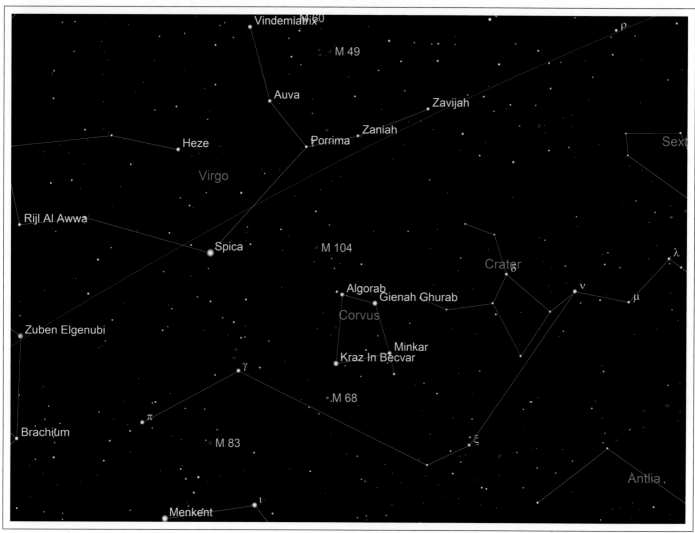

11.33   The Sombrero Galaxy (M104) is found to the west of the bright star Spica

are called "quasars" for "Quasi-Stellar Radio Source." In recent literature, however, it is common to use the term "quasar" for both radio quiet and radio loud QSOs. For some reason, quasars exist only at extreme distances. However, because they are so intrinsically bright, some of them are within range of a backyard telescope!

If you want to see a quasar with your own eyes, I highly suggest locating 3C 273 **FIGURE 11.34**. It is the brightest

quasar in our night sky and one of the closest. Historically, it was the first to be discovered. It is a springtime object located in the constellation Virgo. Since it is radio loud, 3C 273 is a true quasar, and shines at magnitude 13. Its distance from Earth is about 2.4 *billion* light-years, so 3C 273 is the most distant object you will probably ever see, and also the intrinsically brightest.

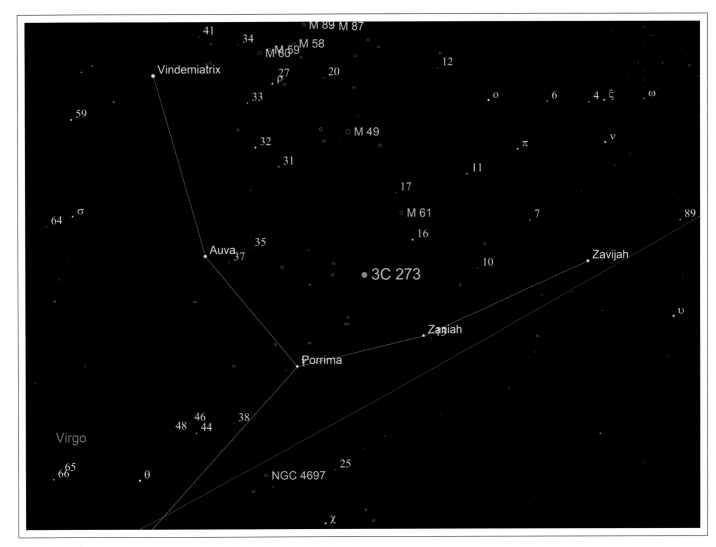

11.34 The quasar 3C 273 is found in Virgo, and appears as a faint star in a backyard telescope under dark skies

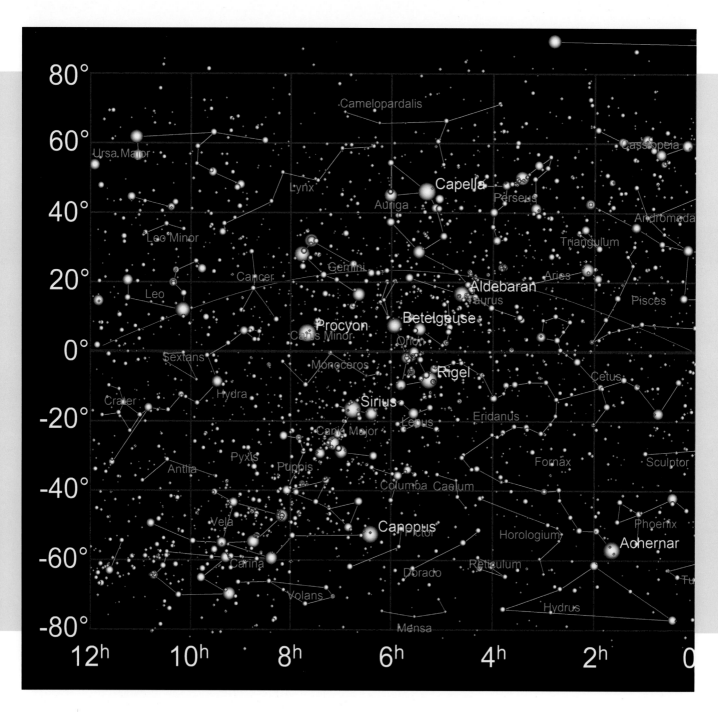

11.35 An all-sky map of the constellations. The brighter stars are labeled.

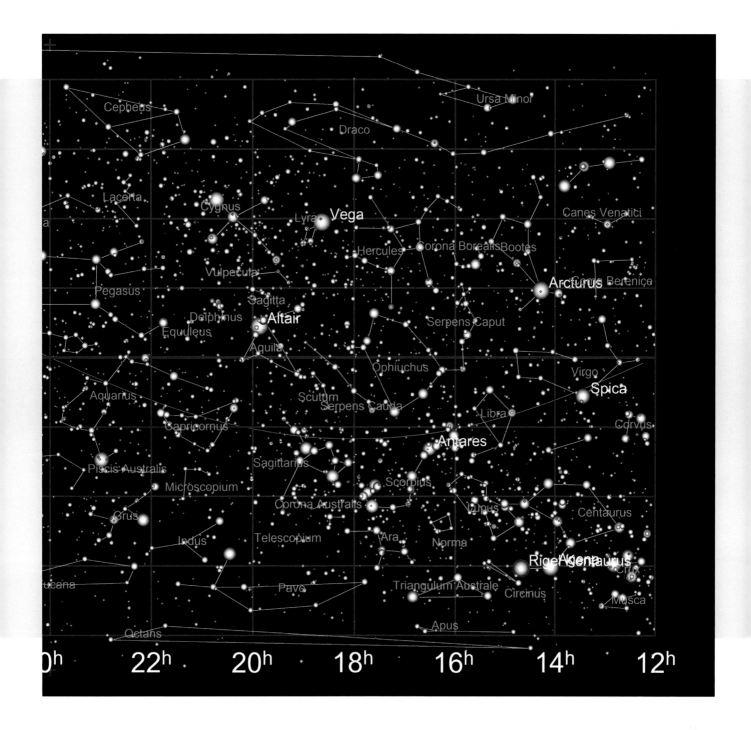

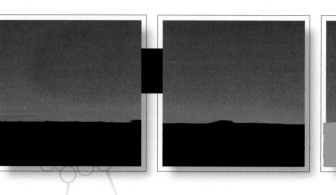

Chapter 12

Astrophotography

Thirty years ago, astrophotography was a pain. You had to worry about film exposure times, getting the telescope exactly polar-aligned, and so on. It was hard, and few people were good at it. Today that has all changed. We are now in the era of digital photography, and what was once difficult is now rather easy. The required exposure times are much, much shorter than they were with film. So you don't have to worry about perfect tracking so much. For that matter, the newer computer controlled telescopes track better anyway, and you never have to worry about wasting film or wondering if the image will turn out. With digital imaging, you have immediate feedback, and if you're not happy with the image, just delete it and try again.

◇Afocal Imaging

A question people often ask is, can you just put your digital camera up to the eyepiece of a telescope and snap a picture? Although it is not the best approach, the answer is: yes, you can. At least with bright objects, this method works pretty well. It's called "afocal imaging." It works best if the camera can be physically mounted to the eyepiece so that it is as steady as possible. You can also take advantage of the camera's optical zoom, and make the image as large as you need. If your camera allows you to adjust its settings, then make the *aperture* as large as possible, and you

may want to increase the *gain* to a larger value. If your camera doesn't have such settings, don't worry about it. You will simply have to experiment with various time-exposure values. I have used this method successfully to image planets. Just be sure to turn off the flash!

There are some drawbacks to using afocal imaging. Digital cameras really weren't designed to work this

A CCD with a focal reducer and a color-filter sliding bar

way and so some problems can arise. Sometimes the field of view will be reduced in the camera, with soft edges that are reduced in brightness relative to the center. This phenomenon is called "vignetting" [vin-yet-ing]. It may not be a problem if you are zoomed in on a small object like a planet, but it could be an issue for larger objects. Changing the camera's optical zoom may help.

Digital cameras are not optimized for low light conditions. Techniques such as dark subtraction and flat fielding (which we will address later) are not generally done with a standard digital camera. There is also a reduction in clarity and brightness due to the fact that the light has to travel through extra lenses. Despite these disadvantages, afocal imaging is easy, and digital cameras are cheap. So give it a try.

A CCD without the focal reducer. This front-on view shows the central chip which records incoming photons.

◇The CCD

The best way to do astrophotography is using a CCD — which stands for "charge coupled device." A CCD is designed for astronomy. If you want the best images, particularly of fainter things like galaxies, consider purchasing a CCD. As of the writing of this book, you can get a decent CCD for a few hundred dollars. And the prices continue to drop.

A CCD is a two-dimensional grid of photoelectric sensors. These sensors convert incoming photons (particles of light) into electric charges that are stored in a bin associated with each sensor. Whenever a particle of light strikes a CCD, a small bit of charge is stored at that location. The more light falls, the more the charge builds. When the exposure is finished, the bins can be sequentially read out to a computer. The row at the edge of the CCD is read first, and then erased. Then all the remaining rows are shifted over one bin, and the new edge row is read out to the computer. The process continues until all the rows have been shifted and read. The process is very fast. The computer then displays a two-dimensional image corresponding to charge on the CCD.

In fact, most digital cameras use a CCD to capture the image, but cameras also have lenses and their CCDs are not optimized for low-light conditions. A CCD of the kind astronomers use has no lenses, because the telescope will act as the lens. When you use a CCD, you remove the eyepiece on the telescope and allow the light to form an image directly on the image sensor. You focus the image by moving the CCD in or out, just as you would an eyepiece. Since there are no extra lenses to get in the way, this produces the sharpest and brightest image. If you want to change the magnification, you must add an extra lens in front of the CCD. Usually you will want to reduce the magnification to increase your field of view. In this case you will want to get a "focal reducer." They are not expensive.

A CCD (of the kind used for astronomy) is optimized for low-light conditions. It will allow you to set the exposure time for each type of object. You will need longer exposure times for fainter objects, so that the scarce photons can build up sufficient charge at each bin in the photoelectric sensor. To focus the image, pick a fairly bright object, a bright star or star cluster for example. That way the exposure time can be very small. You can quickly adjust the focus without having to wait for a long time to see how you did. Take your time and get the focus as sharp as you can. It should remain focused on all subsequent targets. Note that color filters may affect the focus slightly. Some filter sets include a clear filter so that you can focus with that in place, and it will be the same with colored filters.

◇Color vs. Grayscale

Each photoreceptor in a CCD measures only the number of photons that strike it in a given period of time. It does not (as of the writing of this book) measure the energy associated with those photons. In other words, it does not give any information on color. Therefore, CCD images are inherently grayscale. If you don't care about color, then you're all set. After all, many objects in the universe have virtually no color (like the moon), or only muted colors (like some galaxies). But some objects (such as nebulae) have very

striking color, and you may want to see that. If so, there are two ways to produce a color image.

First, you can use color filters. You will need three: usually red, green, and blue if you want the resulting image to look as it would to the human eye. Put the red filter in front of the CCD and take an image. Then remove the red filter and add the green filter and take another image. Then replace the green filter with the blue and take a third image. At this point, you should have three grayscale images of the target. They will all look slightly different because each one was sensitive only to photons in a particular frequency range. Next, you can use computer software to align the three images (in case the telescope drifted a bit between the three exposures). Then you color combine the images, assigning the image taken under the red filter to the red color channel, the green to the green, and the blue to the blue. If successful, you should have a color image of the target. You may then have to adjust the white balance so that the object's color is natural and unbiased.

This is basically the way professional astronomers produce accurate color images. It is not difficult to make a color image using filters, but it does take some time, because for each one color image, you must take *three* time exposures — one with each filter. (That doesn't include dark frames, which will be discussed later.) The following option is faster.

The second way is to use a "single shot color" (SSC) CCD. Some CCDs are designed such that the photo-

A color image of the Ring Nebula (M57) using a 14-inch telescope. This image was produced by taking three greyscale images using red, green, and blue color filters with a standard CCD, and then combining the results.

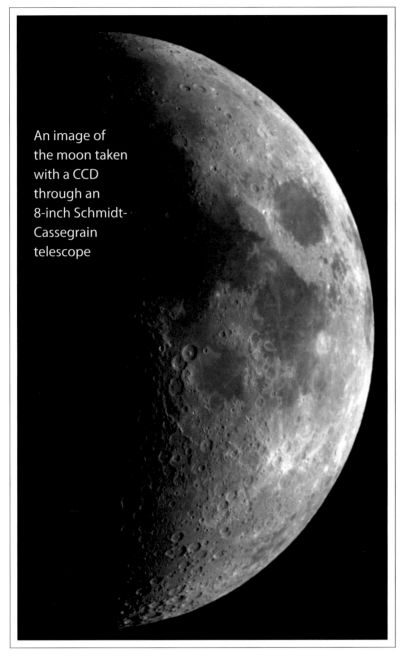

An image of
the moon taken
with a CCD
through an
8-inch Schmidt-
Cassegrain
telescope

to correspond to one pixel on the final image, this means your resolution is reduced by a factor of four. So single shot color CCD images are *half* the width and *half* the height of their non-color counterpart. Also, if you don't care about color, then the color filters do nothing but block precious photons. You will have to take longer time exposures to get a color image than you would a grayscale image. Also, SSC CCDs don't work nearly as well with narrowband filters. You will have to live with the color filters that are built into the CCD.

In deciding which system to use, you must weigh the pros and cons. If you don't care about color, or will only occasionally take a color image, then the standard (grayscale) CCD with color filters is definitely the way to go. You can always create a color image if you want to, and it will be at high resolution. All your images will be twice the size of their color-CDD counterpart. For the best quality images, the standard CCD with color filters is the better choice. If on the other hand you want to take a lot of color images, and don't care too much about having high resolution, and don't want to take the time to take three exposures for every color image, then the single-shot color CCD is the way to go. You won't have to worry about taking three exposures and aligning them every time you want a color image. They will all be in color, and it's automatic.

◇Extending the Range

Recall, in an earlier chapter I mentioned that telescope beginners are often disappointed with views of galaxies and nebulae because such targets are so faint. They look so much less impressive than the images we are used to seeing in textbooks. Well, a CCD changes all that. With a CCD, you will be able to get impressive, highly detailed views of galaxies and nebulae — all with a backyard telescope **FIGURES 12.1, 12.2, 12.3**. Deep-sky objects are no longer little fuzzy blobs — they suddenly become beautiful celestial gems. You can even image targets that are fainter than what the eye can detect in the eyepiece. In this sense, a CCD extends the range of objects that you can observe in a backyard telescope.

receptors are organized into blocks of four (two by two), with a tiny color filter on each one. Each of the four photoreceptors in the block has a different color filter. By comparing the relative intensities of the bins at each block, the computer can calculate not only the brightness but also the color of the image at that point. The advantages of this technique are obvious: you only have to take one exposure to get a color image — not three. You don't have to worry about aligning three grayscale images. It is all done automatically. Most digital cameras use this system.

But there are disadvantages to this system as well. Since it takes a two-by-two block of photoreceptors

12.1 The Whirlpool Galaxy (M51) as imaged through a 10-inch Schmidt-Cassegrain telescope

12.2 Fragment C of comet Schwassmann-Wachmann 3 passing by the Ring Nebula (M57) as imaged through a 12-inch Schmidt-Cassegrain

12.3 A CCD image of globular cluster M13 in Hercules

To make good use of a CCD, your telescope will need to have very good tracking. If your telescope does not have a clock drive, don't invest in a CCD. Get a telescope with a clock drive first. In my experience, computer-controlled telescopes are the best for use with CCDs. They track much more precisely than those you must manually align. The tracking doesn't have to be perfect, but the better it is, the longer-exposure images you can take. Longer exposure translates to better quality images of faint objects.

◇ Flip Mirror

A flip mirror is a very helpful addition for CCD users. Though not essential, it will help you to locate the object you are attempting to view. Essentially, a flip mirror is a single mirror which can be moved into one of two positions. In the "down" position, the mirror is in front of the CCD at a 45-degree angle. This causes the light to be diverted to the side of the telescope

where you can place an eyepiece for direct viewing of the target. In the "up" position, the mirror does not divert the light, so the beam goes directly to the CCD. A flip mirror allows you to quickly check on the target object with your eye, and then quickly switch back to CCD imaging mode.

◇ Time Exposure

The time exposure is the time that will allow light to collect and build up charge on the CCD. The longer you expose the CCD to your target image, the more charge accumulates on the detector. Bright objects require very little time, because they produce lots of photons. Deep-sky objects require longer exposures. Typical time exposures are from a few seconds to a few minutes. With film, a longer time exposure means a brighter image, but with a CCD the image is digital, so you can adjust its brightness to anything you want, *after* the image is taken. Short exposures will tend to have a lot of "noise." That is, they will have a pattern of random static superimposed on the target image. Increasing the time exposure will increase the signature of the target image more than the signature of the noise. It will improve what astronomers call the "signal-to-noise ratio." So if your image looks very grainy, try increasing the time exposure (and make sure you have subtracted the dark frame — as will be discussed below).

It is possible to have a time exposure that is too long as well. In this case, the bins that collect charge become "full" and begin spilling over into adjacent bins. This will tend to produce a vertical or horizontal line on your image that extends from a bright object on the image. If this happens, reduce the time exposure. You may want to take a blank image and discard it to allow the photoreceptors to reset themselves after an over-exposed image. Generally, it is best to have the longest time exposure possible before completely filling the bins. That will give you the highest quality images.

The photoreceptors in most CCDs are very sensitive to red light, and not so sensitive to blue light. (So it is the *opposite* of the rods in your eyes.) This means that if you are taking an image of a blue nebula, then you will have to use a longer time exposure than you would for a red nebula of equivalent brightness in order to get the same quality result. This also means that those faint red nebulae that were challenging to your eyes will be the *best* objects for a CCD. It is important to keep this in mind when producing color images using the three-filter method described above. Using the red filter, a one-minute exposure might be sufficient to get a good image of a galaxy. But when you do the blue filter, it might take twice as long or even longer to get sufficient signal-to-noise.

◇Dark Frame Subtraction

CCDs do not produce perfect electronic representations of the target image. They add a bit of electronic "noise" to the true image. Even when no image falls on the photoreceptors, they generate some charges anyway. So if you take a CCD image of nothing, you'll get an image of something — random static we call "dark current." Essentially, dark current is "junk" that gets added to your image, reducing its quality. Think of it this way: you want an image of your target, but what you are getting is an image plus junk.

There is a clever way of dealing with this. Take an image of nothing. That is, leave the telescope cap on, and take a

CCD image. This is called a "dark frame." If you look at the image, it will be just the "junk" generated by dark current. Now take an image of your target. You will get an image of your target plus the junk. Now, use computer software to subtract the dark frame from the target image. You are essentially subtracting the junk, and leaving a nearly perfect image of your target. The process is called dark frame subtraction. The algorithm to subtract the dark frame from the image will be built into the CCD software. Some programs do it automatically if you have the "dark subtract" option checked.

Note that the dark frame image is dependent on (1) temperature and (2) time exposure. So if you are taking a five-minute exposure of a nebula, you must subtract a five-minute dark frame taken at the same temperature. Always match the time exposure of the dark frame to the time exposure of your image. The temperature can vary slightly and you will be okay, but if it

Proper positioning of the telescope and photography equipment is important to astrophotography

has been an hour or more since you took your last dark frame, and the temperature has changed appreciably, you may want to take some new dark frames because the noise pattern will change.

Dark current is a function of temperature. The higher the temperature, the greater the dark current will be. So CCDs work best at low temperature. Many CCD systems have active coolant systems. Some use liquid nitrogen to reduce the dark current to very low levels. Other CCD systems use other types of electronic cooling systems to reduce dark current. The less expensive CCDs use only passive cooling, so they won't get any colder than the ambient temperature. Even if you use a cooling system to reduce dark current, it is still a good idea to always subtract the dark frame. By combining these two procedures, it is possible to nearly eliminate dark noise.

If you get a CCD with an active cooling system, remember that the dark frame is temperature-dependent. You must wait until the device has reached the desired temperature and stabilized before taking any dark frames. If the CCD is still cooling, your dark frames will be unreliable. If your CCD does not have an active cool-

ing system, that's okay. Just keep track of the ambient temperature. If the temperature changes by more than a few degrees, you will want to take new dark frames.

Keep this in mind when deciding whether to get a single-shot color CCD, or a standard CCD with color filters. With the SSC CCD, you will need to take two images: one dark frame and one of the target. But if you want to assemble a color image using filters with the (higher-resolution) standard CCD, you will need at least four, and perhaps six. You will need three images of the target — one in each color filter — and you will need one dark frame. You can subtract the same dark field from the three different images — but only if they all have the same time exposure. Since CCDs are red-sensitive, you might find that the target requires only a 30-second exposure under the red filter, but perhaps it needs two minutes under the blue or green filter. If that is so, then you will need both a 30-second dark frame and a two-minute dark frame.

Of course, once you take the dark frames, you won't need to take them again unless you change the exposure length, or unless the temperature changes significantly. So when you take an image of another nebula

under three filters with the same exposure time, you don't need to take new dark frames. You can use the ones already saved on the computer. Some computer software will keep track of the dark frames you have at each time exposure within a certain temperature range. You can set the system preferences so that it will automatically subtract the appropriate dark frame, or prompt you if you need to take a new one.

◇Flat Fielding

Dark noise is an additive effect. It adds brightness values to the pixels in your image. That is why you can reduce dark noise by subtracting a dark field. But there is another way in which CCDs produce imperfect images. They also have a multiplicative component. In other words, some photoreceptors in the CCD are more sensitive to light than others. They have different "gain." Perhaps one receptor reports a brightness value of 45 while another reports a brightness value of 35 for stars that have the same true brightness. This cannot be subtracted, because the value is proportional to the amount of light falling on the photoreceptor. If the gain for each photoreceptor were known, you could divide the final image by this value to compensate for the unequal gain of the various pixels. This can be done, and is referred to as "flat fielding."

Here's the good news. If you are just interested in taking pretty pictures, you usually don't need to worry about flat fielding. The gain variation from one photo-receptor to another really isn't all that noticeable. So unless you are doing work that requires scientifically accurate measurements of the pixel values, you can pretty much skip the flat-fielding procedure. *Always dark subtract.* But skip the flat field.

That being said, if you do want to flat field, here's how you do it. You point the telescope at a nearby uniformly illuminated white disk. It needs to be completely featureless, so that the image falling on the CCD is perfectly uniform. Then take an image at a short exposure time. Take a dark frame too (of the same exposure time). Subtract the dark frame from your uniform image, and this will be your flat field. Now take an image of the target. Dark subtract as normal. Now *divide* the resulting image by the flat field image. The result should be a perfectly calibrated image of the target.

For the mathematically inclined reader, each pixel on your computer screen image has a value (let's call it y). Each star in your image has a true brightness value (let's call it x). If CCDs were perfect, then y would be exactly equal to x. So, y=x means that your image is a perfect representation of the target. But in reality, the equation is more like this: y = mx + b. There is a multiplicative component (m) which is different for each photoreceptor. And there is an additive component (b) which is different for each photoreceptor. If you can figure out what m and b are for each pixel, then you can remove them by subtracting b and dividing by m. This is the point of dark-frame subtraction and flat fielding.

When you take a dark frame, the image is nothing (so x = 0 for every pixel). Substituting that in (y = mx + b), we find that y=b for a dark frame. A dark frame is showing you a "map" of the b value for every pixel in your image. To find the m component, we shine a uniform white across the photoreceptors of the CCD — a flat field. So x=1 for every pixel in a flat field. If we subtract the dark frame (b), then the equation becomes y=m. So the flat field is a "map" of the m value for every pixel. By subtracting the dark frame (b), we are removing "b" from the right side of the equation. By dividing by the flat field (m) we remove m from the right side of the equation. And we are left with y=x. That is, we have a theoretically perfect representation of the target.

◇Image Stacking

Faint objects require a longer time exposure than bright ones in order to get sufficient signal-to-noise for a nice image. But longer time exposures are more sensitive to tracking errors than shorter exposures. No telescope tracks perfectly, so the image of the target will tend to drift slightly with time. If it drifts by even one pixel, the resulting computer image will appear smeared. So there is a practical limit on CCD exposure times — it is limited by the quality of your telescope clock drive.

Professional telescopes tend to have exceptionally good tracking. It is common to be able to track for 5 minutes or more without any guiding. However, backyard telescopes are generally not nearly as accurate. You should be able to run time exposures of five seconds with little trouble. However, I have found that most backyard telescopes show visible tracking errors if the exposure times are longer than about ten seconds for a high focal length telescope. Moderate focal length telescopes may track accurately for up to a minute. If yours can go longer, consider yourself blessed with an exceptional telescope.

There is a way to get the quality of long time exposures, even if your telescope tracking isn't that great. It's referred to as "image stacking." Instead of a one-minute exposure, you take 12 five-second exposures. You then select a given star that is visible on each image, and the computer will align the images and add them. The resulting image is the equivalent of a one-minute exposure. It is okay if the tracking isn't perfect, because the computer software will align the images based on the guide star you selected. As long as there

is no noticeable drifting *within* any one image, the computer will shift the images to compensate for any drifting that occurs between any two of them. Image stacking is the best way to get long time exposure images on telescopes that have only mediocre tracking.

There is a drawback to the image-stacking method. Every time the CCD image is transmitted to the computer, there is some random noise that is introduced called "read noise." This is not the same as the dark noise. Read noise has a different cause, and cannot be removed by dark-frame subtracting or flat fielding. There's really no way to get rid of read noise, but fortunately it is fairly small and not normally noticeable. It does happen every time the CCD is read, so it can add up. In our previous example, 12 five-second exposures have considerably more read noise than one one-minute exposure, so it is better to take one long exposure than stacking many shorter ones. But sometimes that

simply isn't possible due to tracking errors, so there is a tradeoff. The quality will be better if you take fewer individual images, thereby reducing read noise. The bottom line is this: make your exposures as long as you can get them without showing tracking errors (even if that's only five seconds). Then use image stacking to increase the effective exposure time beyond that.

If you have a high-magnification spotter (or "guiding") scope, you can also try manually compensating for tracking errors. Many guide scopes have adjustable crosshairs that you can move to a target "guide" star. Then all you have to do is manually keep the guide star in the crosshairs, while you are taking the CCD image, and there will be no smearing. It is also possible to use a second CCD attached to the guider scope to automatically adjust the telescope motion.

◇Hot Pixels and Dead Pixels

A few other imaging problems may arise, and can be ameliorated with software. Hot pixels are spots on the CCD where the value is reported as being very high, even when no light is falling on that spot. Dark-frame subtraction can sometimes deal with these areas, unless the pixel value is really far off. If the pixel value is "off the charts" (due to a damaged photoreceptor, for example) then it may show up as a bright pixel even after dark subtraction. You can use software to deal with this problem. Most programs have a feature to "remove hot pixels," which will analyze the image for anomalously high pixel values, and then replace those values with the average of the surrounding pixels.

A similar problem occurs when pixels have an anomalously low value. Some pixels will report a value of zero, or some small value even when brightly illuminated. When the photoreceptors are not sensitive to light at all, these are said to be "dead pixels." Dead pixels cannot be fixed by dark-frame subtraction or by flat fielding because the brightness information at that location has simply been lost. Fortunately, most CCD programs have a feature to "remove dead pixels" similar to the feature for removing hot pixels. The image

is scanned for anomalously low pixel values, and such pixels are replaced with the average value of the surrounding pixels.

◇The Best CCD Targets

The best target objects for CCD imaging are the worst targets for viewing with the eye and vice versa. Those galaxies that look like nothing more than a fuzzy glow to the eye in a telescope will be delightful on a CCD. Red nebulae that are barely detectable to the human eye will show in glorious detail on a CCD. Conversely, bright planets which look so lovely to the eye in a telescope are notoriously difficult CCD targets. They tend to be too small, and it is hard to pick out any detail.

CCDs are best used (with a focal reducer) to capture large-scale, faint deep-sky objects. But if you want to try some planets too, here are some tips. First, remove the focal reducer. With a planet, you want all the magnification you can get. Second, try using very short exposures to "freeze out" the seeing. The goal here is to capture the planet during a second of good seeing. Therefore, take hundreds of pictures and throw away all but the best few. Since the exposure time is so short (less than a second), you can do this quickly.

A better way to image planets is to use a web cam to record a .avi file. The resulting file consists of thousands of individual images of very short exposures. You can then use various software packages that will automatically select the best images in the series, and stack them. Some of the best images of planets by amateur astronomers are produced by this method. It works really well, but it takes some experience. Remember that planets are also a good target for attempting afocal imaging with a digital camera.

The moon is the one exception that looks both spectacular to the eye and spectacular with a CCD. Just remember to use very short exposure times for the moon, only a fraction of a second. With a CCD, you might have to take several images of various sections of the moon, and then stitch these together in Photoshop to make a mosaic.

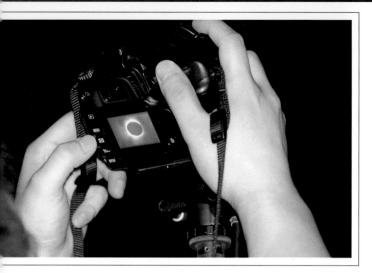

◇ Night Photography

You don't have to be a professional to enjoy taking photos of the night sky – and with an understanding of camera settings and basic photography, you can begin collecting some of your stargazing special events!

The main difference between daytime photography and night time photography is available light. Just before dark, when the first stars and the moon appear, it may take exposure times of a few seconds; a full darkness exposure will be considerably longer. Longer exposures require a solid foundation which makes a steady tripod essential and be sure your tripod is made to securely hold your camera! A remote shutter release will also aid in reducing movement because of your hand.

Practice a little and keep a log of what works – and make notes of what doesn't. Try different times of the night; often just before dawn is the darkest and right at dusk can be great for moon pictures. As with any stargazing, get away from the city lights — deserts, mountains, or rural areas. City lights and other brightly lit areas on the ground cause what's known as light pollution. This shows up as unwanted bright blotches in your photos. Also, count to yourself how long it takes the camera to do a full-darkness exposure – this will highlight the reason that a tripod is a must!

◇ Many Shapes and Sizes

Digital cameras have eliminated the suspenseful wait for film developing to see if your night sky attempts are successful, so you can easily make multiple attempts while you are learning with no costs and the ability to reuse the space on the camera's SD card. Although some great photos can begin with a "point and shoot" model or a smartphone (with the help of some apps and filters), for best results a DSLR (digital single-lens reflex) can be used. Though not made specifically as astronomical cameras, they have proven to be able to capture amazing images with a little patience, skill, and luck!

DSLRs often have a larger sensor than a point-and-shoot, the ability to leave the shutter open for extended times, and features for noise reduction. Get acquainted with your DSLR's advanced settings; that's the secret as there are no automatic or default settings.

Consult your manual to find the bulb, mirror lockup, timer, and noise reduction. The "mirror lockup" locks the camera's internal mirror in the "up" position for a moment before the shutter fires, and this will reduce camera vibration and increase image sharpness. Also, become familiar with your camera's timer function, or as mentioned, use a remote shutter release.

A word of caution! Always consult the manufacturer's specifications for standard acceptable times to leave your shutter open as overheating the sensor can cause damage. This is usually not a problem because ambient light is so dim but ideally you want to take several darker photos and give the camera a bit of a rest between. For instance, take three 10-minute exposures over a period of 45 minutes, and then combine them together with computer software.

◇ Start with the Moon

Because the moon is the brightest object in the night sky, it can be photographed with only slight camera adjustments. A full moon, for example, can be captured with ISO settings of 1600 f/5.6 with shutter speed of 1/20 seconds. The moon's illumination on a partly cloudy night, or a clear night with moon reflection on water, can also be captured. To photograph the moon's surface features, start with ISO 1600 f/36 1/30 second and a 200mm lens. Longer focal length lens, 200mm or longer, will achieve good detail of the moon's craters and ridges.

Capturing a lunar eclipse is also easy. For best results in capturing an eclipse, keep the entire moon framed. Adjust your settings based on the stage of the eclipse.

↘ Event	ISO 200	ISO 400
Full Moon	1/250 f/16	1/250 f/22
Penumbra Shadow	1/60 f/16	1/125 f/16
2nd and 3rd contact	1 f/4	1/4 f/2.8
Totality	2 f/2.8	1 f/2.8

◇Star Trails

A popular and artistic night sky photograph is star trails. These are the tracks, often circular, that appear because of the combination of the Earth's rotation and long exposure setting. For the celestial pole rotation in the northern hemisphere, locate the point that lies near Polaris, the North Star. The shutter will need to remain open for 30 to 60 minutes to capture the streaks of movement. How long the exposure is will depend on many factors including how dark the night is. The f stop should be down to f/2.8 to f/8 and ISO setting at 100. A wide angle lens, tripod and a fixed focal point and these photographs often show the horizon. Set your camera on the bulb setting, if available, per the manufacturer's recommended levels.

◇Stars — Clear Focus

Stars are more of a challenge than the moon. Appearing in the night sky as much smaller than the moon, for the clearest shot, it is best to use an equatorial mount and a motor drive attached to a telescope to prevent the movement of star trails.

You can also mount your camera to a telescope with a "camera-to-telescope" adapter. To focus while using an adapter, try focusing first on a moon crater. Without a telescope and special equipment, a very dark night when the stars are bright is still worth a try. Use a wide aperture setting (f/2.8) and expose for 15 to 30 seconds. Again, practice and keep a log. High-zoom lenses aren't really necessary to capture adequate composition – a medium range, around 80mm, works very well for this application.

◇Meteors

These are among the most fun and rewarding events to try and capture! Pick an appropriate focal point such as Perseids, known to be a prolific meteor shower, appearing to come from the constellation Perseus. Using a wide field of view, keep the shutter open for two to 10 minutes. Start with ISO settings of 800.

Keep in mind, more luck than skill is required. So try and try again. Here are some composition tips:

- Pointing the camera at the North Star, meteors will appear as bright lines streaking across the frame.

- Pointing the camera at the place where the meteor shower is centered, meteors should appear as lines radiating out from the middle of the frame.

- Remember, longer exposures drain your battery power, so be prepared with full charge and/or a backup battery.

Although settings can depend on your camera type and lens, here is a helpful reference to some starter settings:

↘ Quick Settings Chart	tripod	aperature	exposure	ISO
General sky photography	yes	f/2.8-f/4	12 to 30 sec	1600
Moon - full	yes			
star trails	yes	f/4-f/8	30 - 60 min.	100
Stars - clear focus	yes		20-40 sec	1600+
Nightfall	yes	f/2.8	20-40 sec	400
Constellations	yes	f/2.8, f/3.5, to f/4		1600
Milky Way	yes	f/3.5 to f/4	60 sec	1600+

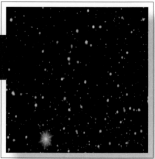

Afterword
The Relevance of Astronomy

I have always loved astronomy, even when I was a little child. As soon as I could read, I would seek out books on outer space. Hopefully my passion for this topic has come across in this book. But what does it all mean? Is the universe simply the result of "chance"? If so, then our appreciation of its beauty has no real meaning. It would simply be one chemical accident interacting with another accident. There would be no intrinsic

value to astronomy, nor any inherent value to human life. If that is the case, then you have wasted your time reading this book. It is all "sound and fury, signifying nothing" (Macbeth, Act V, Scene V).

It is my conviction that the universe is so orderly and beautiful precisely because it is not an accident. It is upheld by the mind of God. I speak not of the whimsical and limited "gods" of Greek or Roman mythology; these have limited power, change their minds, and fight amongst themselves, and therefore cannot account for the consistency and order of the universe. Nor do I speak of the impersonal and inconsistent "god" of Islam, nor the changing "gods" of Mormonism. These are all the product of human imagination. Rather I refer to the sovereign God of Christianity. Only the Biblical God as described in the pages of Scripture can make sense of the universal laws of nature which describe the predictable behavior of the cosmos. Moreover, the fact that such laws can be expressed by mathematical laws (such as F=ma) confirms that the universe was designed to be understood by the human mind. (See *The Ultimate Proof of Creation* for more details on this topic.)

To this end, I have devoted much of my life to studying and teaching science, and showing how the Christian worldview makes sense of science. I have worked at

Dr. Jason Lisle

234

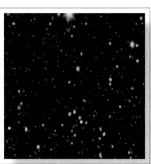

Answers in Genesis, an apologetics ministry that defends the Christian worldview, specializing in the area of origins. The Answers in Genesis ministry is responsible for the Creation Museum, just south of Cincinnati. I was a technical advisor for much of the scientific content throughout the museum. However, my main connection with the museum is the Stargazer's Planetarium and the Johnson Observatory.

The Stargazer's Planetarium is one of the most popular exhibits at the Creation Museum. It uses a Digistar 4 projection system, which provides all-dome digital playback in full-color, ultra-high definition. It was my privilege to write the three shows which are now playing at this planetarium: Worlds of Creation, The Created Cosmos, and The Christmas Star. These shows explore the universe from a Biblical perspective, with dazzling special effects, and are packed full of scientific information.

As telescopes were donated to the Creation Museum, we began a program of stargazer's evenings where we invited the public to come and view the universe through our high-quality portable telescopes. And it has been my delight to lead a number of these. These events have been very popular. Around 2,000 people have participated in these stargazer's events to date, and experienced many of the wonders mentioned in this book.

In 2011, the family of Lyle T. Johnson donated two permanently mounted telescopes to the Creation Museum, which were previously used in The Wilds, a Christian camp in North Carolina. These telescopes are both handmade (one by Johnson himself), with 16-inch diameter instruments that require permanent mounting. I therefore designed the basic layout for an observatory at the Creation Museum to house these telescopes. The design featured a roll-off roof, and two concrete base pillars (one for each telescope) isolated from the building by a small gap and going down to the bedrock for stability. The talented artists at the Creation Museum designed the stunning artistic look of the external portions of the observatory. Other employees worked with outside contractors to construct the building, which is now in use at the Creation Museum.

I would highly encourage readers to visit the Creation Museum. Be sure to see the Stargazer's Room. And if you are staying in the area for more than one day, consider planning your trip to include one of the Stargazer's events listed on the CreationMuseum.org website. Also, check out the www.answersingenesis.org website. It has a host of articles written by myself and others, which confirm the Christian worldview.

Unlike many of my other books, *The Stargazer's Guide to the Night Sky* is not an apologetics book, but I do believe that the heavens declare the glory of God. An understanding of the heavens can only deepen a person's appreciation for the Creator. No one can look into the night sky and honestly deny the Biblical God. In this respect I agree with the famous astronomer Johannes Kepler, that doing astronomy is like "thinking God's thoughts after Him."

The Johnson Observatory at the Creation Museum

◇INDEX

◇Endnotes:

CHAPTER 1

[1] A "great circle" is a circle that occurs on a sphere and in which the center of the circle is the same as the center of the sphere. A great circle is therefore the largest possible circle that can be drawn on a sphere. The earth's equator is an example of a great circle, as are the circles that mark longitude (such as "160° East"). Circles that mark latitude (such as (40° North) are not great circles, because their center is not the center of the earth — except for the equator (latitude 0°). The meridian, the horizon, the celestial equator, and the ecliptic are all great circles that occur on the celestial sphere.

CHAPTER 2

[1] At least, that would be the case if it weren't for other complications, such as the distorting effects of earth's atmosphere. These cause the day and night to be not exactly 12 hours on the equinox, but they are very close.

[2] There are 12 (synodic) months in a year — the moon goes through all its phases 12 times. But phases are relative to the sun, not the stars. The moon actually orbits the earth 13 times in one year — 13 sidereal months. The extra month is because the earth has orbited the sun one time in this period (just as there are 366 sidereal days in a year, one more day than the 365 solar days).

[3] Every ellipse has two "foci" — each one is called a "focus." The foci are such that the distance to each point on the ellipse from one focus plus the distance of that point to the other focus is a constant.

CHAPTER 5

[1] Recently, some astronomers have suggested that the Quadrantid meteor shower, like the Geminids, is also sourced by an asteroid rather than a comet. They suspect that asteroid 2003 EH1 may be the progenitor since its orbit is a close match. Other astronomers disagree and instead identify comet C/1490 Y1 as the likely source for the Quadrantids. This comet was spotted over 500 years ago, and has been lost. It has also been suggested that 2003 EH1 is somehow related to comet C/1490 Y1, the former having broken away from the latter at some time in the past.

CHAPTER 9

[1] The transit happens on the evening of June 5 for observers in North America, and in the morning of June 6 for observers in Europe, Africa, Asia, and Australia.

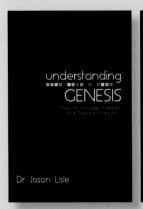

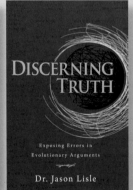
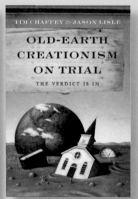
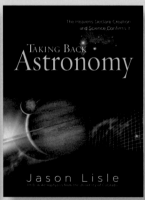